Parks and **Nature Places**
Around Vancouver

Parks and **Nature Places** Around Vancouver

Edited by Alison Parkinson

Harbour Publishing

1 2 3 4 5 — 13 12 11 10 09

Harbour Publishing Co. Ltd.
P.O. Box 219, Madeira Park, BC, V0N 2H0
www.harbourpublishing.com

Additional photography credits: Front cover, Queen Elizabeth Park by Alex Downie; Tiger swallowtail by Al and Jude Grass. Back cover, butter clam by Al and Jude Grass; Nootka rose by Al and Jude Grass; Townsend's chipmunk by Devin Manky; salal berries by James Holkko. Page 1, spotted towhee by Al and Jude Grass. Pages 2–3 Gentian Lake on Hollyburn Ridge by Steve Britten. Page 5, skunk cabbage by Wayne Weber.
Text design and layout by Roger Handling, Terra Firma Digital Arts.
Maps by Rick Danko.
Printed and bound in Canada.
Printed on 10% PCW paper using soy-based inks.

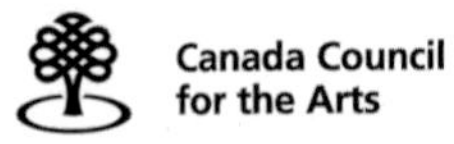

Harbour Publishing acknowledges financial support from the Government of Canada through the Book Publishing Industry Development Program and the Canada Council for the Arts, and from the Province of British Columbia through the BC Arts Council and the Book Publishing Tax Credit.

Library and Archives Canada Cataloguing in Publication

Parks and nature places around Vancouver / edited by Alison Parkinson.

Includes index.
ISBN 978-1-55017-464-9

1. Natural history—British Columbia—Lower Mainland—Guidebooks.
2. Lower Mainland (B.C.)—Guidebooks. I. Parkinson, Alison
QH106.2.B7 P38 2009 508.711'3 C2009-900856-4

Contents

Preface

When the first edition of this book was published, in 1996, gas was 79 cents per litre. Recently it's been twice as costly. In the past many of us hopped into the car to go on a day's outing and didn't give it a single thought. All that is changing, and not a moment too soon. The desire to visit places by public transport or bicycle is growing.

Metro Vancouver is home to many species, including this robber fly. *Les Leighton*

Nature Vancouver (formerly Vancouver Natural History Society) members—volunteers all—have written and illustrated the chapters of this book. All of them know their areas well and spend time birding, botanizing, walking, keeping an eye on changes and developments, leading walks to introduce others to these pursuits and generally taking on a stewardship role in areas they love. They are volunteers and naturalists extraordinaire!

Our Nature Vancouver (VNHS) founder, Professor John Davidson, had an objective in 1918 of "promoting access to, and maintenance of, the natural areas in the vicinity of Vancouver." Ninety years on, this book continues to do just that.

Many thanks to Daphne Solecki, fellow board member, and Alison Parkinson, editor, who have kept the team on task in the production of this book.

Cynthia Crampton, President
Nature Vancouver (VNHS)
July 2008

Acknowledgements

Nature Vancouver (VNHS) would like to thank the many people who have contributed to this book. Conceived as a 90th anniversary venture, it has mushroomed into a far-reaching project involving a considerable proportion of the society's membership. It is not possible to name all the people who have supported the project by making suggestions, answering questions, submitting unpublished photographs and generally helping out, but their support is very much appreciated.

Nature in Vancouver, published by VNHS in 1996, is the inspiration for this new book, *Parks and Nature Places Around Vancouver*. Many of the original authors have again contributed. Its introduction is an adaptation of the one Val Schaefer wrote for the earlier work.

Sheila Byers, David Cook, Al and Jude Grass, Mike Griffin, Bill Kinkaid, Annie Prud'homme Genereux, June M. Ryder, Kelly Sekhon, Jennifer Swanston and Terry and Rosemary Taylor were some of the people involved in compiling the list of 60-plus natural places.

Contributing authors for this edition were Catherine Aitchison, Kristine Bauder, Peter M. Candido, John Chandler, George Clulow, David Cook,

Making friends with a gray jay may be part of your nature excursion. *Ian Lane*

Margaret Coutts, Larry Cowan, Cynthia Crampton, Judy Donaghey, Alex Downie, Elaine Golds, Al and Jude Grass, Eric Greenwood, Will Husby, Louise Irwin, Paul Harris Jones, Douglas Justice and Daniel Mosquin, Bill Kinkaid, Michael Le Geyt, Margo A. Longland, Murray MacDonald, Devin Manky, Pat Miller, Jaideep Mukerji, Viveka Ohman, Alison Parkinson, Juliet Pendray, Bev Ramey, June M. Ryder, Val and Anny Schaefer, Kelly Sekhon, Daphne Solecki, Katharine Steig, Bill Stephen, Jennifer Swanston, Rosemary Taylor, Terry Taylor, Elizabeth Thunstrom, Sheena Vennesland, Geoff Williams, Niall Williams and Robyn Worcester.

Photographs were provided by Steve Britten, Kent Brothers, Sheila Byers, Peter M. Candido, Larry Cowan, Alex Downie, Roy Edgell, Dan Gleadle, Al and Jude Grass, Eric Greenwood, Grouse Mountain Resorts Ltd., Mark Habdas, Peter Hamilton as Founding Director of Lifeforce, Dawn Hanna, Virginia Hayes, Peggy Heath, James Holkko, Will Husby, Paul Harris Jones, Bill Kinkaid, Ian Lane, Michael Le Geyt, Les Leighton, Josh Lewis, Margo A. Longland, Joan Lopez, Devin Manky, Daniel Mosquin, Jaideep Mukerji, Viveka Ohman, Alison Parkinson, John Parkinson, Richmond Nature Park, Ed Robertson, June M. Ryder, Rick Saunier, Val and Anny Schaefer, Kelly Sekhon, Bill Stephen, Jennifer Swanston, Kiyoshi Takahashi, Rosemary Taylor, UBC Botanical Garden, UBC Botanical Garden Archive, Ben VanBuskirk, Ross Vennesland, Wayne Weber, Michael Wheatley, Geoff Williams, Niall Williams, Nancy Wong, Robyn Worcester and Mark Wynja.

All maps were created by Rick Danko.

The Customer Information Department at Coast Mountain Bus Company verified the transit information.

Park visitors who tested the information on location were Judith Allerston and James Chen, Lorna Brown, Angela Dawson, Sandy and Frank Duck, Pat Ishkanian and Pierce Brewster, Marie McConkey and Eva Nagy.

Specialist reviewers included Peter M. Candido and June M. Ryder. Proofreaders and reviewers were Marian Coope, Daphne Solecki and Al and Jude Grass.

Alison Parkinson compiled and edited the submitted material and coordinated the project. John Parkinson provided valuable assistance.

The overall business manager was Daphne Solecki.

Introduction

by Val Schaefer and Alison Parkinson

Parks and Nature Places Around Vancouver is intended to help city dwellers and visitors find the many beautiful natural places within the Metro Vancouver area that it's possible to reach by public transit.

Going out to visit nature is a tonic. Being able to get there without a car is an added bonus for those of us who long to reduce our ecological footprint. This book describes more than 60 natural locations that we can reach by public transportation; it also takes a bicycle to reach a few. All are described by naturalists who want to share their own enjoyment. Not a hiking or walking guide, the book can provide authoritative information about the natural life we can explore, observe and enjoy in these many amazing places.

Nature is All Around Us

Most of us live in cities. We generally do not think of cities as wildlife habitats or as part of a globally important ecosystem. Cities are generally considered to have little or no natural value. Nothing can be further from the truth. Most cities are strategically located at river mouths or at the entrances of straits and fjords. These are often rich with natural productivity and biodiversity.

Vancouver and its neighbouring municipalities extend along the Strait of Georgia, the Fraser River Estuary and Burrard Inlet. This region is on the Pacific Flyway, home to millions of birds that live and breed here or stop over on their way between Northern Canada or Alaska and Central or South America. Millions of salmon fry and smolts feed along the foreshore; the adults themselves travel through the area on their way to spawn in many tributaries of the Fraser River farther inland.

Fishing is a rewarding activity in many parks, including Capilano River Regional Park. *Steve Britten*

Greater Vancouver has many important environmentally sensitive areas, several of which are surviving ecosystem fragments that represent some of the original habitat in the region. Some are now second growth, becoming established after the initial onslaught of logging in the region about a hundred years ago. We also have many artificially created ecosystems such as

Purple sea stars prey on shellfish such as mussels, barnacles, limpets and snails.
James Holkko

our parks, which are exceptional in their beauty and biodiversity.

Even in the heart of the city, nature surrounds us in the most unexpected ways. Flocks of birds may descend on a tree in a small park downtown or use a climbing vine on a wall for shelter overnight. There are stickleback trout in the smallest of ponds next to railway lines. Even a single tree may have a small food chain on its leaves that includes aphids, aphid eggs, ants and ladybugs.

Parks and Nature Places Around Vancouver is a multi-level guide to the natural wonders of Vancouver and surrounding areas. The suggested locations are all accessible by public transit, in some cases with an additional pleasant cycle ride; all present rich opportunities for discovery. We live with nature every day. It does not exist only in far-off places accessible by canoe or backpacking. Nature is here for us to enjoy wherever we are and whenever we want.

Contributing Naturalists

In *Parks and Nature Places Around Vancouver*, more than 40 naturalists describe their favourite haunts so that you can share their pleasure and excitement at being there. From their particular specialty—geology, botany, ornithology, marine life or just everything—they describe the aspects of the park that interest them the most. You will probably see much more than they describe; it is impossible to give a full account of a park in just a couple of pages.

These diverse aspects offer lively reading and the opportunity to explore particular concepts in more detail. For example, the Stanley Park Seawall section emphasizes its geology; the description of Garry Point Park in Steveston gives a wonderful account of its plant life; and the Iona Beach Regional Park entry describes mainly birds. All biological specialties are interwoven closely, and it is fair to assume that at all locations there will be plenty to interest any nature lover.

Fly amanita delivers water and nutrients to a nearby tree and receives sugar in return.
James Holkko

The descriptions are further enhanced by hundreds of photographs and maps contributed by naturalists who have the knowledge, patience and artistic eye to record images that you can peruse, enjoy and learn from at your leisure.

The authors and photographers who have contributed to this book are all nature enthusiasts and experts in their fields. Some of them manage the parks they describe, while others have led nature walks for years. They are familiar with the types of questions that people ask about the parks.

Transit to Nature

Transit information is ever-changing. Routes, schedules, transit modes and fares are constantly being updated as the Metro Vancouver transit system develops. So while the book does describe current routes, it minimizes changeable details such as schedules. But be assured that current public transit passes within a few minutes' walk of 54 of the 61 nature destinations described and within a few kilometres' cycle ride of the other seven.

Preserving our Parks

by Bev Ramey

This book describes 61 nature locations that you can visit and enjoy, but not take for granted. If you think that a park is permanently protected, think again. Numerous examples exist of habitat loss in areas that people had thought were protected in a park. This loss happens because many people in our society, including decision makers, do not value forested areas, old field grasslands or other natural areas.

For those of us who value nature, this is difficult to comprehend, but the reality is that many people see natural habitats as wastelands or under-utilized land. Remember the saying "Beauty is in the eye of the beholder." Undeveloped parkland may even appear threatening to some people because there are no buildings or pavement, and others do not like to have their view blocked by trees. Some developers consider natural parklands the least expensive option to build upon.

For over 20 years, groups lobbied to preserve Maplewood Conservation Area. *Al and Jude Grass*

Parks are Fragile

A compilation of the threats to parks in the Lower Mainland over the past half-century, and stories of the groups rallying to protect land that had been designated as parks, would fill the pages of several books. Such a compilation is not the purpose of *Parks and Nature Places Around Vancouver*, but one of our goals is to remind you of the fragile nature of our beloved parks. They are fragile not just because of the sensitive ecosystems that they contain, but also because of human decisions.

Public effort and outcry has defeated a few of these threats over the years:

- Road expansion – the current Gateway proposal along the edge of Burns Bog Nature Conservancy
- Golf course proposals – several were proposed in parks, especially in the 1980s, but most were defeated, including those at Boundary Bay Regional Park, Crippen Regional Park, Mundy Park and Colony Farm
- Beach volleyball courts in old field habitat – defeated at Jericho Beach Park
- Dog walking trails – recently turned down at Maplewood Conservation Area

- Sports playing field – proposed for rough grasslands and forest at Vancouver's 37th Ave. and Oak Street Park
- Outright development of parkland – potential at Hastings Park Conservancy and Pacific Spirit Regional Park
- Ski resort expansion – proposed at Cypress Provincial Park
- Deletion of parks – proposed at Pinecone Burke Provincial Park to accommodate a transmission line from a run-of-river project – subsequently defeated following large public outcry
- Hardening of natural shorelines and marina construction – ongoing proposals along the Fraser River and ocean foreshore

Development is Highly Organized and Funded

Proposals to develop or remove land from natural parks arise with great force because their proponents are organized and often paid through commercial or industrial ventures. Meanwhile, those who support retaining natural habitats are generally not as well organized or funded. People who appreciate natural habitats usually do so in an unstructured way through quiet walks, alone or in small groups, observing nature in a variety of ways and at a variety of times throughout the day. Incidentally, such nature walks are now showing up repeatedly in scientific literature as being extremely beneficial to human physical and mental health!

Be Alert and Involved

It is important for all of us who appreciate nature to become knowledgeable about our favourite natural habitats beyond casual visits. As well, we should notice changes and bring them to the attention of others. We can learn of threats to parks and join with others as part of a local club to speak up in support of nature.

If you are already a member of a nature club, get involved! If not, consider joining the club near you: Alouette Field Naturalists, Bowen Nature Club, Burke Mountain Naturalists, Central Valley Naturalists, Delta Naturalists' Society, Friends of Semiahmoo Bay Society, Langley Field Naturalist Society, Little Campbell Watershed Society, Nature Vancouver (VNHS), Royal City Field Naturalists, Stoney Creek Environmental Committee and White Rock and Surrey Naturalists. Contact information for all these clubs and other stewardship groups is available at www.bcnature.ca.

Trip Tips

When you visit a local park, you can probably just walk or catch a bus or SkyTrain and enjoy your visit without much preparation. If you feel more adventurous and want to travel farther afield, some planning can prevent frustration when you meet unfamiliar situations. For your personal safety, it's a good idea to have company on your trip, especially if you visit the more remote locations. Otherwise leave some indication of where you are planning to go in case you have an unexpected problem.

Transportation

Check transit routes and schedules ahead of time, particularly the details of your return trip. Many parks are in quiet rural areas where transportation is infrequent, and a wonderful day can be easily spoiled by a long wait for a bus on your return.

Transportation information changes often. Park transit directions may remain valid, but routes and schedules will likely alter. Public transit will improve each year, we can hope, with more convenient routes and schedules as the demand increases.

Also check the best fares for your expedition; there may be day passes that work for your group. If you are bringing a wheelchair, check that the transit vehicle can accommodate it.

Cyclists take a break near Lost Lagoon in Stanley Park. *Steve Britten*

For transit information, contact TransLink at 604-953-3333 or at www.translink.ca.

If you are travelling by BC Ferries as a foot passenger, you currently need to be at the terminal at least 10 minutes before sailing time, preferably earlier. For information contact BC Ferries at 1-888-BCFERRY (1-888-223-3779) or *BCF (*223) or www.bcferries.com.

Bicycles

Seven of the nature destinations are not currently within walking distance of public transit, but they are quite close. By bringing your bicycle on the transit vehicle, you can complete your journey with a pleasurable cycle ride of, in most cases, just a few kilometres. Directions for the cycle ride are provided in each entry. Check with transit that the vehicle can accommodate your bicycles. Also, bring locks to secure your bicycles while you explore the park on foot.

If you plan to bring your pet along, carefully check dog access and leash regulations.
Steve Britten

Maps

Each park description includes a map that shows its general location and another map that focusses on its immediate vicinity, showing the nearby transit stop and the park entrance. Along with your own Lower Mainland street map, this should equip you to find your way to the park entrance.

Most parks have notice boards at their entrance that display detailed information and usually maps for the park. In addition there may be brochures containing maps that you can pick up and carry with you, though the supply can run out during a busy visiting period.

Information, including maps, is usually available from the Internet, by telephone or from government offices. For further details, check the More Information sections at the end of each park description.

Park Facilities and Entrance Fees

Wheelchair facilities are improving; dog access and on-leash and off-leash areas are continually fluctuating as administrators listen to and act on different viewpoints; bicycle and skateboard rights keep changing; and lifeguard schedules are inconsistent. If these considerations affect your agenda, you can check them out ahead of time. Fines can be substantial for running off-leash dogs in on-leash areas.

Most provincial and regional parks have no food services. Municipal park concessions, where they exist, are often only available in summer. It is a good idea to pack your own food and take drinking water along. Some parks do not have washrooms, so be prepared for that as well.

Park facility and opening time information is usually available on the Internet or by telephone. Currently most parks have no admission charge; the exceptions are Grouse Mountain, UBC Botanical Garden, VanDusen Botanical Garden, Bloedel Conservatory and George C. Reifel Migratory Bird Sanctuary. You may want to check out the current charges for nearby facilities such as museums or swimming pools.

Tide Tables

If you are planning to beachcomb, you can check that the tides will be reasonably low by consulting the tide tables at www.waterlevels.gc.ca.

Nature Identification Handbooks

Notice boards and brochures at the park often provide interesting information about the natural life you'll find there, but there will always be additional sightings that will keep you guessing. Books that you can purchase and take with you will help you identify plants, fungi, birds, marine life and geological features.

Plants of Coastal British Columbia, Revised, by Jim Pojar and Andy MacKinnon [eds], Lone Pine Publishing, 2005.

The New Savory Wild Mushroom, by Margaret McKenny, Daniel E. Stuntz and Joseph F. Ammirati, Douglas and McIntyre, 1994.

Field Guide to the Birds of North America, by Jon L. Dunn and Jonathon Alderfer [eds], National Geographic, Fifth Edition, 2006.

Marine Life of the Pacific Northwest, by Andy Lamb and Bernard P. Hanby, Harbour Publishing, 2005.

Vancouver, City on the Edge, by John Clague and Bob Turner, Tricouni Press, 2003.

BC Wildlife Watch Website

The BC Wildlife Watch website provides useful information about viewing wildlife in many locations in BC, including several places that are featured in this book. Organized by geographical region, it offers bird checklists, information on fish viewing and highlights of other wildlife and viewing.

Visit the BC Wildlife Watch website: www3.telus.net/driftwood/bcwwhome.htm.

Don't Forget

Take a cell phone along in case you get lost or need assistance during your expedition. And remember your binoculars or spotting scope and a camera!

Viewing Ethics and Suggestions

Viewing Ethics for Conservation

Wildlife viewing demands courtesy and common sense. For the well-being of the wildlife and habitats, please follow these guidelines.

Respect wildlife

Keep your distance and use binoculars or a spotting scope. This enables you to observe wildlife without causing stress to animals.

Respect habitat

Plants and the landscape are important parts of fish and wildlife habitats. Do not damage or remove them or pick flowers and berries.

Control pets

Pets can harm wildlife and hinder viewing opportunities. Keep pets safe and under control by putting them on a leash.

Do not approach young wildlife

Young animals are rarely abandoned or lost. The adult is usually at a safe distance waiting for you to leave.

Viewing Suggestions for Wildlife Viewers

These tips will improve your chances of seeing wildlife in its natural habitat. Remember that wildlife is wild and may choose not to be seen.

Choose the right season and time of day

Many species are most active during the cooler morning and evening hours. A hot, dry, sunny afternoon is usually not the best time to look for wildlife.

Move slowly and reduce your visibility

Wildlife usually senses your presence long before you sense its presence. Most animals have a keen sense of hearing and smell, and most birds and large mammals have sharp eyesight.

Be patient and be quiet

Wildlife may be difficult to observe, even though you have heard animals or detected their signs. Remain still and quiet, so that the wildlife will determine that you are no threat and may become active and more visible.

Use binoculars or a spotting scope

Visual aids help you scan wide areas, increasing your chances of observing wildlife without disturbing it.

Metro Vancouver Transit

by Margaret Coutts

The inspiration for *Parks and Nature Places Around Vancouver* is that it is possible to visit many Lower Mainland parks and natural areas using public transportation. We have included, along with each nature place description, local transit route information. It indicates a transit route that passes close to the nature destination and the closest transit stop for convenient access.

A SkyTrain line passes by Sapperton Landing Park.
Mark Habdas

Vancouver and the surrounding region does have an ever-improving system of public transportation, so current transit routes may soon be superseded by expanded ones. As well, transit schedules continually change, even with the seasons. In this morphing world, we cannot emphasize too strongly that before you start your trip, you need to check all transit information using the websites or phone information lines. In the rural areas where many of the parks are located, buses may run less frequently, so it is particularly important to have the correct information.

TransLink Travel Modes

TransLink plans and manages the public transit system in Metro Vancouver. There are several integrated travel modes that connect at transit exchanges and stations so that you can easily transfer from one route to another.

Trolley buses and diesel buses provide regular bus service in urban areas.

However, in recent years more types of buses have been introduced. On heavy commuter routes, large-capacity articulated B-Line buses provide fast limited-stop transportation. In quieter areas, community shuttle minibuses connect to the regional transit network.

Currently SkyTrain provides automated light rail transport in Vancouver, Burnaby, New Westminster and Surrey on two lines: the Expo Line and the Millennium Line. The Canada Line is fast developing to Richmond. As well, the SeaBus provides a shuttle service across the waters of Burrard Inlet between downtown Vancouver and North Vancouver in twin-hulled catamarans.

Fares

Metro Vancouver is divided into three fare zones. Your fare will depend on how many zones you visit, your age, the day, the time of day and the method of payment. For each fare TransLink provides up to 90 minutes of travel with unlimited transfers between buses, the SkyTrain and the SeaBus.

There are several ways to pay your fare. If you travel fairly frequently, you may choose to buy a book of 10 FareSavers in advance at a discount. These are sold at FareSaver outlets, which are usually drug stores, convenience stores or supermarkets. You can use FareSavers as you need them on any transit vehicle. Alternatively, you can buy DayPasses, which may be more economical for a day of unlimited travel. When boarding transit with a new FareSaver, you must get it validated by the bus driver or—at a SeaBus or SkyTrain station—by a machine.

Crossing Burrard Inlet by SeaBus is a quick way to downtown from the North Shore. *Steve Britten*

For the SkyTrain and SeaBus, before you enter the fare paid zone, buy tickets and DayPasses from nearby vending machines that provide change. To pay cash for your fare on a bus, you must tender the correct fare with coins as you enter; no change is available. Remember to ask the bus driver for a transfer ticket if you plan to continue your journey on another transit vehicle.

Wheelchairs and Bicycles

SkyTrain, SeaBus, B-Line buses, community buses and many other buses are wheelchair accessible. SkyTrain and SeaBus carry bicycles in a designated location. Many buses have bike racks, though some buses do not carry bikes at night. There is a limit to the number of bicycles that can be carried.

Getting TransLink Information

TransLink provides two options for obtaining transit information. Trip Planning can be accessed on its website, www.translink.ca, or by telephoning its information line at 604-953-3333. In almost all cases, cross streets must be given for destinations. For the parks in this book, this information is provided in the park descriptions.

Another useful source of TransLink information is its transportation map and guide *Getting Around*. You can buy it for a couple of dollars at TransLink FareSaver outlets. This Metro Vancouver map shows all the transit routes and makes it easier to plan your route—though you still need to check schedules.

Many buses are equipped with bike racks. *Steve Britten*

BC Ferries

BC Ferries provides transportation between coastal locations in the province. In Metro Vancouver there are two ferry terminals, both served by TransLink transportation: Tsawwassen terminal and Horseshoe Bay terminal in West Vancouver. Ferries to Bowen Island dock at Horseshoe Bay terminal.

Walk-on passengers must arrive at the ferry terminal in plenty of time for their ferry, currently at least 10 minutes before sailing; BC Ferries is unyielding on this requirement. Bicycle riders wait by the car deck entrance and enter or leave the ferry just before the cars.

For ferry information, access BC Ferries at www.bcferries.com or by telephone at 1-888-BCFERRY (1-888-223-3779) and *BCF (*223) from a cell phone on the Rogers or Telus mobility network.

Enjoy!

We hope you will find pleasure in exploration and in travelling to these parks and natural areas. Using public transit reduces your ecological footprint, which may in turn increase your enjoyment of these places.

Nature Vancouver (VNHS)

by Daphne Solecki

Nature Vancouver, founded as the Vancouver Natural History Society (VNHS), has a long tradition; 2008 marked its 90th anniversary. The publication of *Parks and Nature Places Around Vancouver* is one of the activities in which many of the society's approximately 750 members participated to celebrate this important milestone.

In 2006 the VNHS changed its name to Nature Vancouver, which more readily conveys the essence of the society. It also reflects our connection with the national organization Nature Canada and our provincial counterparts such as Nature Saskatchewan and Nature New Brunswick. Both names are still valid. As Nature Vancouver, the society will continue to enjoy the outdoors, educate members and the public on the natural history of the province and press for the preservation of wildlife and natural areas in the Metro Vancouver area and throughout BC.

John Davidson, an ardent naturalist, was the founder of Nature Vancouver (VNHS).
UBC Botanical Garden Archives

Early History

Nature Vancouver (VNHS) was originally a section of the Vancouver Mountaineering Club, founded in 1907, which became the BC Mountaineering Club (BCMC) in 1909. The BCMC's focus was to explore and map the local mountains. As the only organized group in Vancouver actively enjoying the outdoors, BCMC membership swelled, and in 1911 members added a botanical section, an entomological section and a geological section. One of the charter members of the botanical section was a newly arrived Scot, John Davidson, who was the eventual founder of the VNHS.

Professor John Davidson, as he became, had been a member of the botany department of the University of Aberdeen in Scotland. Frustrated in his desire to rise to the position he felt he deserved in that university and needing to live in a less harsh climate, he emigrated to BC in 1911. He wasted no time in establishing himself so that he could bring his family to Vancouver. He was appointed to conduct a botanical survey of BC, the first such survey in Canada. He was also the first appointee to BC's new university. Shortly afterward he was named provincial botanist, began a plant collection that was to become the BC Provincial Herbarium and Botanical Garden, organized the Arbor Day Association to promote tree planting in public spaces, started teaching evening botany classes and made many friends in the burgeoning naturalist movement.

When John Davidson joined the BCMC and launched the natural history section, his energy and enthusiasm drew so many new members that the naturalists soon outnumbered the climbers. On May 10, 1918, VNHS—with an initial membership of seventy—was formed by splitting off the BCMC natural history section and melding it with the Arbor Day Association. Three days later the new society held its first field trip, visiting Burnaby Lake and Deer Lake. By 1921 membership had grown to 200.

While the wording has changed over time, the objectives of Nature Vancouver have remained essentially unchanged since 1918: to enjoy, study and protect nature in Vancouver and throughout BC. A major component of the society's activities has always been education of both members and the public. Exploratory field trips, nature study, camps, lectures, publications and briefs to government are some of the ways this is achieved.

Conservation

Throughout its history, VNHS made some of its top priorities the conservation of wildlife and natural areas. As early as the 1920s, the society campaigned against the bounty system, in which the government rewarded the killing of animals they termed noxious predators, including wolves, foxes, cougars, coyotes, birds of prey and even robins and squirrels. While the society's campaign was not entirely successful, it reduced the number of animals killed.

In 1924 John Davidson presented a speech, "The Handwriting on the Wall or Wake Up! Vancouver." It condemned the devastation of trees in the Vancouver area, specifically in the Capilano watershed. The subsequent investigation resulted in a logging phase-out, and by December 1933 it was reported that the last log had been taken out and that the watershed would from that day forward be out of bounds.

This vigorous emphasis on education, conservation and protection of species and habitats has continued to this day. Field trips and section meetings remain a constant draw for members, and the knowledge gained through these activities form the foundation for conservation efforts. Some recent Nature Vancouver conservation successes include the preservation of Terra Nova Natural Area in Richmond and the Maplewood Conservation Area in North Vancouver. Other important achievements for the society are the restoration of Camosun Bog in Pacific Spirit Regional Park, the restoration of the marsh for yellow-headed blackbirds in Iona Beach Regional Park and the protection of Hollyburn Mountain from downhill ski development.

Current conservation concerns for the society are UBC Farm preservation,

BC provincial parks management and funding, the protection of Boundary Bay, the Deltaport expansion, Pinecone Burke Provincial Park, Hastings Park Sanctuary and Pacific Spirit Regional Park.

Nature Vancouver birders enjoy a New Year's Day excursion to Richmond.
Kelly Sekhon

Education

Nature Vancouver has pursued its education goals through its role in the establishment and development of the Nature House at Lost Lagoon in Stanley Park and the Young Naturalists' Club of British Columbia. On a continuing basis the society conducts workshops on topics such as bird identification and nature photography, weekly field trips and public lectures. Activities include habitat restoration, the Christmas Bird Count, the Raptor Survey, the Coast Bird Survey and the Wildlife Tree Stewardship program.

Recent VNHS publications include *Nature West Coast: As seen in Lighthouse Park* (1973, republished 1988), *Nature in Vancouver* (1996), *The Birder's Guide to Vancouver and the Lower Mainland* (2001), *Wilderness on the Doorstep: Discovering Nature in Stanley Park* (2006) and several bird checklists.

Objectives

Nature Vancouver's objectives are to:

- promote the enjoyment of nature
- foster public appreciation of nature
- encourage the wise use and conservation of natural resources
- work for the protection of endangered species and ecosystems
- promote access to local natural areas around Vancouver and maintain them

Parks and **Nature Places** Around Vancouver

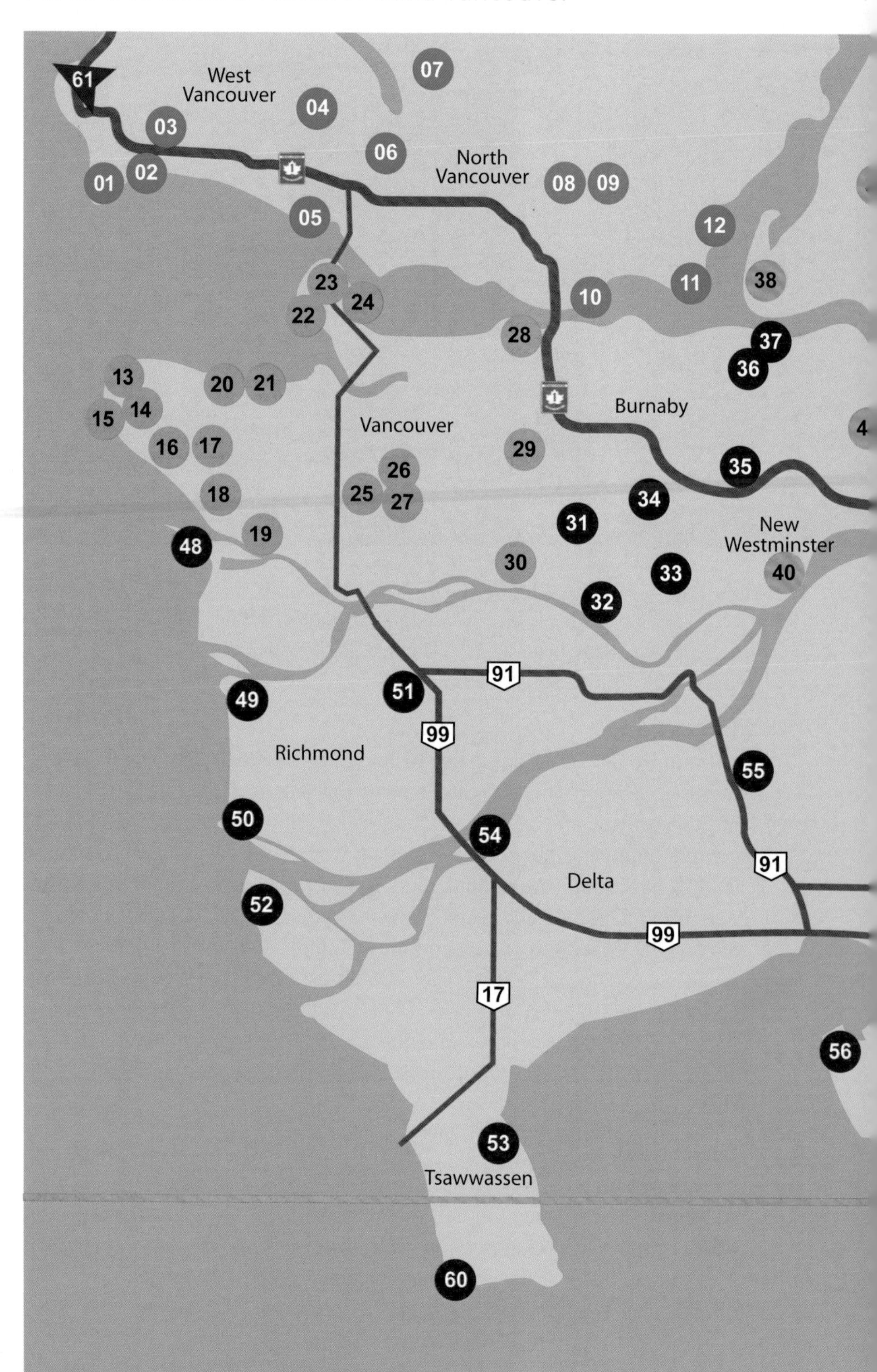

Map of the 61 Nature Places

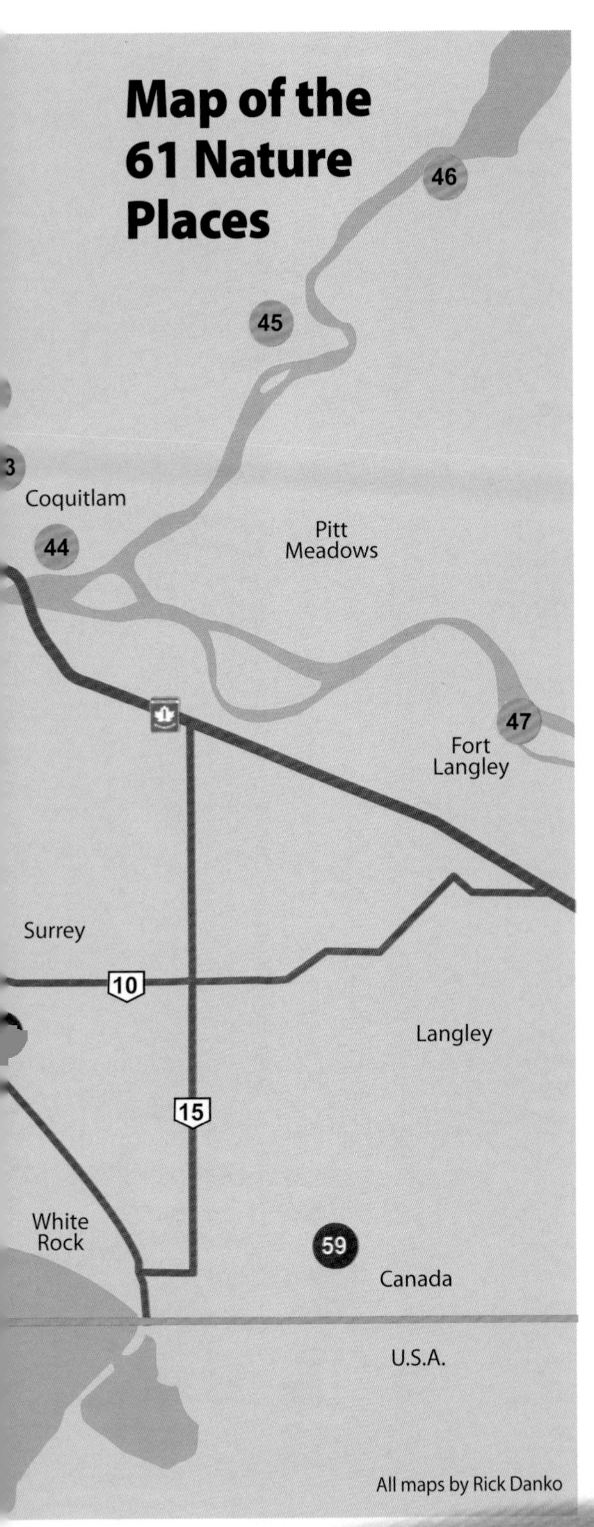

All maps by Rick Danko

North Shore

1 Lighthouse Park
2 Caulfeild Park
3 Cypress Falls Park
4 Hollyburn Ridge
5 Ambleside Park
6 Capilano River Regional Park
7 Grouse Mountain
8 Lynn Canyon Park
9 Lower Seymour Conservation Reserve
10 Maplewood Conservation Area
11 Cates Park
12 Deep Cove

Vancouver City

13 UBC Campus: Cecil Green Area
14 UBC Campus: UBC Farm
15 UBC Botanical Garden
16 Pacific Spirit Regional Park
17 Camosun Bog
18 Musqueam Park
19 Southlands
20 Jericho Beach Park
21 Point Grey Foreshore
22 Stanley Park: West
23 Stanley Park: East
24 Stanley Park Seawall
25 VanDusen Botanical Garden
26 Queen Elizabeth Park
27 Bloedel Conservatory
28 Hastings Park Sanctuary
29 Renfrew Ravine Park
30 Everett Crowley Park

Burnaby City

31 Central Park
32 Burnaby Fraser Foreshore Park
33 Byrne Creek Ravine Park
34 Deer Lake Park
35 Burnaby Lake Regional Park
36 Burnaby Mountain Conservation Area
37 Barnet Marine Park

East of Vancouver

38 Belcarra Regional Park
39 Buntzen Lake Recreation Area
40 Sapperton Landing Park
41 Shoreline Park, Port Moody
42 Como Lake Park
43 Mundy Park
44 Colony Farm Regional Park
45 Minnekhada Regional Park
46 Grant Narrows Regional Park
47 Brae Island Regional Park

South of Vancouver

48 Iona Beach Regional Park
49 Terra Nova Natural Area
50 Garry Point Park, Steveston
51 Richmond Nature Park
52 George C. Reifel Migratory Bird Sanctuary
53 Boundary Bay Regional Park at Centennial Beach
54 Deas Island Regional Park
55 Delta Nature Reserve, Burns Bog
56 Blackie Spit Park
57 Serpentine Wildlife Management Area
58 White Rock Pier and Promenade
59 Campbell Valley Regional Park
60 Lighthouse Marine Park, Point Roberts, WA

Over the Water

61 Crippen Regional Park, Bowen Island

north shore

Previous page: Kayakers discover that navigating Capilano Canyon waters is a thrilling experience. *Steve Britten*

Above: Point Atkinson Lighthouse sits at the tip of the forested Lighthouse Park peninsula. *James Holkko*

Lighthouse Park

by David Cook

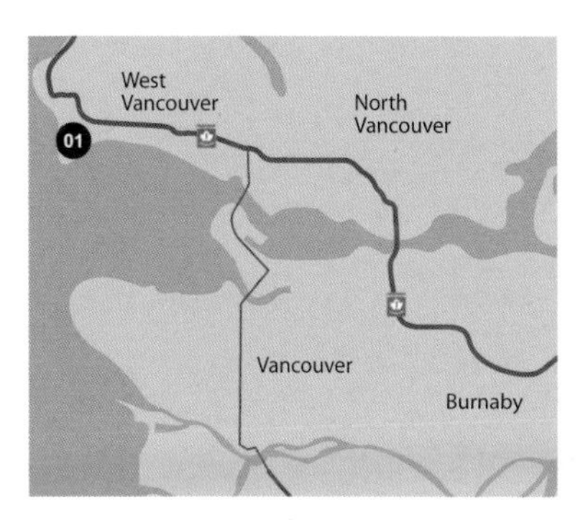

Old-growth forest on a rocky headland with high biodiversity

Location

Lighthouse Park is in southwest West Vancouver at the end of Beacon Lane off Marine Dr.

Transit Information

From downtown Vancouver, board the #250 Horseshoe Bay bus and alight at the Marine Dr. and Beacon Lane stop. For up-to-date information, contact TransLink at www.translink.ca or 604-953-3333.

Introduction

Lighthouse Park is 75 hectares (185 acres) of natural forest set aside in 1881 as a dark backdrop to the Point Atkinson lighthouse, now automated. The park, owned by the federal government, is leased and managed by the District of West Vancouver.

The main trail will take you down through towering Douglas-fir and western redcedar to the lighthouse. There you will encounter the other big attraction of Lighthouse Park, its setting on a rocky peninsula with scenic views west across the mouth of Howe Sound, south across Burrard Inlet to Point Grey and southeast to Stanley Park and Burnaby Mountain.

The park forest is an isolated fragment of the coastal western hemlock biogeoclimatic zone and has retained many characteristics of an old-growth forest.

Natural History Visit

From the bus stop, walk down Beacon Lane to Lighthouse Park and proceed through the parking lot to the

The living stump is grafted to the roots of the big tree but has no leaf growth. *James Holkko*

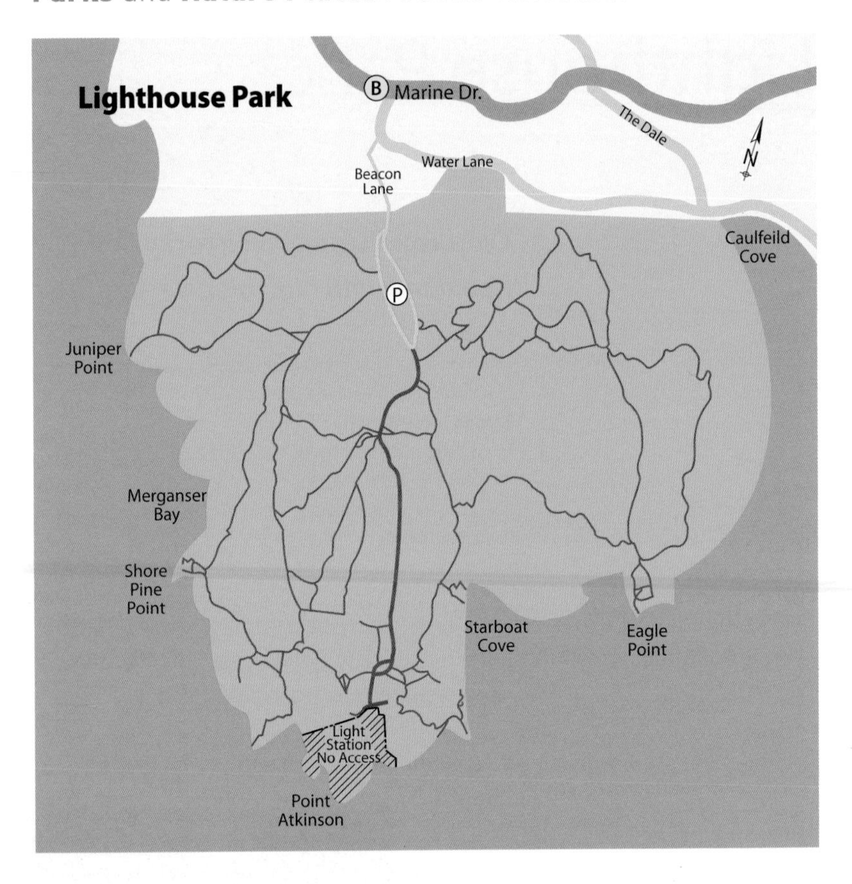

main trail down to the lighthouse. Several smaller trails lead off into the forest on either side. The main trail is easy to walk on, but for the side trails we recommend good gripping shoes for hiking over tree roots and rocky outcrops and climbing some of the steep inclines.

The Lighthouse Park peninsula lies at the entrance to Howe Sound, one of North America's most southerly fjords. The fjord and the peninsula were shaped by glaciers that advanced and retreated many times during the last two million years. Various features left here on the rocks by the moving ice are polish, flutes, grooves and striations. One location to see polish and striations is the lighthouse viewpoint.

In many places in Lighthouse Park, the granitic rocks have been intruded by dark-coloured basalt dikes. Two excellent locations to view a dike are West Beach and East Beach.

The highest point of the park is 119 metres (390 feet) at the northern end. Because of this elevation gain, various sections of the park receive annual rainfall ranging from 1,270 millimetres (50 inches) at its lowest elevation to 1,580 millimetres (62 inches) at its highest. The rugged topography contains a high diversity of habitats and therefore species.

The main trail leads through huge Douglas-fir and western redcedar to the lighthouse.
James Holkko

In the coniferous forest, huge old-growth Douglas-firs and western redcedars tower over the more numerous western hemlocks. The understory is mainly sword fern and salal; deer fern grows in the moister sites. Two western redcedar trees, culturally modified by the removal of bark strips, grow on the Shore Pine Trail between the Jack Pine Lookout and the connection with the Juniper Loop Trail.

Kinnikinnick and coastal reindeer lichen grow together on a low rocky face.
James Holkko

BC's only broad-leaved evergreen, the arbutus, and the drought-resistant shore pine grow on the rocky headlands and outcrops. Rocky surfaces without soil are covered in crustose lichens and some mosses. Where a little soil can develop, look for a number of lily species, blue-eyed Mary, saxifrage, Wallace's selaginella, gumweed and the fragile and beautiful reindeer lichen.

On shaded and humid rock cliffs, maidenhair fern, licorice fern and many flowering plants find conditions to their liking. In a wetland along the Juniper Loop, skunk cabbage and Pacific water parsley thrive.

With its forest, headlands, seashore and open water, Lighthouse Park provides habitat for many bird species. Bald eagles occasionally nest in an

The basalt dike (centre of photo) has eroded faster than the surrounding granite rock.
James Holkko

old-growth Douglas-fir; seabirds such as Barrow's goldeneyes and surf scoters in rafts of up to 2,500 birds thrive offshore; in wildlife trees, pileated woodpeckers have made holes looking for ants and grubs. In these holes—as they rot and get larger—wood ducks, nuthatches and chickadees as well as raccoons, squirrels and mice make nests, shelter and store food. The park handbook currently lists 171 species of birds.

Visit year-round. May to September is best for birds; spring and early summer are best for flowering plants.

Nearby Locations

- Caulfeild Park is a 0.5-kilometre (0.3-mile) walk to the east along Water Lane

Some Alerts

- bluffs with steep slopes to the water are slippery and very dangerous, particularly after rain
- rough and slippery trails in many places

More Information

West Vancouver map and guide: www.westvancouver.ca/Government/maps/municipal-map/dwv-municipal-map.htm

West Vancouver Municipal Hall: 604-925-7000 or http://www.westvancouver.ca

Nature West Coast: As Seen in Lighthouse Park, by Kathleen M. Smith, Nancy J. Anderson, and Katherine I. Beamish, Nature Vancouver (VNHS), 1988.

Phyl Mundy Nature House is located in the park and operated by the West Vancouver Girl Guides

Caulfeild Park

by David Cook

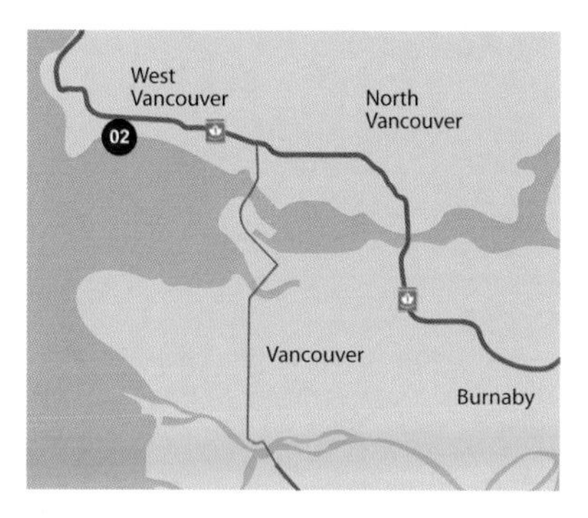

Rocky bluffs, renowned geology and a historical village

Location

Caulfeild Park is in southwest West Vancouver on Pilot House Rd. off Piccadilly South and Marine Dr.

Transit Information

From downtown Vancouver, board the #250 Horseshoe Bay bus and alight at the Marine Dr. and Piccadilly North stop. For up-to-date information, contact TransLink at www.translink.ca or 604-953-3333.

Introduction

Caulfeild Park, at 3.6 hectares (8.9 acres), is one kilometre (0.6 mile) of linear waterfront along the shore of the charming English-style village of Caulfeild. The village was created by Francis Caulfeild a century ago and still has a village green, lych-gate and church near the Caulfeild Cove boat dock. There is a commemorative plaque with an anchor in the park. The park is managed by the District of West Vancouver.

This rocky shoreline park offers scenic views across Burrard Inlet to Stanley Park and Point Grey and is the perfect place for a picnic. The shoreline is mostly rocky bluffs and large flat rock surfaces between two small coves: Pilot Cove with its small sandy public beach to the east and Caulfeild Cove. There is also woodland.

Caulfeild Park is internationally renowned among geologists as a site that helps to demonstrate how granitic rocks are formed. On the rocky bluff southeast of the anchor, there is a spectacular example of a granite intrusion into the dark gneiss rock. You can see rounded masses of the gneiss that were melting in the granite magma. Caulfeild Park also includes remnants of a coastal bluff ecosystem that is vulnerable to the human footprint.

Spots on a Columbia (tiger) lily are guide marks to attract pollinating insects. *Wayne Weber*

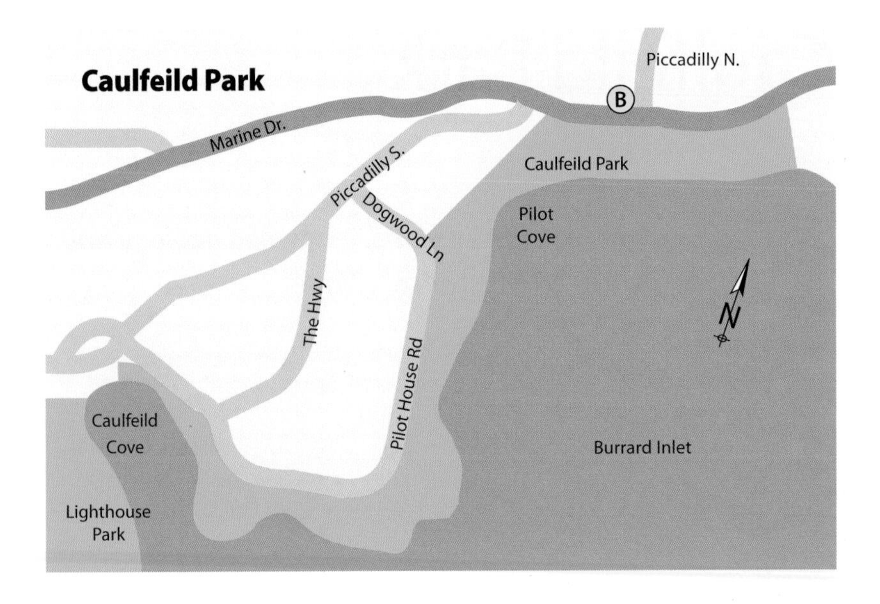

Natural History Visit

From the bus stop, walk half a block west along Marine Dr. toward Piccadilly South. Just before the intersection, turn left down off the road toward the water. Walk across the rock face and down the stone staircase on your right to the park path and the sandy beach below at Pilot Cove. Then walk along the path through the woods to the rocky headland and Caulfeild Cove.

Within the dark Caulfeild gneiss, you can see a paler intrusion of molten rock.
James Holkko

Over the rock surface, crustose lichens cling, and mosses that require little or no soil grow as poorly attached sheets. The mosses can be stripped off in minutes by careless walking, and the lichens are slowly worn away by human feet, never to re-establish themselves unless the area is fenced off.

White fawn lily and Columbia (tiger) lily, chickweed, monkey-flower, camas, harvest brodiaea, kinnikinnick or bearberry, false box, saxifrage, western trumpet honeysuckle, broad-leaved stonecrop, gumweed, Pacific crab apple and Wallace's selaginella grow on the open areas by the rocks. Away from the rocks Douglas-fir, shore pine, salal, arbutus, Saskatoon berry, salmonberry, Pacific dogwood and juniper grow.

When the tide is out, the area below the cliff face on the west side of

Caulfeild Cove is a good place to view intertidal life zones: the uppermost splash zone, upper intertidal zone and mid-littoral zone. Mahogany clams, heart cockles and Manila clams live in the sand and gravel along the shoreline. Red coralline algae thrive on rocks around the sandy beach. At the municipal dock you may see all kinds of sea stars attached to the pilings.

Birds that frequent the park include towhees, robins, crows, song sparrows, black-capped chickadees, great blue herons, gulls, Barrow's goldeneyes and common mergansers.

The rock bluffs and coves of Caulfeild Park have been shaped by the action of ice over the last two million years. Wave action and atmospheric weathering since the ice left about 12,000 years ago have given the final touch to their forms.

Two principal types of rock make up the rocks and bluffs of Caulfeild Park: a dark-banded metamorphic rock called the Caulfeild gneiss and a younger light-

The rocks at Caulfeild Park make a perfect place for exploration and a picnic.
John Parkinson

An oystercatcher uses its long red bill to pry mussels and limpets from rocks. *Mark Habdas*

coloured granitic rock with a salt and pepper appearance.

Other types of rock in the park are pegmatite (large crystals of quartz, feldspar and white mica) and aplite (very small crystals of quartz and feldspar). These constitute dikes within the granitic rocks.

Visit anytime but especially when the lilies and camas are blooming in April or May. Remember the saying "Leave them be for others to see."

Nearby Locations

- Lighthouse Park is a 0.5-kilometre (0.3-mile) walk to the west along Water Lane
- Cypress Falls Park is a 1.5-kilometre (0.9-mile) uphill walk along Piccadilly North and Caulfeild Dr.

Some Alerts

- slippery trails
- rough, rocky terrain

More Information

West Vancouver map and guide: www.westvancouver.ca/Government/maps/municipal-map/dwv-municipal-map.htm

West Vancouver Municipal Hall: 604-925-7000 or www.westvancouver.ca

Caulfeild Walk from the West Vancouver Archives: www.westvancouver.ca/Residents/Level2.aspx?id=608

Cypress Falls Park

by Juliet Pendray

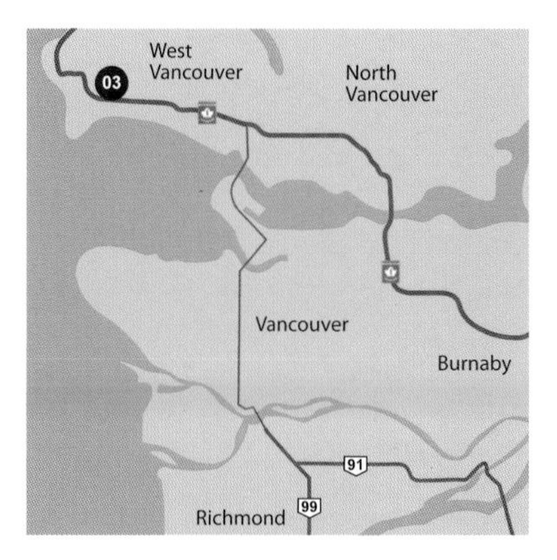

Hidden, forested, waterfall wilderness in a pocket canyon

Location

Cypress Falls Park is in northwest West Vancouver at the end of Woodgreen Place off Woodgreen Dr.

Transit Information

From downtown Vancouver, board the #253 Caulfeild bus. Soon after you pass under the Upper Levels Hwy., alight at the Woodgreen Place and Woodgreen Dr. stop. Note that on your return you must flag the bus driver to stop.
For up-to-date information, contact TransLink at www.translink.ca or 604-953-3333.

Introduction

Cypress Falls Park, administered by the District of West Vancouver, is easily accessible from the city, but being there feels as if you are out in the wilds. Visit this unspoiled old-growth forest oasis with spectacular waterfalls for an hour or two or explore its attractions and wildlife for most of a day.

While the park is large—32.4 hectares (80 acres)—the boundaries help to keep a new visitor from getting lost. Currently the trail signage is poor, and there is no map at the entrance, but there are plans for improvement. Cypress Creek bisects the park north-south; human habitation lies to the west and south, and to the north there is a gravel road. Elevation ranges from 167 to 290 metres (548 to 951 feet). Trails are packed dirt, bumpy with roots and rocks, easily walked on and varying from flat to steep. In summer, parts of the river are accessible for a dip in the cold mountain water. Good riverside spots for lunch include the area by the wooden bridge and the upper part of the park, in sight of the upper waterfalls. Always keep an eye out for bears.

A pair of lightning bugs mate. This type of firefly does not emit light. *James Holkko*

Natural History Visit

From the bus stop, walk downhill a few metres and take a left onto Woodgreen Place into the parking lot. The trailhead is at the far end. It takes three minutes to get this far.

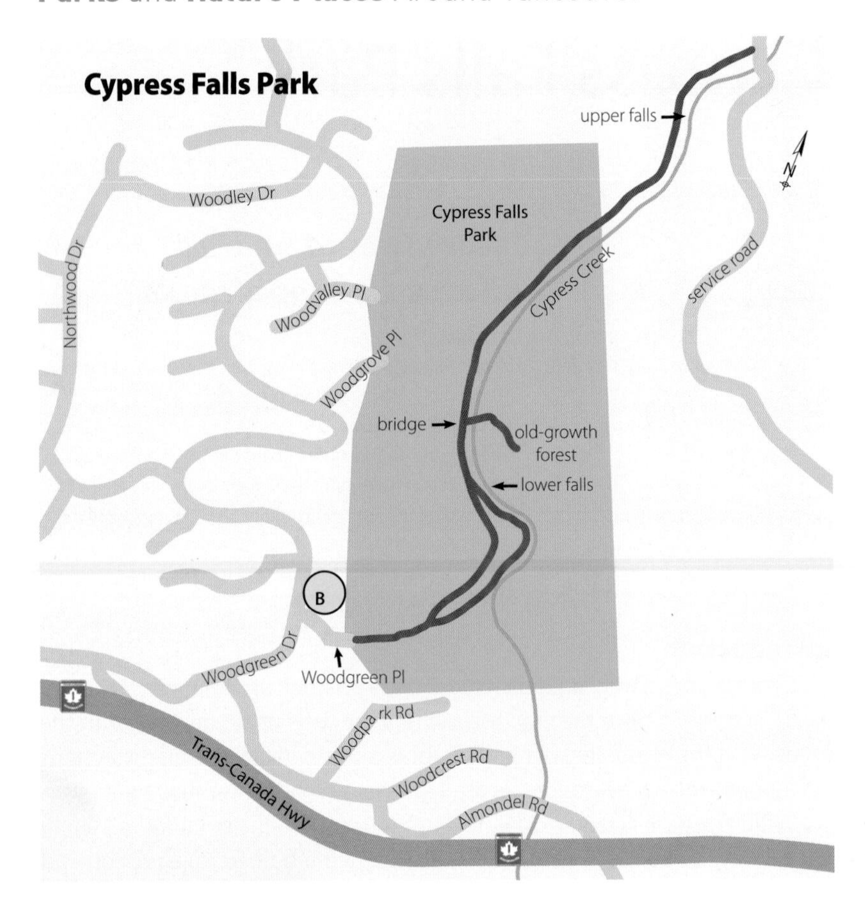

Gnome-plants have no chlorophyll. They steal nutrients from underground fungus.
James Holkko

Soon after the trailhead, you have a choice of trails. Take the left trail that follows a higher route up the west side of the creek. It passes the lower waterfalls and a bridge, then climbs to the upper waterfalls just beyond a fence marking the park boundary. After you enjoy the falls, return on the same trail to the bridge. You can cross it for a short side trip over the river and up the bank to visit the old-growth forest to the east. Return over the bridge to the west bank to follow the lower trail, which lies closer to the creek, back to the trailhead. A fast walk from the upper waterfalls directly back to the trailhead takes about 30 minutes.

Along the trail are old-growth and second-growth western redcedar, western hemlock, Douglas-fir and a few western white pines. Some ancient Douglas-firs are up to 8 metres (26 feet) around and over 400 years old!

Scars from fires show how the thick, corky bark defends a Douglas-fir from flames.

The trails weave among giant boulders and nurse logs draped with lush mosses and liverworts. Fallen trees and stumps nourish the forest plants; they also feed and provide homes for birds, insects and the fungi needed to complete the ecological cycle of this healthy forest.

Woodpeckers have been at work on trees bordering the trail to Cypress Falls.
James Holkko

In summer, pink coralroot orchids and white Indian-pipe, also called ghost flower, bloom near the trail. In the river gorge itself, graceful fronds of maidenhair fern reach out to the spray from the waterfalls. Riverside, you can find small flowering plants like saxifrage and small-leaved chickweed. Between June and August salmonberry, huckleberry and Oregon grape cycle from flower to fruit throughout the park.

In late summer and early fall, the brittle-gill russula mushrooms bloom from the ground with caps coloured bright red, purple, green, pink, black, white or yellow. Deadly but beautiful white-flecked amanita mushrooms break out of their half-buried egg-like encasings, and in the later fall, shiny orange jelly mushrooms adorn wet logs.

Cypress Falls Park is also popular with animal life. Chittering squir-rels, rotund winter wrens, raven pairs, chickadees, sapsuckers and pine siskins thrive in the treetops. Huge green and black slugs undulate fearlessly across the trails in search of anything edible that can't run away.

The west side of the park is a slightly drier and warmer habitat, favoured by white pines, arbutus trees and other plants more characteristic of a Gulf Islands type habitat. Also on the west side, a small wetland hosts bright green skunk cabbages and other wet-loving plants.

Of geological interest in the area of the upper waterfalls are the many inclusions—rounded chunks of dark-coloured rock averaging about 10 centimetres (3.9 inches) in diameter—of metamorphic rocks that were intruded

The rushing waters of Cypress Creek flow into Burrard Inlet just east of Caulfeild. *James Holkko*

by granitic magma approximately 100 million years ago. Also, there is an interesting plunge pool at the base of the upper waterfalls.

Early summer to mid-fall is the best time to visit. The river receives the most sunshine between about 12 p.m. and 2 p.m. The park has attractions in all seasons, but the rainy seasons make the trails muddy and the river high, fast and inaccessible.

Nearby Locations

- Caulfeild Park is a 1.5-kilometre (0.9-mile) downhill walk along Caulfeild Dr. and Piccadilly North
- Cypress Provincial Park trail system: an open gate just before the upper waterfalls indicates the park boundary. Trails from here and the park's east side lead into the provincial park trail system. These are very long hikes, and there is no public transit to and from the provincial park.

Some Alerts

- bears
- poor signage on the trails; use the river as your guide
- steep drops at the side of some trails; do not go off the trail, as the crumbling cliff edge could be very dangerous
- fast-flowing river

More Information

West Vancouver map and guide: www.westvancouver.ca/Government/maps/municipal-map/dwv-municipal-map.htm
West Vancouver Municipal Hall: 604-925-7000 or www.westvancouver.ca
Map of Cypress Provincial Park: www.env.gov.bc.ca/bcparks/

Hollyburn Ridge

by Katharine Steig

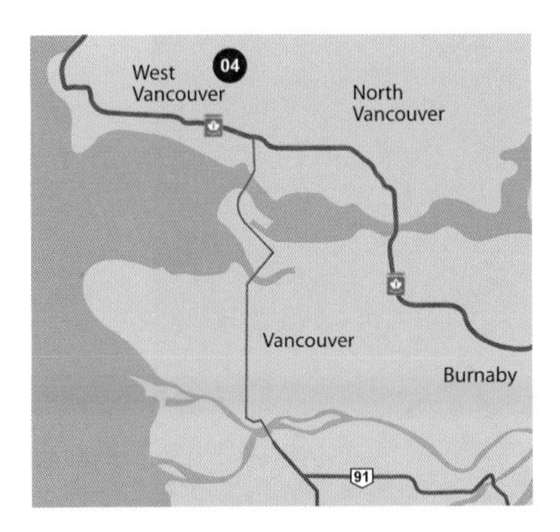

Peaceful, forested, mountainside trail leading to a fast-flowing creek

Location

Hollyburn Ridge is in northeast West Vancouver at 1121 Millstream Rd. just east of Henlow Rd.

Transit Information

From downtown Vancouver, board the #254 British Properties bus to the British Properties and alight at the Eyremount Dr. and Crestwell Rd. stop.

For up-to-date information, contact TransLink at www.translink.ca or 604-953-3333.

Introduction

Hollyburn Ridge refers to the more than 970 hectares (2,396 acres) of forested land on the lower slopes of Hollyburn Mountain above the residential development in West Vancouver. The ridgeline, with Hollyburn Peak rising behind it, is clearly visible from Vancouver. The lower part of Hollyburn Ridge is on undeveloped British Pacific Properties land, the middle section is owned by the District of West Vancouver and the upper part extends into Cypress Provincial Park.

The distinctive vase-shaped woolly chanterelle grows near Douglas-fir trees. *James Holkko*

Hollyburn Ridge has a rich natural and cultural history and is treasured by those who value its wilderness ambience so close to the city. Its numerous trails and appealing destination points make possible a great variety of hikes, both short and long. The beauty of its forest is a constant delight, with several small lakes and streams adding special interest. Although most of lower Hollyburn Ridge was logged from the late 19th to the mid-20th century, the forest is regenerating. There are old-growth stands higher up the mountainside.

This description focusses primarily on the Brothers Creek Fire Rd., and we suggest some additional hiking destinations. Bring a map on your hike, since there are several trail options in this area.

The Brothers Creek waterfall is a refreshing place to rest while hiking up Hollyburn.
James Holkko

Natural History Visit

From the bus stop above Eyremount Dr., walk one block up Crestline Rd. to Henlow Rd., then left one block on Henlow Rd. and right one block on Millstream Rd. to 1121 Millstream, where the trailhead is located.

The Brothers Creek Fire Rd. leads gently uphill from the trailhead, at an elevation of 380 metres (1,246 feet), and continues up the far east side of

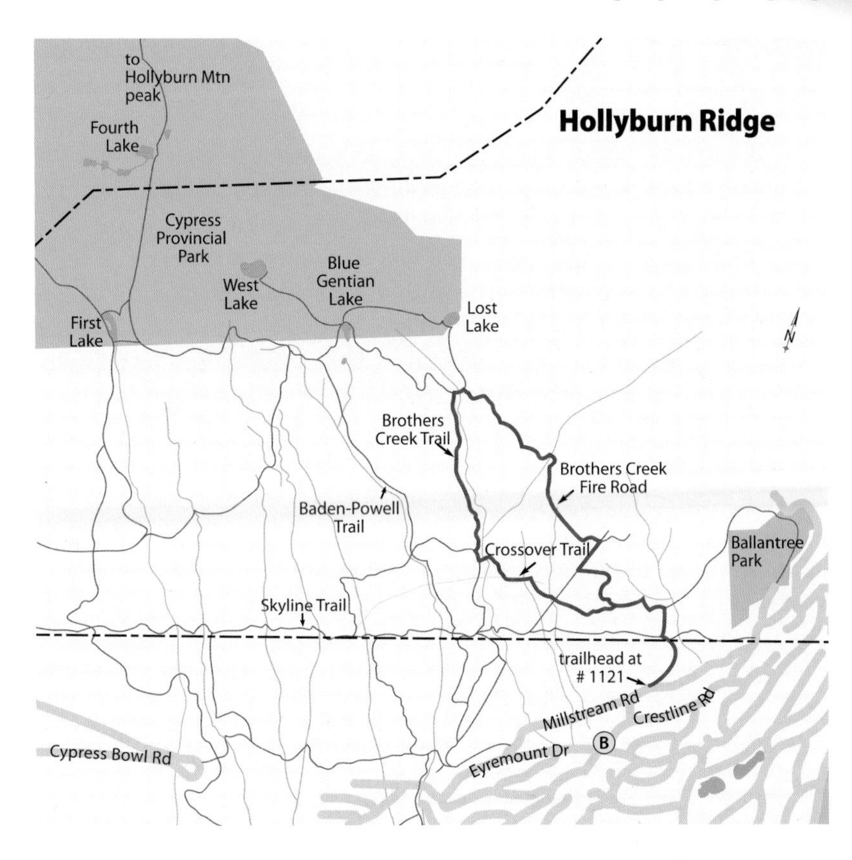

Brothers Creek. The first section passes through an attractive regenerating second-growth forest of western hemlock, western redcedar, red alder and Douglas-fir with an understory of salal, Oregon grape, salmonberry, thimbleberry, red huckleberry and other shrubs. The ground is covered with sword and deer fern, foamflower, bunchberry, coast boykinia and many other forest plants. Small streams flow alongside or across the trail in several places.

A short distance above the intersection with the Skyline Trail, a 200-tonne (220-ton) glacial erratic lies stranded on the slope to the right, evidence of a glacier that left the area about 12,000 years ago. Numerous large western redcedar and Douglas-fir stumps have springboard notches from old-time logging. Posts with numbers refer to West Vancouver's forestry heritage brochures.

Farther along the understory becomes increasingly lush with devil's club, the pleasantly pungent stink currant, blueberry bushes, false azalea, skunk cabbage, Pacific bleeding heart, queen's cup lilies, clasping and rosy twistedstalk, false lily-of-the-valley, five-leaved bramble and yellow wood violets. Large, awe-inspiring western redcedars attract attention along the trail. Amabilis firs begin to appear as you climb. Mountain hemlock and yellow-cedar cones now mingle with the cones of western hemlock and redcedar on the forest floor. In autumn many different species of fungi make a colourful show.

Winter wrens, Swainson's thrushes, golden-crowned kinglets, bushtits, red-breasted nuthatches and other forest dwellers serenade hikers. You may also hear a pileated woodpecker or small Douglas squirrel.

About two hours up the trail, you will encounter the sound of a rushing waterfall and then a bridge over the creek at an elevation of 720 metres (2,362 feet). Here you can cross the bridge and take the rather rough Brothers Creek Trail down the west side of the creek, passing near the falls and enjoying more ancient trees, clusters of scraggly yews, and in early summer, stands of western coralroot orchids. A second bridge takes you back to the east side of Brothers Creek and along the Crossover Trail to reconnect you with the Brothers Creek Fire Rd. and the trailhead.

Other options from the top of the Brothers Creek Fire Rd. are to continue up the east side of Brothers Creek to Lost Lake or to cross the bridge and head up to Blue Gentian Lake and beyond to West and First lakes. King (blue) gentians bloom at Lost, Blue Gentian and First lakes in late August. On warm summer days you can sample wild blueberries and swim at West Lake with northwestern salamanders.

Hollyburn Ridge can be hiked at any time of year, although snow at higher elevations in winter can be a serious hazard. The best times are spring through late fall.

Nearby Locations

- Cypress Provincial Park: the upper part of Hollyburn Ridge extends into the provincial park, but there is no public transportation from this destination

Some Alerts

- Bears and, rarely, cougars
- Hollyburn Ridge is a large wilderness area with many different trails; bring a good trail map or hiking guide and calculate beforehand the distance you plan to hike to avoid getting lost
- rough, rooty, slippery trails sometimes blocked by trees; parts of some trails are near drop-offs above creeks

More Information

West Vancouver map and guide: www.westvancouver.ca/Government/maps/municipal-map/dwv-municipal-map.htm

West Vancouver Municipal Hall: 604-925-7000 or www.westvancouver.ca

"Shakes, Shinglebolts and Steampots" and "Lawson Creek Forestry Heritage Walk," two self-guiding forestry history brochures, are available at West Vancouver Municipal Hall.

Map of Cypress Provincial Park: www.bcparks.ca

Ambleside Park

by Sheena Vennesland

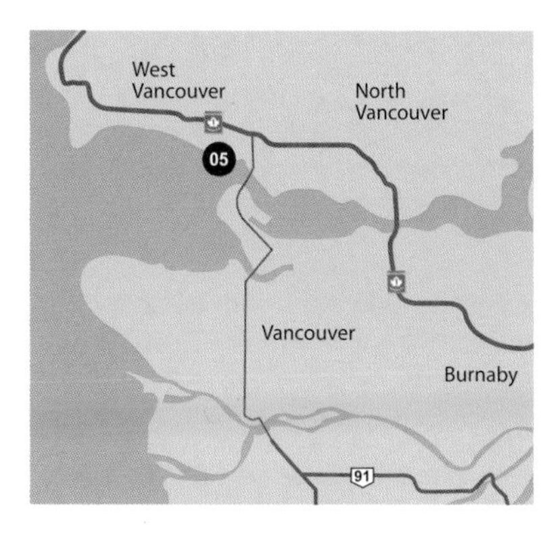

Passing cruise ships, sandy beach and a bird refuge

Location

Ambleside Park is in southeast West Vancouver at Marine Dr. and 13th St.

Transit Information

From downtown Vancouver, board the #250 Horseshoe Bay bus, the #251 Queens bus or the #252 Inglewood bus and alight at the Marine Dr. and 13th St. stop.

For up-to-date information, contact TransLink at www.translink.ca or 604-953-3333.

Introduction

Ambleside Park, managed by the District of West Vancouver, is 25 hectares (62 acres). Its setting, on the shores of the First Narrows sea lane to Vancouver's bustling inner harbour, is unique at any time of the year and hard to beat in summer. It is close to the graceful span of Lions Gate Bridge, the estuary of the Capilano River and the steep cliffs of Prospect Point across the channel. Ambleside is a great place for recreation and bird watching, and also to watch in close-up the fascinating business of the sea. Coastal marine traffic—tugs, barges, tankers and pleasure boats—move nimbly with the tide compared to the heavy ocean-going freighters and many-decked Alaska cruise ships, which approach the bridge with notable caution.

Part of Ambleside Park is the ancestral land of First Nations, who call it Ch'tl'am. Don't miss the impressive *Spirit of the Mountain* sculpture by Rick Harry of the Squamish Nation at the entrance to the park. Also visit the huge carved *Squamish Nation Welcome Figure* at the end of the rocky promontory.

A belted kingfisher is ever ready to catch a fish in the water below.
Ed Robertson

Natural History Visit

From the bus stop walk down to the park at the foot of 13th St.; there you have a choice of pathways. Either walk along the popular seaside route beside the ocean and the Capilano River or take a quieter path nearer the railway tracks.

Among the peaceful byways and treed trails on the east side of Amble-

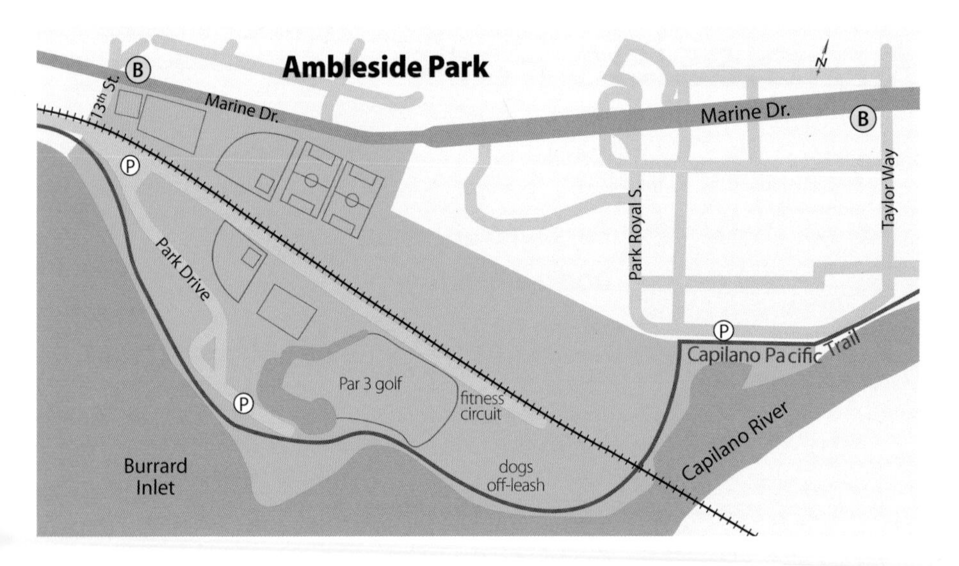

side Park, many visitors, including keen birders and nature photographers, prefer the tranquility of the pond, screened from park activity by trees and native shrubs. There the fall and winter peak population of some 300 wild ducks gradually disperses through spring and early summer to nesting grounds elsewhere. They leave the pond to residents such as mute swans, great blue herons, belted kingfishers with their rasping call, and of particular delight to children, numerous turtles basking on floating logs when the weather is warm.

Dog owners are encouraged to take pets to the dog park rather than natural areas. *John Parkinson*

Seasonal migrants—among them green herons, colourful warblers and red-winged blackbirds—arrive in spring and early summer from southern wintering grounds. They join the all-year population of towhees, juncos, sparrows and chickadees. On the neighbouring wetland north of the pond, brilliant dragonflies flit about, beavers tend their dams, and near the mouth of the Capilano River, otters roll and play in warm summer waters.

You may see a variety of diving ducks offshore on undulating ocean swells; these may include occasional common or red-breasted mergansers, Barrow's or common goldeneyes, surf scoters or seagoing cormorants. Watch too for an osprey or bald eagle patrolling high above First Narrows for its next meal. You may see a breakneck dive and—if it's successful—the great bird's steady climb, up, up and away with a substantial fish secured in its powerful claws.

A sociable place, the park also provides many opportunities for informal

The Ambleside duck pond is a haven for a wide variety of overwintering waterfowl.
John Parkinson

recreation: a combined basketball-skateboard court, tennis courts, volleyball on the beach, picnic tables in sun or shade at the concession near the children's playground, swimming in calm waters on a designated sandy beach and summertime Par 3 mini-golf on a pretty landscaped course.

The fitness circuit east of the golf course is little used because most people prefer to walk or jog on the uninterrupted ocean and riverside trail, part of it an off-leash area and designated swimming beach for the dogs.

The best time to visit depends on the taste and inclination of each visitor. Though summer is by far the most popular, there are fewer wild waterfowl.

Nearby Locations

- the John Lawson Park locale is a short walk to the west on Argyle St.; if you walk farther, you will reach a restored salmon-bearing creek and the Centennial Sea Walk, which extends along the shore to the pier at 25th St.
- Capilano Regional Park is a short walk to the north

Some Alerts

- slippery rocks if you climb down to the river's edge

More Information

West Vancouver map and guide: www.westvancouver.ca/Government/maps/municipal-map/dwv-municipal-map.htm
West Vancouver Municipal Hall: 604-925-7000 or www.westvancouver.ca
Cruise ship schedule: www.portmetrovancouver.com/vanAlaCruise

Capilano River Regional Park

by Jennifer Swanston

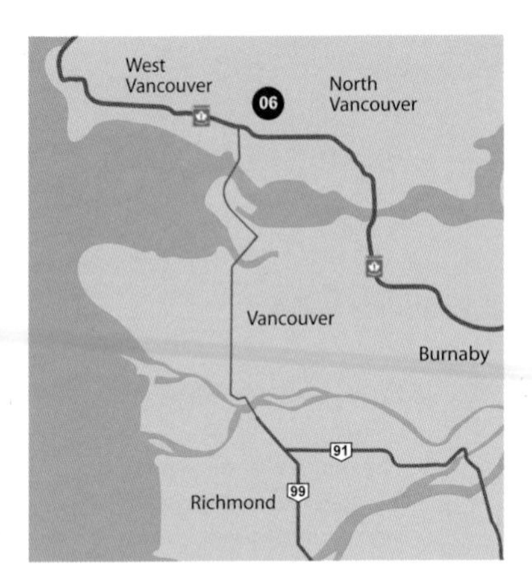

Salmon hatchery in a deeply carved river canyon

Location

Capilano River Regional Park is at the west side of North Vancouver at Capilano Rd. and Capilano Park Rd.

Transit Information

From the Lonsdale Quay SeaBus terminal, board the #236 Grouse Mountain bus and alight at the Capilano Rd. and Mount Crown Rd. stop. Alternatively, continue up to the Nancy Greene Way and Prospect Ave. stop and enter the park near Cleveland Dam.

For up-to-date information, contact TransLink at www.translink.ca or 604-953-3333.

Introduction

Capilano River Regional Park, occupying 160 hectares (395 acres), covers a large area of canyon carved out by the Capilano River. Sheltered beneath a temperate rainforest canopy, the park is home to the river and its populations of salmon and trout, the Capilano Hatchery and the Cleveland Dam.

American dippers stand and bob on rocks, then plunge underwater for insects and fish. *Les Leighton*

Walk the beautiful forest trails that wind along the cliffs above the Capilano River, stopping at viewing platforms to enjoy spectacular views of the river racing through its canyon, salmon darkening the river in their numbers during fall spawning, huge old-growth coniferous trees and water cascading over the Cleveland Dam. Walk across the paved top of the Cleveland Dam and gaze out over Capilano Lake, one of three dam reservoirs that provide drinking water for Metro Vancouver. If the weather is clear, admire beautiful views of the Skyride on the side of Grouse Mountain and the two mountain peaks that make up The Lions at the head of the lake.

Natural History Visit

From the Mount Crown Rd. bus stop, cross to the west side of Capilano

Coho and chinook salmon and steelhead raised at Capilano Hatchery go downriver to sea.
Steve Britten

Rd., then walk down Capilano Park Rd. and leave the world of city streets behind. Enter a green, fresh place that's lush with towering trees and mossy cliffs. As you walk down Capilano Park Rd. you will descend into the Capilano Canyon. Notice how the air cools and feels moist against your cheek. After about 15 minutes you pass on your left Camp Capilano, a facility nestled in the heart of the forest.

The road ends at the Capilano Hatchery, where a visitor centre managed by Fisheries and Oceans Canada is open year-round to the public free of charge. If you visit in the late summer or fall, you can view masses of coho salmon entering the hatchery via a fish ladder. From the hatchery, views out over the river may include merganser duck mothers gathering their chicks up on their backs for safety or little grey American dippers bobbing beneath the water in search of aquatic insects, fish eggs or small fish to eat.

If you leave the bus at the Cleveland Dam, walk across the top of the dam and thrill at the views of water cascading down the spillway on one side and Capilano Lake with its mountain backdrop on the other. Take the Capilano Pacific Trail down the west side of the river toward the hatchery. After about 10 minutes, you'll see a trail marker on the left for the Giant Fir Trail. This leads past massive Douglas-fir and western redcedar trees, several of them more than 500 years old. One spectacular example is Grandpa Capilano, a

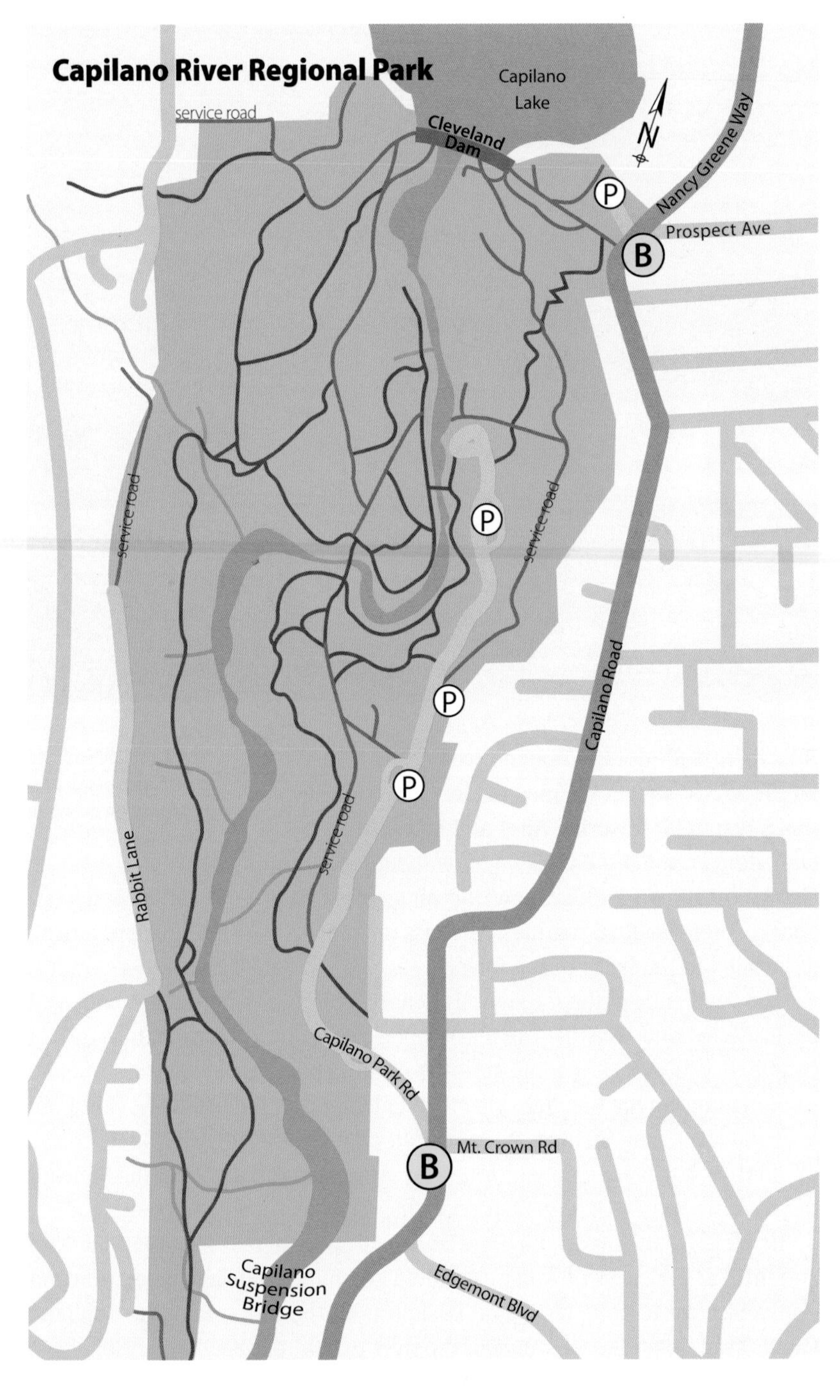

huge Douglas-fir tree said to be the largest remaining in the park. The tallest tree, near the parking lot at the fish hatchery, is over 61 metres (200 feet) tall and 1.8 metres (5.9 feet) thick.

Continue along the Giant Fir Trail to a fork. The left fork leads to a viewing platform built out over the river with a view up to the dam spillway. When the water is high, this spot is a whirlwind of mist and spray. The right fork of the trail leads to the Cable Pool Bridge and over to the hatchery. During summer when the water is low, you can often observe kayakers from this bridge.

If you stay on the west side of the river, the wonderful canyonside 30-minute Coho Loop walk takes you along the river and over the Pipeline Bridge then back up the east side to the hatchery. This bridge is built on top of a pipeline system that has been carrying drinking water to the city since the late 1800s. From here, river views are enhanced by lush plant life such as delicate maidenhair ferns visible on the dripping canyon walls.

Deeply grooved bark encases Grandpa Capilano, the largest Douglas-fir in the park.
Steve Britten

Visit year-round. In late summer and fall, view returning spawning salmon in the hatchery. In winter and spring, high water often cascades over the dam and roars down the canyon. In Capilano River Regional Park you and your family will visit the heart of the temperate rain forest and leave with misty memories of swirling water and giant trees.

Nearby Locations

- Capilano Suspension Bridge is to the south; access it from Capilano Rd.
- Ambleside Park is to the south; enter by walking farther down the river
- Grouse Mountain Skyride is to the north

Some Alerts

- bears
- steep cliffs
- footbridges and viewing decks are slippery when wet

More Information

Metro Vancouver Regional Parks:
www.metrovancouver.org/services/parks_lscr/regionalparks/Pages/default.aspx
Metro Vancouver Regional Parks West Area Office: 604-224-5739
Capilano Salmon Hatchery: 604-666-1790 or
www-heb.pac.dfo-mpo.gc.ca/facilities/capilano/capilano_e.htm

Grouse Mountain

by Devin Manky

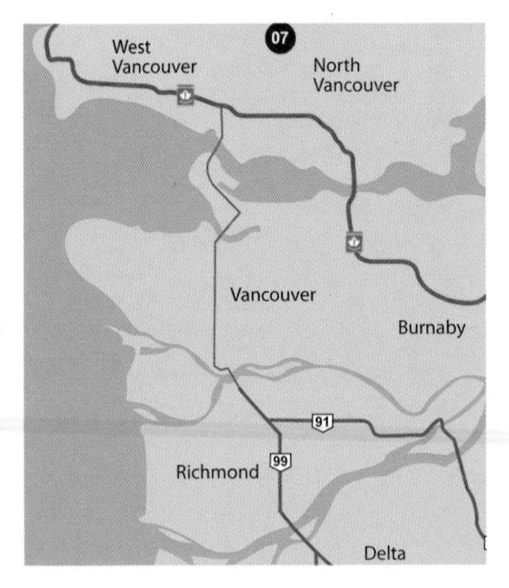

Hike or Skyride to alpine mountaintop trails and vistas

Location

Grouse Mountain is in northwest North Vancouver at the end of Nancy Greene Way off Capilano Rd.

Transit Information

From the Lonsdale Quay SeaBus terminal, board the #236 Grouse Mountain bus and alight at the final stop at Grouse Mountain Skyride.

Then either board the Grouse Mountain Skyride to the mountaintop or hike one of the trails up the mountain and perhaps ride down.

For up-to-date information, contact TransLink at www.translink.ca or 604-953-3333.

Introduction

Grouse Mountain was named by the first recorded hikers to reach the summit in October 1894. In those days, climbing Grouse Mountain was a three- or four-day epic journey; there was no bridge across Burrard Inlet and no road to the base. Along the way, the climbers hunted a blue grouse (now called sooty grouse) and honoured the plentiful game bird by calling the peak Grouse Mountain. Soon after this first ascent, Grouse Mountain began attracting hundreds of intrepid hikers.

At the alpine plateau, the elevation is 1,128 metres (3,700 feet) and the views go on forever! Summertime activities include guided eco-walks,

A Townsend's chipmunk feeds on mountain-ash berries. *Devin Manky*

The Skyride is an easy way to ascend Grouse Mountain.
Grouse Mountain Resorts Ltd.

lumberjack shows, falconry demonstrations and wildlife interpretation at the Refuge for Endangered Wildlife. Wintertime activities include ice-skating, snowshoeing, skiing and snowboarding.

There is a significant charge for riding the Skyride up and down; it costs less to ride down only. It is a good idea to check this beforehand. Annual memberships are also available.

Natural History Visit

After arriving at the base of the mountain, you can choose to either ride the Grouse Mountain Skyride or hike to the mountaintop. If you are hiking up Grouse Mountain, head to the east side of the parking lot to find the entrance to the popular Grouse Grind Trail or the British Columbia Mountain Club (BCMC) Trail. Make sure you have sturdy footwear and are carrying water. The Grouse Grind Trail is 2.9 kilometres (1.8 miles) long and gains 853 metres (2,800 feet). The average completion time is about 1.5 hours. Note that the Grouse Grind Trail is generally closed during winter and in inclement weather. If you hike up the mountain, you may want to ride the Skyride back down to the parking lot.

Once on the mountaintop you'll see a variety of plants and animals. Mountain hemlock, yellow-cedar and amabilis fir dominate the mountain-top. Scattered around are numerous blueberry and huckleberry bushes, and in the spring and summer a variety of flowers grow in the subalpine

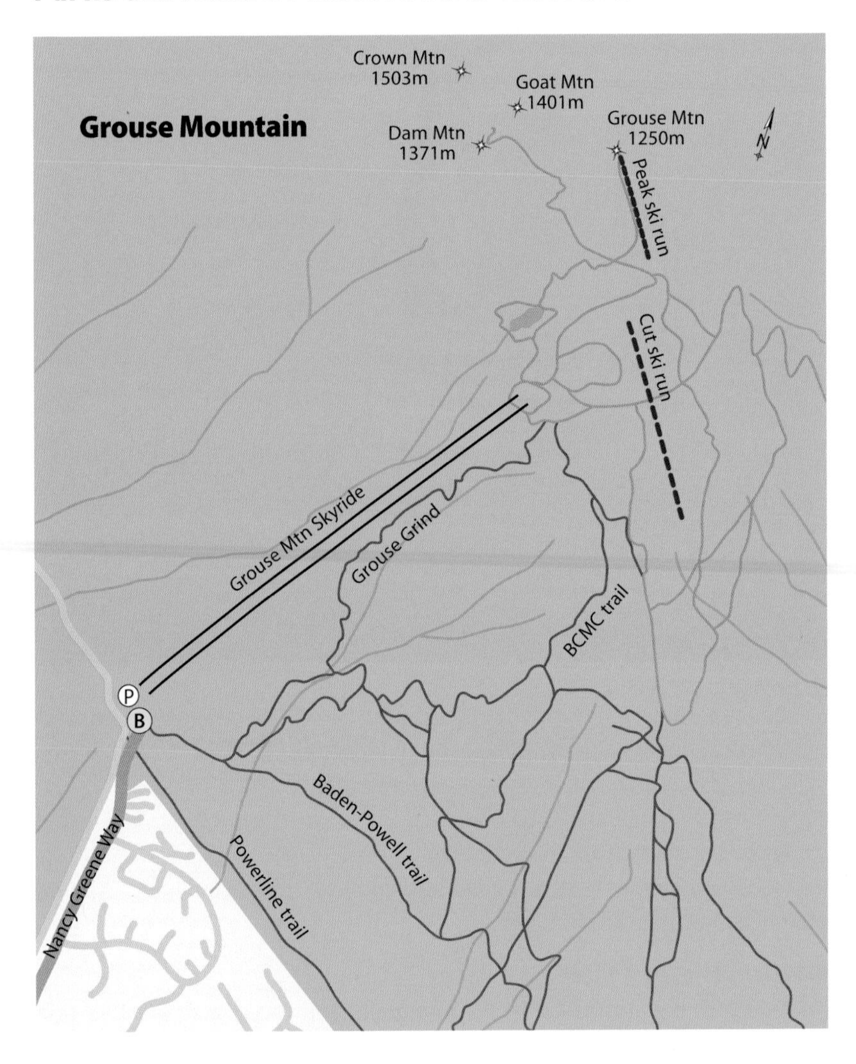

meadows. On Grouse Mountain the snow usually lasts until early summer, so bushes may not have leaves until then.

Native mountaintop wildlife is plentiful, and it is not uncommon to see small herds of black-tailed deer grazing within a few feet of the pathways. Black bears, pine martens, Douglas squirrels, lynx, snowshoe hares and coyotes are just a few of the mammals that you may see while hiking around Grouse Mountain. Bird species are also there in abundance. Flocks of dark-eyed juncos, red crossbills and white-crowned and golden-crowned sparrows are a common sight, and you can see Steller's jays and gray jays throughout the year. Over 60 common ravens have been counted in a single day on the mountaintop plateau. Raptor species seen include bald eagles, red-tailed hawks, Cooper's hawks, sharp-shinned hawks, merlins, kestrels, peregrine falcons, barred owls, great horned owls and northern saw-whet owls.

Just outside the main chalet you can find the entrance to the eco-trails. Here you can take either a guided or a self-guided walk around the man-made Blue Grouse Lake and the *híwus* First Nations feasthouse. On this trail you may find in season the flowering copperbush, false azalea and white-flowered rhododendron.

When the breeding season starts, a male sooty grouse displays his colourful throat patch.
Mark Wynja

At the end of the walk you exit near the grizzly bear habitat, part of the Refuge for Endangered Wildlife. At the refuge be sure to visit orphaned grizzly bear cubs that are being given a second chance at life.

Finally Grouse Mountain is also the starting point for many ventures into Vancouver's backcountry region. Many hikers use the plateau as a starting point for trips to Dam, Goat and Crown mountains as well as the Haynes Valley route to Lynn Valley.

It's always a good time to visit Grouse Mountain. However, most organized activities are geared around the summer season from May until the Thanksgiving weekend in October and the winter season from November until April.

Nearby Locations

- Capilano River Regional Park and Capilano Suspension Bridge are to the south

Some Alerts

- bears and cougars
- steep drop-offs away from the trails
- rapidly changing mountaintop weather—if you are hiking, make sure you are well equipped and have appropriate maps and guidebooks
- sturdy footwear and water bottles are essential

More Information

Contact: 604-984-0661 or www.grousemountain.com

Lynn Canyon Park

by Bill Stephen

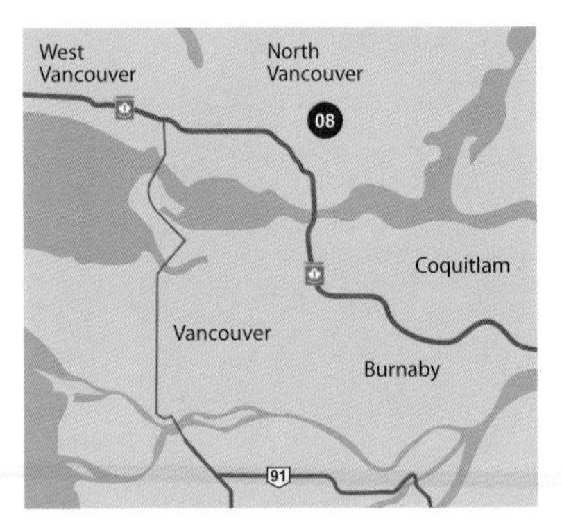

Mountain river thundering through rocky canyon walls

Location

Lynn Canyon Park is in the centre of North Vancouver at the end of Peters Rd. off Lynn Valley Rd.

Transit Information

From the Lonsdale Quay SeaBus terminal, board the #229 Westlynn/Phibbs Exchange bus and alight at the Peters Rd. and Duval Rd. stop.

For up-to-date information, contact TransLink at www.translink.ca or 604-953-3333.

Introduction

The brightest jewel in the crown of the District of North Vancouver's park system is the 250-hectare (618-acre) Lynn Canyon Park. It is a popular summer attraction for folks seeking a break from the summer heat or the stress of the city. An educational Ecology Centre is open to the public on a donation basis and hosts many splendid nature exhibits and activities designed for all ages. A prominently situated café welcomes visitors.

BC's largest woodpecker, the pileated woodpecker, excavates tree trunks for insects. *Mark Wynja*

Lynn Canyon Suspension Bridge provides an exciting wobbly trip high above the river.
Bill Stephen

The remainder of the park provides an excellent day-hiking experience with plenty of nature served up in a dramatic fashion.

Natural History Visit

From the bus stop it is a short walk along Peters Rd. into the park, located at the edge of the beautiful historic community of Lynn Valley. Inside the park the landscape plunges suddenly into an evergreen world of lush temperate rain forest and pristine waterfalls. The sounds of the town fade, the

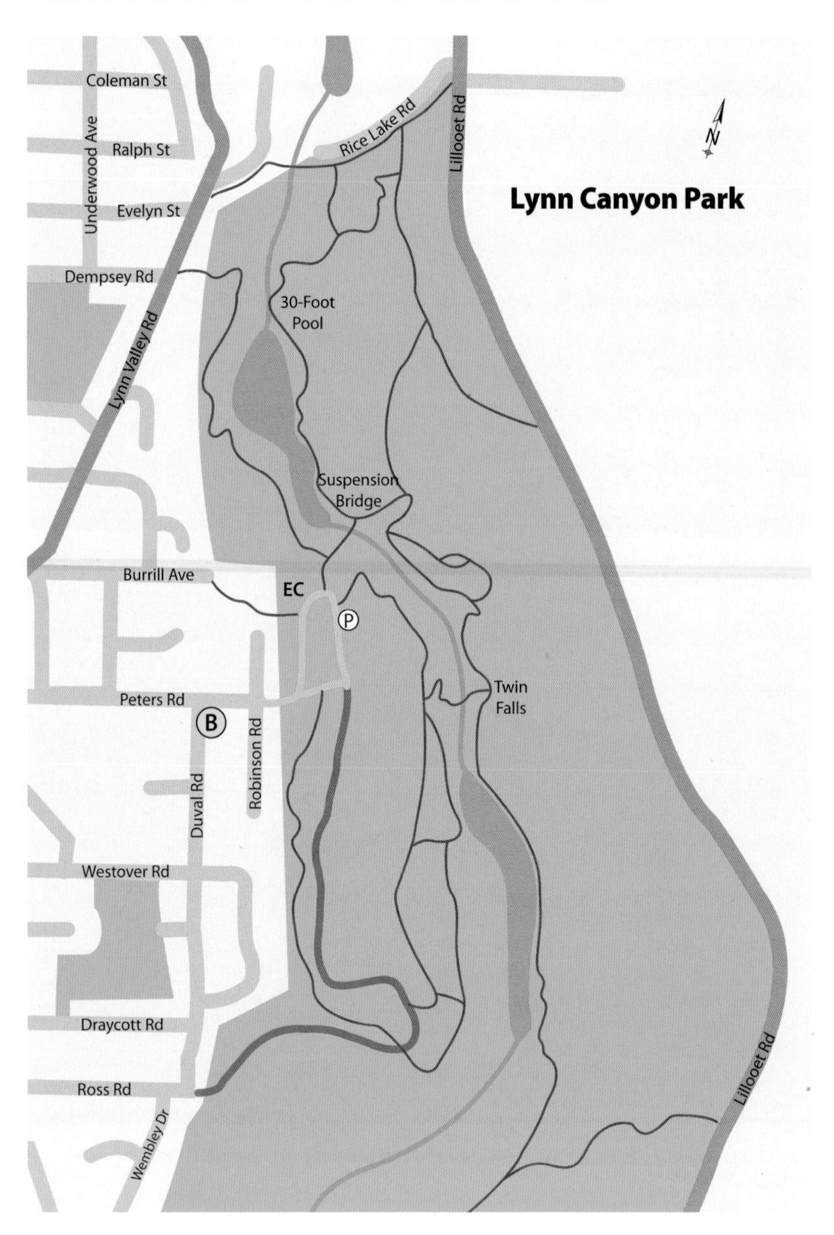

air immediately freshens and an explorer's mood will mellow on entering the park's western gate. Gravity and the roar of the river will draw you first to the main attraction, the suspension bridge. Its dizzying height over the sharply cut canyon makes most visitors hesitate before stepping out, but the realization of its perfect safety calms those willing to have a little faith in human engineering. From your perch in the middle of the gently swaying bridge, you can look down upon two 15-metre (49-foot) waterfalls descending into churning pools of flotsam and froth.

The buff-coloured stomach identifies a Douglas squirrel, native to BC. *Wayne Weber*

Take your choice of trails that amble downward in all directions from the bridge. Clear signage will enable you to find your way deep into the canyon. Notice as you pass the eroded slopes; they relate the passage of immense time. They tell a story of how Lynn Creek or the neighbouring Seymour River flooded, was buried and recarved the landscape over multiple periods of glaciation. The canyon has ground itself through a bedrock fracture in the geologically brief time of 12,000 years since the end of the last ice age.

The park was logged over a century ago, as the massive stumps show. However, rich soils and plentiful rainfall have produced a replacement forest of giant trees. The trails, descending southward from either end of the suspension bridge, meander through especially impressive stands of Douglas-fir. Sheltered from the wind, many have attained heights of over 60 metres (197 feet). Salal, sword ferns and deer ferns blanket the forest floor. Look carefully for the delicate maidenhair fern clinging to cliff faces in the spray and spume of the canyon. Licorice ferns nestle in the thick moss coating the hardwood trees.

Local mammals sometimes seen in the park include Douglas squirrels, black bears and coyotes. Birds frequenting the area are chestnut-backed chickadees, hairy and pileated woodpeckers, varied thrushes, winter wrens, belted kingfishers and Steller's jays. Lucky visitors will notice a small drab grey bird flitting from boulder to boulder in the river during the winter high water; the American dipper astonishes observers when it dives into the rushing torrent to feed on the aquatic insects that shelter beneath the rocks.

Above: A boardwalk leads through deciduous trees beside Lynn Creek. *Steve Britten*

Left: Lynn Pool is a cool place to be on a hot summer day. *Bill Stephen*

On the trail, watch out for giant banana slugs and their black relatives.

Any time of year is good to visit, but a trip after a week of heavy rains is particularly exciting.

Nearby Locations

- Deep Cove: the Baden Powell Trail passes through the park, leading walkers 12 kilometres (7.5 miles) eastward to Deep Cove
- Lynn Headwaters Regional Park or the Lower Seymour Conservation Reserve: trails heading north from the park connect directly to these areas, but there may be no public transportation from these destinations

Some Alerts

- steep trails cover a challenging range of elevation
- swimming and cliff diving are forbidden; these activities are extremely dangerous and claim one or more lives every year

More Information

Lynn Canyon Park: www.lynncanyonparkguide.bc.ca/
Lynn Canyon Ecology Centre: 604-990-3755 or www.dnv.org/ecology
District of North Vancouver: 604-990-2311 or www.dnv.org
District of North Vancouver Park Rangers: 604-981-3149

Lower Seymour Conservation Reserve

by Jennifer Swanston

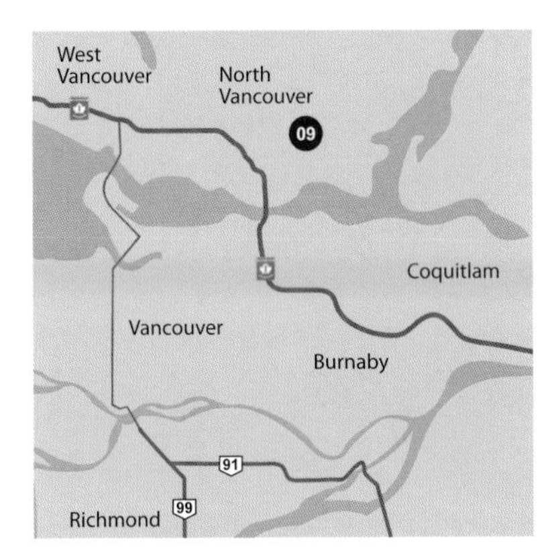

Mountain fishing lake, dense forests and logging artifacts

Location

Lower Seymour Conservation Reserve is in the north part of North Vancouver at the end of Rice Lake Rd. off Lynn Valley Rd.

Transit Information

From the Lonsdale Quay SeaBus terminal, board the #228 Lynn Valley bus to the final stop at Lynn Valley Rd. and Dempsey Rd.

For up-to-date information, contact TransLink at www.translink.ca or 604-953-3333.

Introduction

Sandwiched between Lynn Headwaters Regional Park and Mount Seymour Provincial Park, the 5,668-hectare (14,000-acre) Lower Seymour Conservation Reserve (LSCR) is a wonderful place for families to experience the mountainous terrain of the North Shore. It occupies approximately one-third of the 18,000-hectare (44,460-acre) Seymour Watershed. This watershed area is managed by the Metro Vancouver watershed division.

Black bears are a common sight on the North Shore. Keep your distance. *Mark Habdas*

The LSCR is technically not a park but an area being managed by Metro Vancouver for potential water use. The Seymour River is dammed to the north of this area, and the Seymour Reservoir provides drinking water for Vancouver. The area below the dam, the LSCR, is managed as a multi-use area while being reserved for future water use.

The area is popular for recreational activities such as hiking on the 25-kilometre (15.5-mile) network of forest trails and mountain biking on many of them. Biking or in-line skating is popular on the 11-kilometre (6.8-mile) paved Seymour Mainline Trailway that runs north toward the mountains and is accessible at the park entrance. Along the way you can view

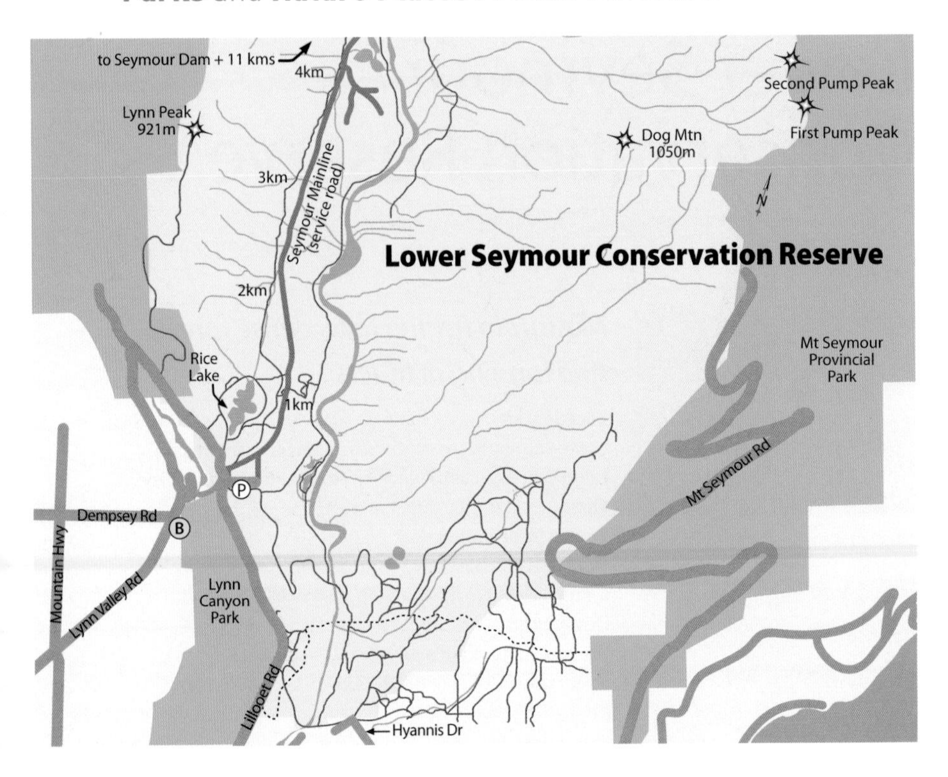

Mount Seymour and surrounding mountain peaks, and a steady breeze blows through the valley even in the heat of summer.

Rice Lake, once a source of water and a storage area for log shingle blocks, is now encircled by a lovely trail and stocked annually with rainbow trout. Fishing is popular at the Douglas Mowat Special Fisheries project, a wheelchair accessible floating dock. Trails lead through diverse forest habitats, over streams and along rushing waterways. Habitats within the reserve include a variety of forest types, river flood plain and alpine meadows.

Natural History Visit

From the bus stop, walk one block north up Lynn Valley Rd., then take the east branch to your right along the gravelled Rice Lake Rd., cross Lynn Creek Bridge and climb the path up the east side of Lynn Creek to the main gate area for the LSCR.

From the Learning Lodge near the main gate, a trail connects to the Rice Lake Loop. As you walk down this trail, note the reconstructed log flume on your left. In the past, logs cut here were transported down to waiting ships in these water-filled chutes. Continue along the trail for another few minutes and link up with the trail circling Rice Lake. Head right and walk briefly down the path to a clearing with a bench overlooking the lake. This spot provides a beautiful view of the lake with its mountain backdrop, and there

Douglas Mowat floating dock on Rice Lake is a great place to fish for rainbow trout. *Steve Britten*

is always a collection of mallard ducks here hoping for some seeds.

Continue around the lake until you reach the floating Douglas Mowat Special Fisheries wharf. The wheelchair accessible dock is a great spot for trying your luck at fishing, but remember to bring your fishing licence. Rice Lake is stocked annually with over 5,000 rainbow trout. If you are on the dock in spring or early summer, try looking down through the water to the bottom of the lake. Search for caddis fly larvae, snails, larval amphibians, tadpoles and a variety of aquatic insects roaming over the lake bottom in search of food.

Rice Lake is a sanctuary for summer-breeding waterfowl such as mallards. *Robyn Worcester*

As you continue the loop trail toward the northern end of the lake, notice the large submerged boulders along the lake edge. Watch for the small dragon-like bodies of rough-skinned newts swimming among the rocks. Continue meandering along the lake edge and listen to the variety of bird calls filling the air. Just before you close the loop trail at the south end of the lake, take the short spur trail to the right and walk up to the huge boulders. The writing on the rocks commemorates a plane crash on April 28, 1947, just west of Lake Elsay and high on the ridge that you can see from this spot. The main gate is a few hundred feet from here. As you

Hikers set off on an outing though the extensive LSCR trail system. *Steve Britten*

return across the Lynn Creek Bridge, stop once more to admire the beauty of this canyon carving its way through the North Shore mountains and the surrounding forest.

Visit year-round. In spring enjoy an overhead lattice of green leaves and the calls of many birds; in summer savour the scent of the dry forest floor. In fall watch for black bears searching for berries, and in winter enjoy the misty swirling rush of Lynn Creek.

Nearby Locations

- Lynn Headwaters Regional Park: at the foot of Rice Lake Rd. on the west side of Lynn Creek Bridge, the lovely Varley Trail meanders northward beside the clear, rushing waters of Lynn Creek for about 1.5 kilometre (0.9 mile) to the park
- Lynn Canyon Park is a 1-kilometre (0.6-mile) walk south along the Suspension Bridge Trail

Some Alerts

- bears and cougars
- it is important to stay on the trails to avoid getting lost
- bring a fishing licence if you plan to fish

More Information

Metro Vancouver Regional Parks:
www.metrovancouver.org/services/parks_lscr/regionalparks/Pages/default.aspx
Metro Vancouver Regional Parks West Area Office: 604-224-5739
LSCR Education Programs: 604-987-1273 or lscr_ed@metrovancouver.org

Maplewood Conservation Area

by Al and Jude Grass

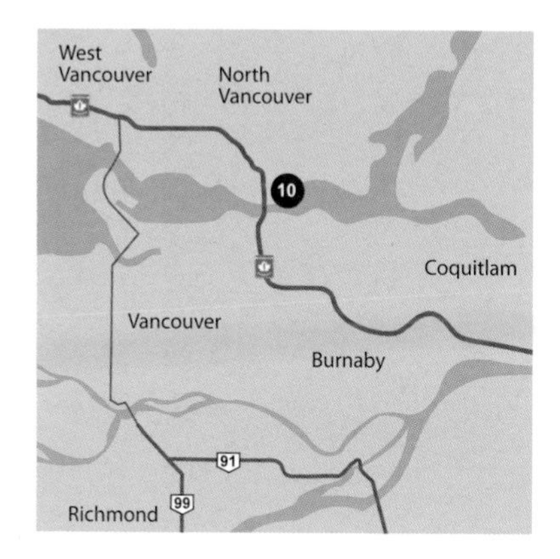

Numerous bird habitats in a small waterside sanctuary

Location

Maplewood Conservation Area is in the south part of North Vancouver at 2645 Dollarton Hwy. just east of Forester St.

Transit Information

From the Lonsdale Quay SeaBus terminal, board the #239 Park Royal/Phibbs Exchange/Capilano College bus to Phibbs Exchange. Then transfer to the #212 Deep Cove bus and alight at the Dollarton Hwy. and Forester St. stop.
For up-to-date information, contact TransLink at www.translink.ca or 604-953-3333.

Introduction

Maplewood Conservation Area is just east of the Ironworkers Memorial Second Narrows Crossing. It is a nature sanctuary, not a park, and is managed by the Wild Bird Trust of British Columbia. There are no entrance fees, but donations are welcome.

The sanctuary of 28 hectares (69 acres) features habitats including salt marsh, forest, hedge, meadow, tidal flats and both open salt water and fresh water. This variety is reflected in its rich diversity of bird life; more than 240 species have been reliably reported from the site.

The North Shore's last significant salt marsh habitat is off-limits to visitors. *Al and Jude Grass*

Volunteers staff the sanctuary office of the Wild Bird Trust of British Columbia. A receptionist is always available on Saturdays, and you can purchase membership and checklists.

Natural History Visit

From the bus stop on Dollarton Hwy., look for the Maplewood Conservation Area and Pacific Environmental Science Centre (PESC) signs. Go through the pedestrian portal at the gateway and proceed all the way past the PESC building on your left to the Maplewood Sanctuary office and notice

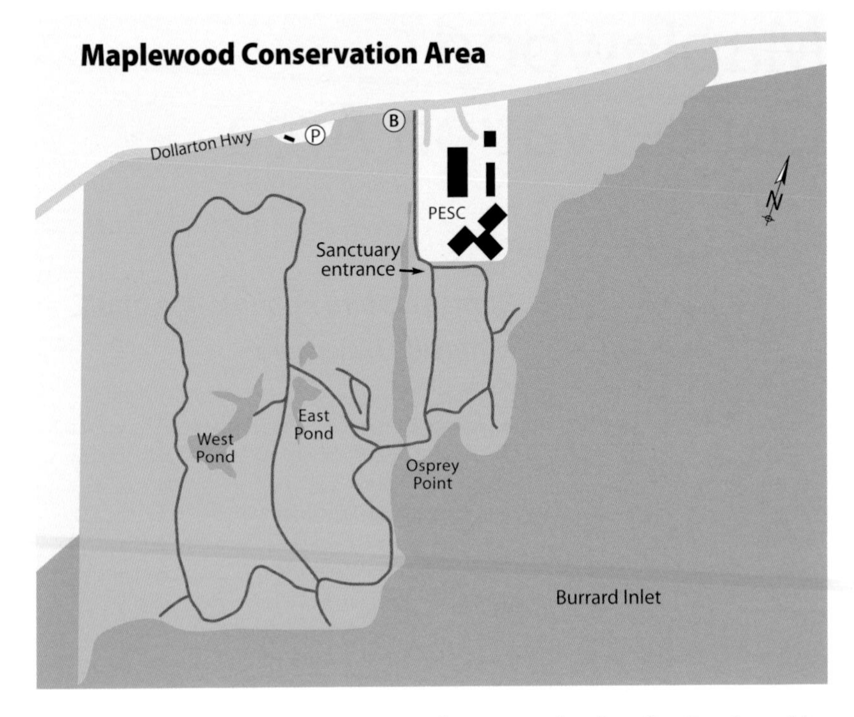

boards. These show the sanctuary's fine network of trails. On the white board on the south side of the office, look for a list of birds and other wildlife seen recently.

The recommended walking route is to turn left just before the main notice board onto the trail leading to and around the flats. As this route returns you to the main trail, you come to a bridge over the Barge Channel at Osprey Point. After crossing the bridge, keep to the left side trail, which heads to the shore of Burrard Inlet and includes Otter Point. The trail passes by excellent meadow habitat.

A male mallard in flight shows off the brightly coloured bands on his wings.
Al and Jude Grass

At the West Pond, the largest freshwater body in the sanctuary, look for mallard, wood duck and pied-billed grebe. In winter it is one of the best Lower Mainland sites to view ring-necked ducks. There are benches at various locations along the trail where you can sit and enjoy the peace and beauty here. Year-round, keep a look out for deer, river otters and harbour seals.

The Barge Channel bridge connects the western woodland to the eastern tidal flats. *Al and Jude Grass*

The West Pond is also an excellent site to view dragonflies and damselflies; more than 20 species have been observed here. Common whitetails, blue-eyed darners, cardinal meadowhawks and four-spotted skimmers are commonly seen.

The trail then winds back to the ponds through a forest of red alder, black cottonwood and scattered western redcedar and western hemlock. Woodpeckers, vireos, warblers and other forest birds dwell in the greenery. From time to time a great horned owl, northern pygmy-owl or barred owl is spotted here. Take the side trail up to the lookout to see down onto the ponds through the trees.

Eventually the trail loops back to the bridge at Osprey Point, an excellent place to view ospreys, purple martins or an offshore dolphin. The purple martin colony is the Lower Mainland's largest and one of BC's largest colonies. It is a remarkable conservation success story.

In spring to late summer, at the Danny Grass Memorial Butterfly Garden located at Osprey Point, sit on the bench to enjoy fine views of Burrard Inlet and watch for species including the western tiger swallowtail, Lorquin's admiral, Milbert's tortoiseshell and red admiral. You may also see hummingbirds.

Maplewood is excellent for observing butterflies such as the tiger swallowtail.
Al and Jude Grass

Maplewood Conservation Area is a year-round sanctuary; every season has its own special rewards. See purple martins in late spring and summer and ospreys from late spring to fall. Winter is best for viewing the maximum diversity of waterfowl and raptors.

Nearby Locations

- Cates Park is 3 kilometres (1.9 miles) to the east by bus or on foot

Some Alerts

- bears
- stay on trails; the mud flats are dangerous and footprints can damage the delicate ecosystems

More Information

Wild Bird Trust of British Columbia: 604-922-1550 or www.wildbirdtrust.org/

Cates Park

by Geoff Williams

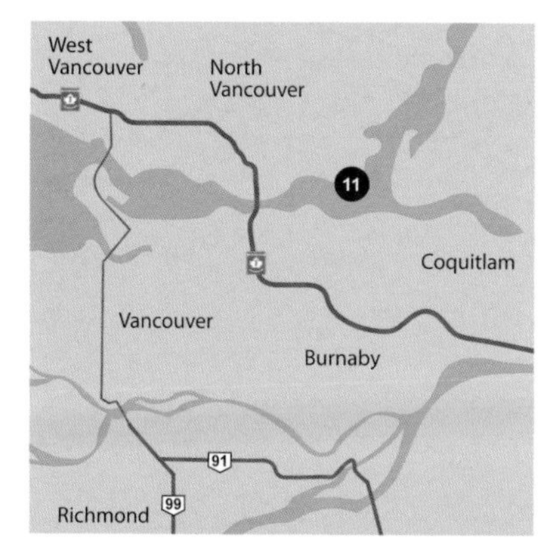

Beaches, meadows and a seashore woodland trail

Location

Cates Park is in southeast North Vancouver on Dollarton Hwy. just east of Roche Point Dr.

Transit Information

From Lonsdale Quay SeaBus terminal, board the #239 Park Royal/Phibbs Exchange/Capilano College bus to Phibbs Exchange. Then transfer to the #212 Deep Cove bus and alight at the Cates Park stop on Dollarton Hwy.

For up-to-date information, contact TransLink at www.translink.ca or 604-953-3333.

Introduction

Cates Park is a municipal park administered jointly with the local First Nations band, now known as the Tsleil-waututh First Nation. The park's alternative name is Whey-ah-wichen, which means "facing the wind." There is a totem pole and the original 50-foot (15-metre) war canoe, hand-carved by Chief Peter George in about 1920 and donated by his widow. These are located close to the beginning of the Malcolm Lowry Walk.

This huge western redcedar stump nurtures ferns and mosses. Douglas-fir stumps rot faster.
Geoff Williams

Cates Park is about 22 hectares (54 acres) and is irregular in shape. It provides public access to the waterfront, both on Burrard Inlet proper and on Indian Arm. This scenic fjord, popular with boaters and sightseers, extends to the north for about 14 kilometres (8.7 miles) into the mountains. Roche Point has a light to assist shipping, sandy beaches and a swimming area that is sometimes supervised. Nearby are a food concession, a playground, washroom facilities and large grassy meadows suitable for picnicking.

Natural History Visit

From the bus stop, walk down the park road past the floral display area, the large rhododendrons in the median and the boat launching ramp to

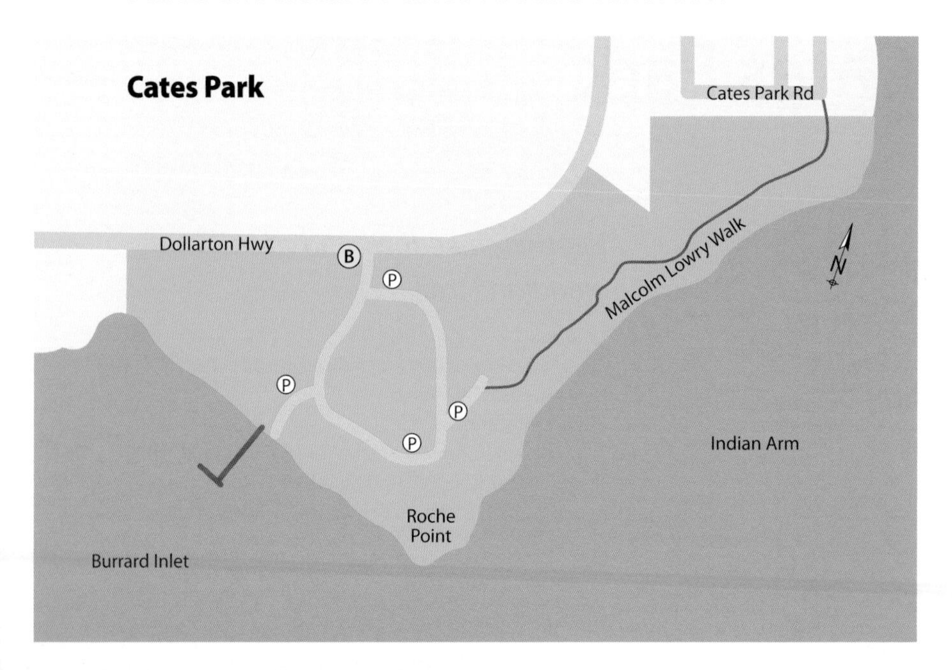

Looking toward Indian Arm, you can see Belcarra on the opposite shore. *Steve Britten*

A maturing red rock crab sheds its outgrown shells. Look for the discarded shells on the beach.
Sheila Byers

Roche Point. Beyond the parking area a path leads to a grassy area and steps down to the beach. From Roche Point you can see the Ironworkers Memorial Second Narrows Crossing and ships riding at anchor waiting to enter Port Moody. Look across the inlet to Burnaby Mountain, the 350-metre (1,148-foot) plateau on the other side.

The Malcolm Lowry Walk is a wide, smooth gravel path that starts at the east side of the Roche Point parking lot, where it is clearly marked with a sign. It commemorates author Malcolm Lowry, whose famous book *Under the Volcano* was said to have been written here. He lived in one of the squatters' cabins in this area before it was developed by the District of North Vancouver.

Along the trail you'll see many native trees including western redcedar, western hemlock, Douglas-fir, bigleaf and vine maple, red alder, bitter cherry and hazel, as well as introduced trees such as pines. About halfway to the wooden footbridge, skunk cabbage, also known as swamp lantern, has colonized some waterlogged ground on the left. In early spring the plant—named for its unpleasant odour—is quite spectacular, with its large yellow spathes or bracts and basal leaves. All over the wooded area, native Indian-plum trees flower at the same time as the skunk cabbage, putting on a beautiful show of flower clusters hanging like jewels. Most of the familiar native plants grow here, including bleeding heart, miner's-lettuce and sword fern. Some non-native plants such as spunge-laurel and English holly are also present; they may be garden escapes that have naturalized. The English daisies in the grassed areas probably came as seed but any daffodils you see in the spring were planted by the Parks Department.

A First Nations totem pole and war canoe are not far from the Malcolm Lowry Walk. *Steve Britten*

Beyond the wooden footbridge over a creek the path divides. Turn right to stay close to the beach. The main Malcolm Lowry Walk leads eventually to a large grassed area with children's play equipment, known locally as Little Cates. Nearby are the foundations of a waste-wood burner and a big patch of Himalayan blackberry.

To make a round trip, walk inland around the tennis courts at Little Cates and return by the Upper Trail through the wooded area. Alternatively, return along the pebbly beach if the tide is out.

Dead trees attract woodpeckers and sapsuckers, but most of the birds you are likely to see are sea birds. In addition to gulls and cormorants, you may see a great blue heron standing on a rock. Cates Park also has its share of raccoons, skunks and squirrels.

Visit Cates Park at any time of year. However, the skunk cabbage and Indian-plum are most showy in the spring, when other wildflowers such as bleeding hearts are also in flower.

Nearby Locations

- Deep Cove is about 3 kilometres (1.9 miles) north by bus or along side roads

Some Alerts

- occasional tree roots project through the surface

More Information

District of North Vancouver: 604-990-2311 or www.dnv.org
District of North Vancouver Park Rangers: 604-981-3149

Deep Cove

by Al and Jude Grass

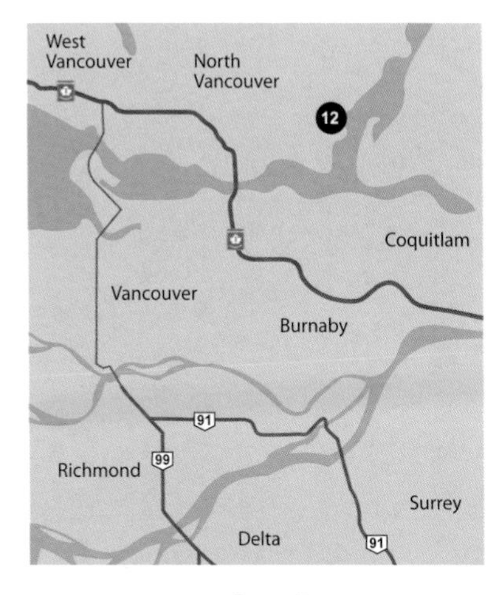

A transition between seashore and cool mountain forests

Location

Deep Cove is in southeast North Vancouver at Deep Cove Rd. and Panorama Dr.

Transit Information

From the Lonsdale Quay SeaBus terminal, take the #239 Park Royal/Phibbs Exchange/Capilano College bus to Phibbs Exchange. Then transfer to the #211 Seymour bus and alight at the final stop at Banbury Rd. and Gallant Ave. Alternatively, transfer to the #212 Deep Cove bus and alight at the final stop at Panorama Dr. and Naughton Ave.

For up-to-date information, contact TransLink at www.translink.ca or 604-953-3333.

Introduction

Deep Cove lies at the eastern end of the North Shore where Burrard Inlet ends and Indian Arm begins, near the southern end of Mount Seymour Provincial Park. The cove has a beautiful setting, surrounded by mountains and facing the inlet spotted with islands, and is a popular kayaking area. It features a sandy beach, grassy slopes and many boating facilities. At Deep

From this bench you may see otters, harbour seals or sea ducks. Look for eagles overhead.
Steve Britten

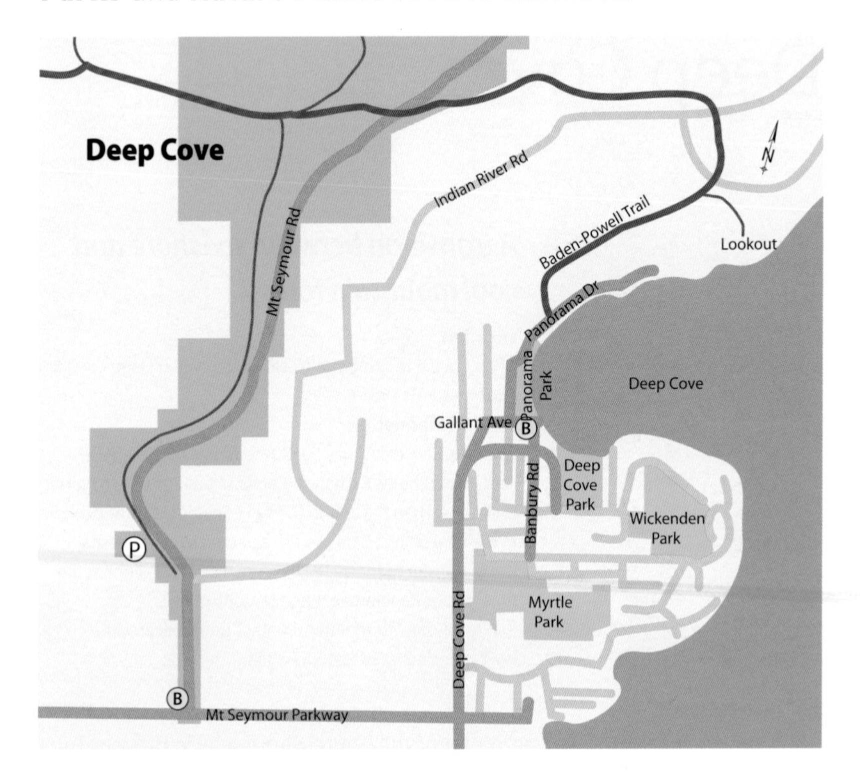

Cove urban life ends and the wilderness begins.

From Deep Cove you can easily access two natural areas. Right on the waterfront, Panorama Park is a 2.4-hectare (6-acre) park managed by the District of North Vancouver. It has many facilities and provides trails along the waterfront. Close by is the start of the 42-kilometre (26-mile) Baden Powell Trail, a popular hiking and walking trail along the North Shore mountain slopes from Deep Cove to Horseshoe Bay. When it was built in 1971 by Boy Scouts and Girl Guides to mark the BC Centennial, it was intended as a set of short hikes between its many access points. The first stretch out of Deep Cove is a lovely forest walk to the beautiful lookout overlooking Indian Arm.

Natural History Visit

From the bus stop, cross Gallant Ave. to Panorama Park. There you can watch for a variety of waterbirds that in winter include common mergansers, Barrow's goldeneyes, common goldeneyes, harlequin ducks and buffleheads. Year-round, look for pelagic and double-crested cormorants. Bald eagles often circle over bluffs near the village, and turkey vultures fly around the ridge toward Mount Seymour. You may see harbour seals out in the water. Try your hand at beachcombing, which is popular here.

To access the Baden Powell Trail from the back of Panorama Park, walk

Visit the Lookout Rock for magnificent views of Burrard Inlet and Burnaby Mountain.
Steve Britten

along Panorama Dr. to the start of the 2500 block. The well-labelled trail entrance is up the hill on the left and continues up a steep staircase into the woods. It is 1.9 kilometres (1.2 miles) to the remarkable Indian Arm Lookout, from which you can return to Deep Cove or go farther along the trail.

The northern pygmy-owl lacks ears. Black marks on the back of its neck resemble eyes.
Al and Jude Grass

On the trail you will pass through a mixed forest of western hemlock, red alder, Douglas-fir, bigleaf maple and rare western yew. Shrubs include salal, false azalea and red huckleberry. In early spring the exotic-looking palmate coltsfoot, with its whitish to pink-tinted flower clusters and large maple-shaped leaves, can be up to 60 centimetres (2 feet) across. Watch for neat rows of small holes pecked in bark, especially of western hemlock; this is the work of a beautiful red-breasted sapsucker woodpecker. Also look for squarish holes excavated in dead trees, which are a sure sign of the spectacular pileated woodpecker, our largest woodpecker, whose loud laughing call echoes through the forest.

Nurse logs are a beautiful feature, and gardens of mosses, liverworts, ferns and fungi thrive on them. Blobs of what looks like egg yolk are a slime mould called scrambled-egg slime. Slimes are strange organisms that show both animal and plant characteristics, depending on their life stage.

Fungi are an important feature of all forests, and this is an excellent route to find and photograph a fine variety. Note that collecting is not permitted in BC provincial parks. Red belt fungus, a bracket type, is commonly seen on dead hemlock trees along the trail. Look, too, for the beautiful turkey tail fungus on dead alders. Its banded pattern and colours may remind you of a rainbow.

In spring and early summer, listen for the low hoots of the sooty grouse, formerly called the blue grouse. This species was recently split into two; the other species is the dusky grouse found in the interior of BC. Other spring bird specialties along the trail include western tanagers, Pacific-slope flycatchers, Cassin's vireos, warbling vireos, orange-crowned warblers and Swainson's thrushes. Winter wrens, varied thrushes, chestnut-backed chickadees and sooty grouse are examples of year-round residents of the park.

Look for small piles of cone scales on stumps and logs; these are telltale signs of a Douglas squirrel feeding on cone flakes. Listen for its chattering call. You may also see coast black-tailed deer and coyotes, and a black bear sighting is also possible.

The best time to see plants and birds at Deep Cove is mid-spring to early summer. Fall is best for a variety of fungi. Warm summer evenings are excellent, too, for this is when deer come out to forage along the roadside and the Swainson's thrushes sing their beautiful flute-like song.

Nearby Locations

- Baden Powell Trail: the trail continues west from the Indian Arm Lookout to the next access point 1.6 kilometres (one mile) away at Mount Seymour Rd. Then you must walk about 3 kilometres (1.9 miles) down Mount Seymour Rd. to Mount Seymour Parkway to get the #211 bus home.
- Cates Park is a 3-kilometre (1.9-mile) walk or bus ride south from Deep Cove

Some Alerts

- bears and occasional cougars
- slippery trails, especially when wet
- water from local creeks is unsafe; giardiasis (beaver fever) is possible
- be cautious on the lookout rock

More Information

District of North Vancouver: 604-990-2311 or www.dnv.org
District of North Vancouver Park Rangers: 604-981-3149
BC Parks website: http://www.bcparks.ca
Deep Cove information: www.deepcovebc.com

vancouver city

Preceding page: Foreshore and forests are not far from downtown Vancouver. *James Holkko*

Above: A hairy woodpecker excavates a nesting cavity. *Mark Habdas*

UBC Campus: Cecil Green Area

by June M. Ryder

Cliff-top haven for diverse and unusual bird species

Location

Cecil Green Area is at the west side of Vancouver at NW Marine Dr. and Cecil Green Park Rd.

Transit Information

Take a bus to the UBC bus loop. Then either walk to the Chan Centre or take the #C20 Totem Park bus and alight at the NW Marine Dr. and Crescent Rd. stop.

For up-to-date information, contact TransLink at www.translink.ca or 604-953-3333.

Introduction

UBC Campus occupies a spectacular site on the tip of Point Grey, the western extremity of Vancouver. It is surrounded on three sides by precipitous cliffs that descend to narrow beaches and the sea and on the fourth (east) side by the forests of Pacific Spirit Park. The campus area is underlain by sediments of the last great glaciation, including thick, white sand, stony glacial deposits and beach sand.

When Captain Vancouver visited Point Grey in June 1792, it was completely forested, with Douglas-fir 50 to 60 metres (164 to 197 feet) high in drier areas and western redcedar and western hemlock on moister soils. No remnants of this original forest have survived, although these tree species still predominate in the small patch of woodland at the western end of the Cecil Green area. Red alder and bigleaf maple are also common here with understory vegetation such as Oregon grape, salal, sword fern and invasive species such as blackberry and thistle.

The main pathway winds between the Museum of Anthropology and the cliffs.
June M. Ryder

The informally named Cecil Green Area is a narrow strip of land along the top of the cliffs on the northern side of the campus.

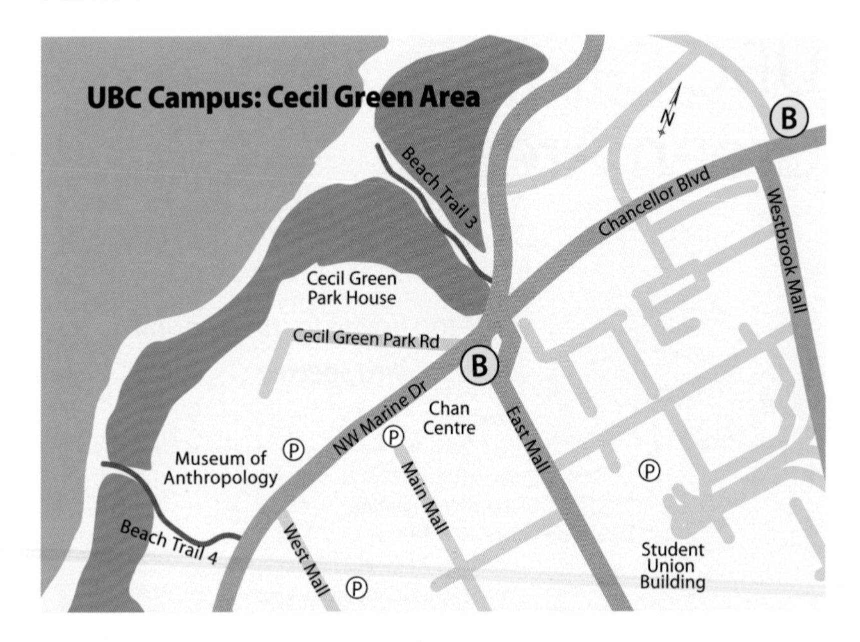

It extends for about half a kilometre (0.3 mile) between Green College just west of Beach Trail #3 and the head of Beach Trail #4 near the Museum of Anthropology. You can follow Beach Trail #3 or #4 down to the shore. Beach Trail #4 descends to clothing-optional Wreck Beach. The Cecil Green area encompasses Cecil Green Park around Cecil Green House and the grounds of the Museum of Anthropology, including the outdoor totem collection and the UBC Anthropology Department.

A secretive forest bird, Hutton's vireo is a challenge to observe.
Peter M. Candido

Cecil Green Area is famous among both local and visiting birders for the numbers and diversity of birds that pass through during migration. This is possibly because it is an attractive landing site next to a wide stretch of open water. Many rarities have been seen, and one local birder has personally observed over 156 species here, including barn owls, rough-legged hawks and whimbrels.

Natural History Visit

From the bus loop, head north to NW Marine Dr. near the Chan Centre. Then cross NW Marine Dr. and follow signs to either the Museum of Anthropology or to Cecil Green Park House on Cecil Green Park Rd.

Stroll along the pathways that traverse the Cecil Green Area; some are gravelled walkways, some are just narrow footworn trails. You can find small patches of dense woodland at the western end of the area and clumps

Lighthouse Park and the mountains of Howe Sound lie northward across Burrard Inlet.
Steve Britten

of trees surrounded by dense shrubbery along the cliff top. Open meadows represent natural habitat near the outdoor totem poles at the museum and alongside the main path farther east. Enjoy the spectacular views to Howe Sound and the Strait of Georgia. The gardens of Cecil Green Park House are also open to the public, but be courteous and avoid any private garden party that may be in progress.

For the best chance to see numerous and unusual birds, visit Cecil Green Area during spring migration from April to May or fall migration from mid-August to early October. In winter look for ducks, grebes and gulls.

Nearby Locations

- Pacific Spirit Regional Park, Wreck Beach and Tower Beach
- Museum of Anthropology: requires an entry fee although the grounds do not
- woodland and gardens around the Asian Centre
- remnants of UBC arboretum around the First Nations Longhouse
- Nitobe Memorial garden: a Japanese garden, requires an entry fee

Some Alerts

- access to the cliffs is prevented by a tall fence; do not climb over it

More Information

UBC Directions, Maps and Tours: www.ubc.ca/about/directions.html

UBC Campus: UBC Farm

by June M. Ryder

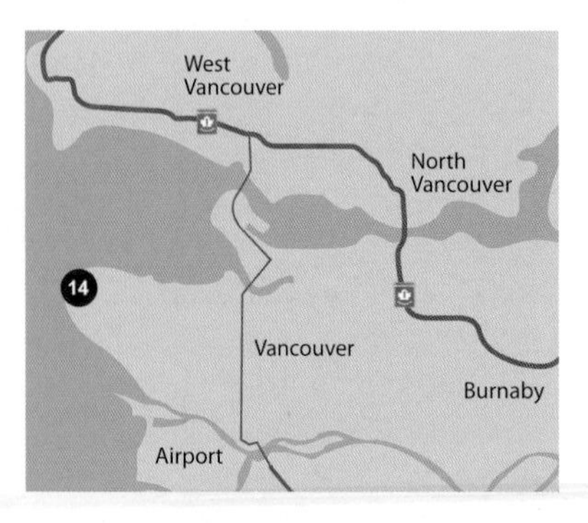

Agricultural land managed for both food crops and wildlife

Location

UBC Farm is at the west side of Vancouver at 6182 South Campus Rd. off Wesbrook Mall.

Transit Information

Take the #25 UBC bus or the #41 UBC bus to UBC. Alight at the W 16th Ave. and Wesbrook Mall stop.

For up-to-date information, contact TransLink at www.translink.ca or 604-953-3333.

Introduction

UBC Farm on South Campus occupies about 24 hectares (59 acres) of gently sloping to flat terrain underlain by thick glacial drift. Managed by students, it is a teaching, educational and research facility and the only working farmland within Vancouver. Objectives include sustainable (organic) agriculture, innovation and integration with the local community. In addition the site is managed to maintain different types of habitat for the abundant local wildlife.

In the flower garden, insects and seed heads draw sparrows, finches and other birds.
June M. Ryder

The farm area includes several hectares of second-growth forest with native trees, shrubs, ferns and herbaceous plants, a market garden, a medicinal garden, agricultural fields, hens, bees, patches of dense conifers that were once plantations, an old arboretum with 47 species of native and non-native trees and wild areas of long grass and blackberry. As well, edge habitats are widespread on the farm. In these boundaries between different types of habitat, such as forest alongside grassy fields, birds and other wildlife may be particularly abundant.

Natural History Visit

From the bus stop, walk 0.7 kilometre (0.4 mile) south along Wesbrook Mall then turn right onto South Campus Rd. for 0.4 kilometre (0.2 mile) to the farm gate at 6182 South Campus Rd. Farm opening times vary with the

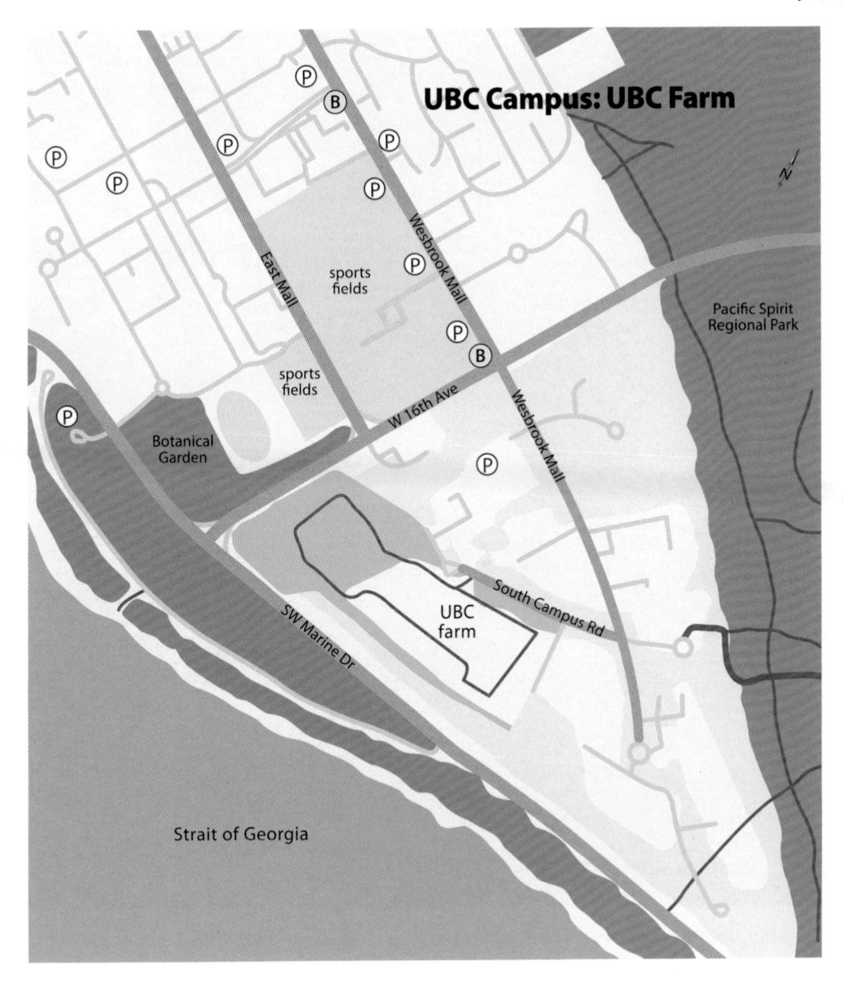

season, so check before you go. The farm is usually closed on Sundays and in winter.

You can explore and find your own way around the farm, staying on pathways and grassy areas. However, a good route to follow that crosses several types of habitat, is the one used on monthly Nature Vancouver (VNHS) bird surveys. This route is marked by posts at the nine birding stops. At the farm entrance you can pick up a Nature Trail Guide, which provides a map showing the stops and a description of the natural life you may find there.

From Stop 1 at the farm entrance gate, follow the gravel road that swings to the right and winds northwest past several buildings. After passing the Landed Learning Garden on your left and the Farm Centre with washrooms on your right, you will reach Stop 2 on the edge of the forest. This is a good spot to see birds emerging from the forest. You may see pine siskins, cedar waxwings, house finches, American robins and dark-eyed juncos year-round.

The interpretive Agroforestry Trail winds through a second-growth forest. *June M. Ryder*

Follow the meandering Agroforestry Trail into the mixed second-growth forest; here the footing is more uneven, and you must negotiate over logs. Students developed this Agroforestry Trail as an interpretive trail, so information signs are posted along the way. This forest has not been managed and so has much more downed wood and more standing snags than nearby Pacific Spirit Park. Consequently wildlife here differs slightly from that of Pacific Spirit Park; for example, there are more woodpeckers. At Stop 3 in the forest, look for chickadees and woodpeckers year-round and kinglets in winter. At the end of this trail, you will emerge from the forest at Stop 4, where you may see a brown creeper.

Keep bearing right along the path and heading generally northwest through deciduous shrubs at the edge of the forest. Soon you'll get close to SW Marine Dr. with its loud traffic noise as you come out onto an old road at Stop 5. This is a clearing where you can scan the surrounding tree canopy for small birds.

Now turn left along the old road until you come to the edge of an open field. Here take a side trip to your left to Stop 6, beside blackberries and farm fields, where you may see Anna's hummingbirds and fox sparrows in winter and song sparrows year-round. Return to the perimeter old road and continue along the perimeter through deciduous forest to Stop 7, then Stop 8 at the corner of the field. Behind this stop, outside the perimeter, you can take a side trip along a meandering trail that leads to a large arboretum containing massive rhododendrons and other unusual trees. After returning to Stop 8, continue around the perimeter of the fields, passing Stop 9 on your way back to the farm entrance gate.

White-crowned sparrows feed on seeds and insects in the flower garden. *Al and Jude Grass*

Visit in spring, summer and fall. Look for uncommon migrant birds during April and May and from mid-August to early October. On Saturday mornings in summer, you can combine a walk with a visit to the farm market. The farm is closed on Sundays and in winter.

Nearby Locations

- Pacific Spirit Park
- UBC Botanical Garden
- UBC Campus: Cecil Green Area

Some Alerts

- respect the farmland by staying on pathways and grassy areas; don't walk across bare soil or crops
- do not pick vegetables or flowers; instead visit the farmer's market
- do not disturb any apparatus or equipment that you find; it is being used for research

More Information

UBC Farm: 604-822-5092 or www.landfood.ubc.ca/ubcfarm
UBC Directions, Maps and Tours: www.ubc.ca/about/directions.html

UBC Botanical Garden

by Douglas Justice and Daniel Mosquin

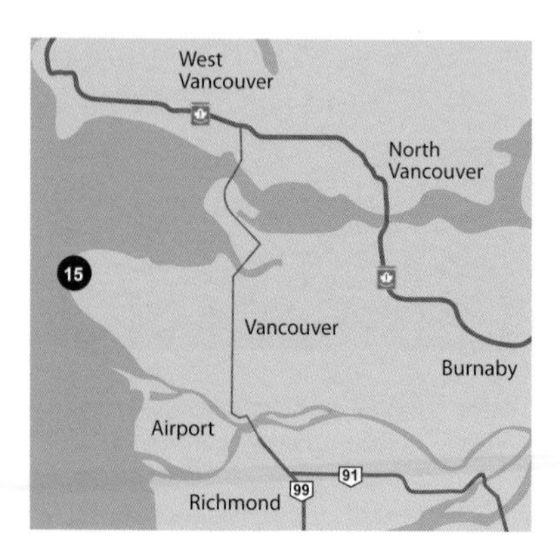

Richly diverse and colourful plant collections and a forest canopy walkway

Location

UBC Botanical Garden is at the west side of Vancouver at SW Marine Dr. and West Mall.

Transit Information

Take a bus to the UBC bus loop, transfer to the #C20 Totem Park bus and alight at the West Mall and Stadium Rd. stop. For up-to-date information, contact TransLink at www.translink.ca or 604-953-3333.

Introduction

The 44-hectare (109-acre) UBC Botanical Garden is open to the public year-round and has richly diverse and colourful plant collections set in a number of separate gardens. These include a food garden, physic (apothecary's) garden, extensive alpine-rock garden, BC native plants garden and its largest feature, a 15-hectare (37-acre) Asian plant garden. The Carolinian Forest, Garry Oak Meadow and Woodland Gardens are new features currently being developed.

Walkers can enjoy more than 5 kilometres (3.1 miles) of paths and trails through gardens and forest.

In the Asian Garden you can see plants from Tibet, Japan, China, Korea and Manchuria.
Daniel Mosquin

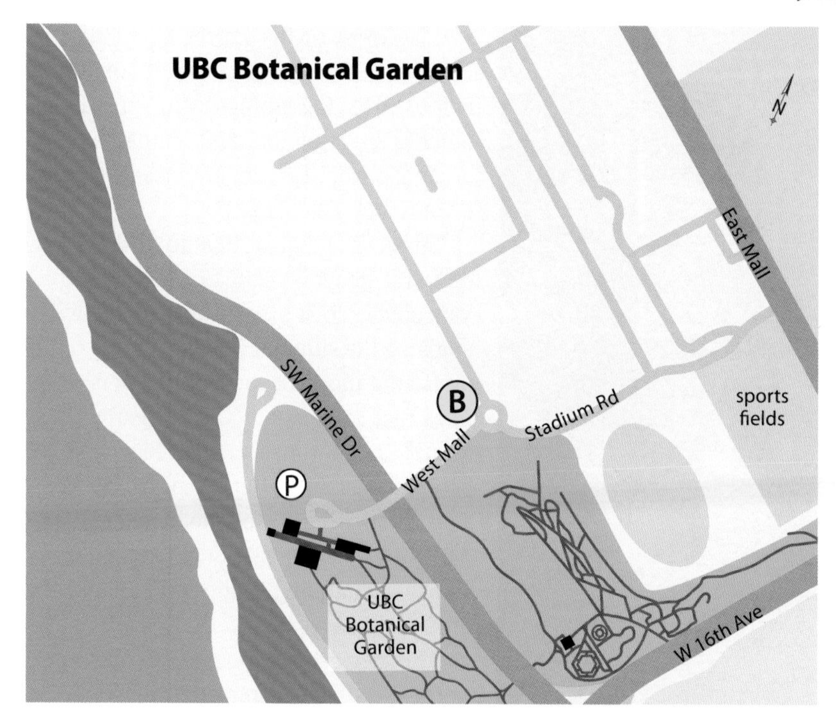

Many paths are wheelchair accessible. Nitobe Memorial Garden, a traditional Japanese tea and stroll garden, is one kilometre (0.6 miles) north along NW Marine Dr. and is administered by the Botanical Garden.

In both gardens, admission is charged year-round and discounted double-entry tickets and interpretive audio-guides are available. There is a separate fee for the canopy walkway.

Visit the extensive UBC Botanical Garden where plants from all over the world thrive.
Daniel Mosquin

Natural History Visit

From the bus stop it is a short walk across SW Marine Dr. to the garden entrance. The garden extends on both sides of SW Marine Dr.; a tunnel under the road connects the two parts. The garden is on the UBC campus, 100 metres (328 feet) above the Strait of Georgia on the south side of Point Grey, the westernmost tip of the city of Vancouver. The garden and surrounding area are well known for bird life, including woodpeckers, owls and numerous other forest-dwellers. Raptors are regularly seen soaring above the cliffs immediately to the west.

A family group crosses the Greenheart Canopy Walkway high above the trees. *Josh Lewis*

Like most of the Lower Mainland, the Point Grey forest was clear-cut some time before 1920. Big stumps with springboard notches are common, and remnants of the original cover also remain; these snags are favoured by bald eagles.

Summer is a great time to visit the garden. It is generally 2°C to 5°C cooler than Vancouver, so it's easy to cool off while enjoying the summer flowers. Spring offers by far the most for lovers of flowers. Peak flowering for magnolias is in early April, for rhododendrons in early May and for perennials in June, but the pleasures don't stop then. Because of the Botanical Garden's diversity of plantings and the mild climate, something is flowering almost any time of the year.

The newest addition to the Botanical Garden is the Greenheart Canopy Walkway. Dubbed UBC's "canopy classroom," this 310-metre (1,017-foot) walkway gives visitors, students and researchers unparalleled access to the mid-canopy ecosystem 17.5 metres (57.4 feet) above the ground and spectacular views of the native forest, the Asian Garden and the Strait of Georgia beyond. A wheelchair specially designed to fit the canopy walkway is available for persons with mobility problems.

Nearby Locations

- UBC Museum of Anthropology: to the west, across the street from the Nitobe Memorial Garden
- Pacific Spirit Park, the UBC Campus and Vancouver's famous clothing-optional Wreck Beach are only minutes away by foot

Some Alerts

- sturdy footwear is required for visitors to the Greenheart Canopy Walkway; no narrow heels or open-toed sandals permitted

More Information

UBC Botanical Garden: 604-822-9666 or www.ubcbotanicalgarden.org

UBC Directions, Maps and Tours: www.ubc.ca/about/directions.html

Pacific Spirit Regional Park

by Terry Taylor

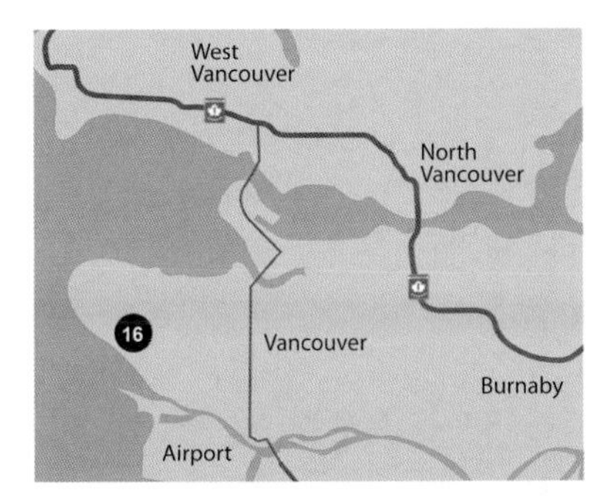

Bedstraw seeds, spread by rodents, have little hooks that catch on animal fur.
James Holkko

Kilometres of gentle trails traversing upland forests and shoreline

Location

Pacific Spirit Regional Park is in southwest Vancouver at W 16th Ave. and Blanca St.

Transit Information

The #17 UBC bus travels along W 10th Ave. The closest stop is at W 10th Ave. and Blanca St. for the W 12th Ave. and Blanca St. park entrance.

The #25 UBC bus travels along W 16th Ave. The closest stop is at W 16th Ave. and Tolmie St. travelling east and W 16th Ave. and Sasamat St. travelling west for the W 16th Ave. and Sasamat St. park entrance.

The #41 Crown/UBC bus travels along W 41st Ave. The closest stop is at W 41st Ave. and Crown St. Walk one block west to the W 41st Ave. and Camosun St. park entrance.

For up-to-date information, contact TransLink at www.translink.ca or 604-953-3333.

Introduction

This 700-hectare (1,730-acre) Metro Vancouver park is on Point Grey adjacent to UBC, west of the City of Vancouver. It contains upland forest and the shoreline below the campus, including the clothing-optional Wreck Beach and the western end of Spanish Banks at Acadia Beach. The park is traversed by 50 kilometres (31 miles) of well-maintained trails through mature second-growth coniferous and deciduous forest.

There are many access points into the park, but the most easily accessible by public transit are probably the trails beginning at W 12th Ave. and Blanca St., W 16th Ave. and Sasamat St. or W 41st Ave. and Camosun St.

Point Grey is underlain by the Quadra sands, which were deposited about 20,000 years ago by meltwater streams from a huge glacier advancing southward down the Strait of Georgia. They are visible in the cliffs at the western end of Spanish Banks. The Admiralty Trail runs along the crest of this sand cliff and affords beautiful views across English Bay to the North Shore mountains.

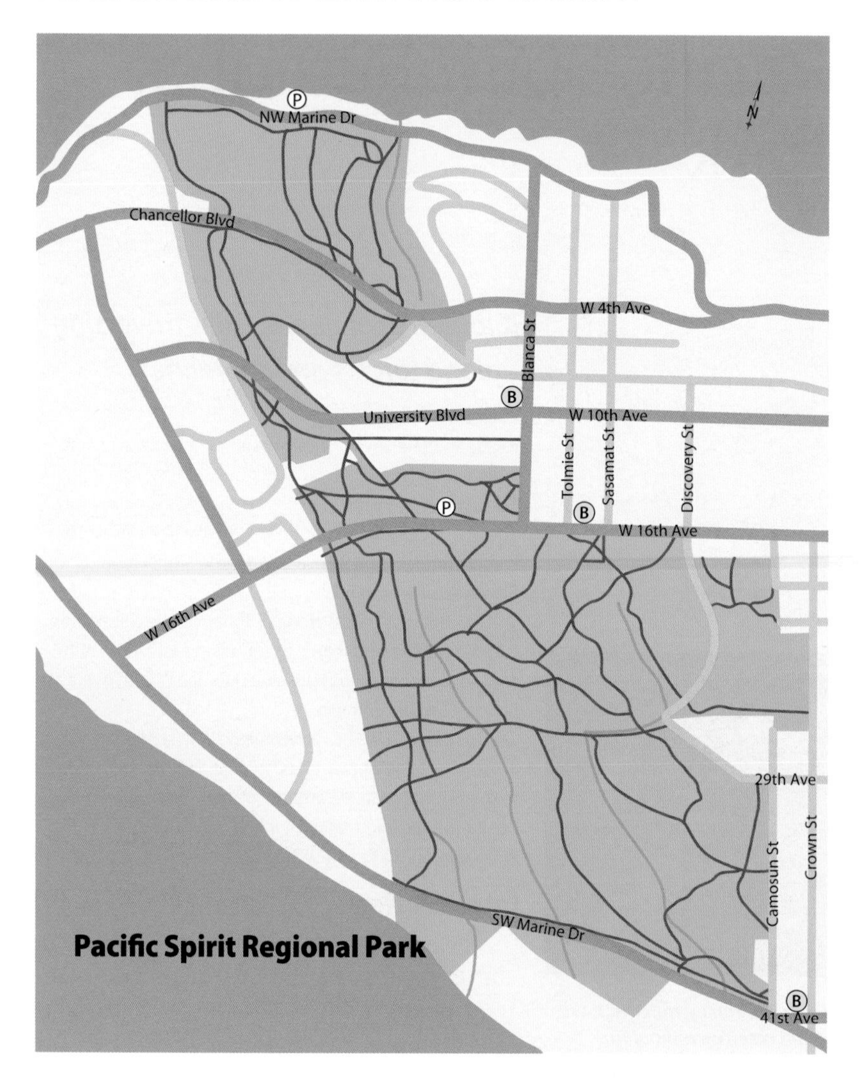

Natural History Visit

Most of the park is covered by coniferous forest including Douglas-fir, western hemlock and western redcedar. However, the section bounded by University Blvd. and Chancellor Blvd. is red alder forest that was established here after logging in about 1950. There is an understory of salmonberries here as well as some large cottonwoods. Because of the open deciduous habitat, this is the best part of the park for songbirds.

In contrast large coniferous trees cover the southern portion of the park, logged in the 1890s. In the southwest corner you can find some of the best examples of Sitka spruce still surviving in the Lower Mainland.

Pacific Spirit Park is a good place to see mushrooms during the autumn, but remember that picking is prohibited in parks. Impressive clusters of

From the northeast part of the park, downtown Vancouver is visible over Spanish Banks.
James Holkko

poisonous fly agarics often grow with the cottonwoods north of University Boulevard, while fairy helmets and brittlegills grow in the coniferous areas.

Near the east end of Imperial Trail are some large bigleaf maples, densely covered in mosses. Because of their rough, nutrient-rich bark, these maples support more mosses and more kinds of mosses than any other native tree.

Remnants of the previous old-growth forest are represented by the numerous rotten stumps that dot the forest floor. Some of these still have the springboard holes from the days of handlogging. Old conifer stumps are brown because fungi have removed the cellulose from them, leaving lignin, which acts as the glue holding wood fibres together. This compound is very resistant to decay and oxidizes to the rich rusty brown shade that is so characteristic of our coniferous forests.

Many trails, a number of them suitable for wheelchairs and strollers, wind through the park.
Steve Britten

Visit the park any time of year.

Nearby Locations

- Spanish Banks Beach is north of the park
- the Botanical Garden, Cecil Green Area and UBC Farm are nearby at UBC

Some Alerts

- cyclists and horses on multi-use trails
- avoid the cliff edge along Admiralty Trail
- watch the tides if traversing the beach below the cliffs of Wreck Beach

More Information

Metro Vancouver Regional Parks:
www.metrovancouver.org/services/parks_lscr/regionalparks/Pages/default.aspx
Metro Vancouver Regional Parks West Area Office: 604-224-5739

Camosun Bog

by Terry Taylor

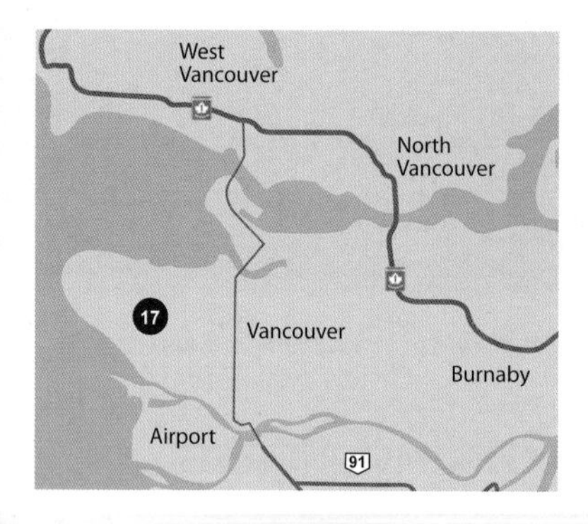

A green moss garden, a place of tranquility

Location

Camosun Bog is in southwest Vancouver at W 19th Ave. and Camosun St.

Transit Information

Take the #25 UBC bus along W 16th Ave. and alight at the W 16th Ave. and Camosun St. stop.

For up-to-date information, contact TransLink at www.translink.ca or 604-953-3333.

Introduction

This beautiful example of a true peat bog is part of Pacific Spirit Regional Park. Approximately a city block in area, it comprises a central pond and surrounding sphagnum bog that is encircled by a boardwalk trail. Over the last 10 years the Camosun Bog Restoration Group has restored the bog to its original state. This is the only successful bog reclamation in the Lower Mainland.

The round-leaved sundew's sticky red glands curve to entrap insects, then digest them. *James Holkko*

The surrounding forest shields Camosun Bog from external sounds and the nearby residential area. This silence, combined with the subtle hues of the sphagnum moss carpet, produce a place of remarkable peace and tranquillity.

Camosun Bog is about 2,000 years old. It was formed by the gradual infilling of a small lake that was probably similar to Beaver Lake in Stanley Park. The small pond within it is a remnant from that time.

Natural History Visit

From the bus stop on W 16th Ave., walk south along Camosun St. to the entrance trail that begins just south of W 19th Ave. This will take about five minutes.

The acidic nature of sphagnum mosses creates an ecosystem different from other habitats, and the plant species found here are uniquely adapted

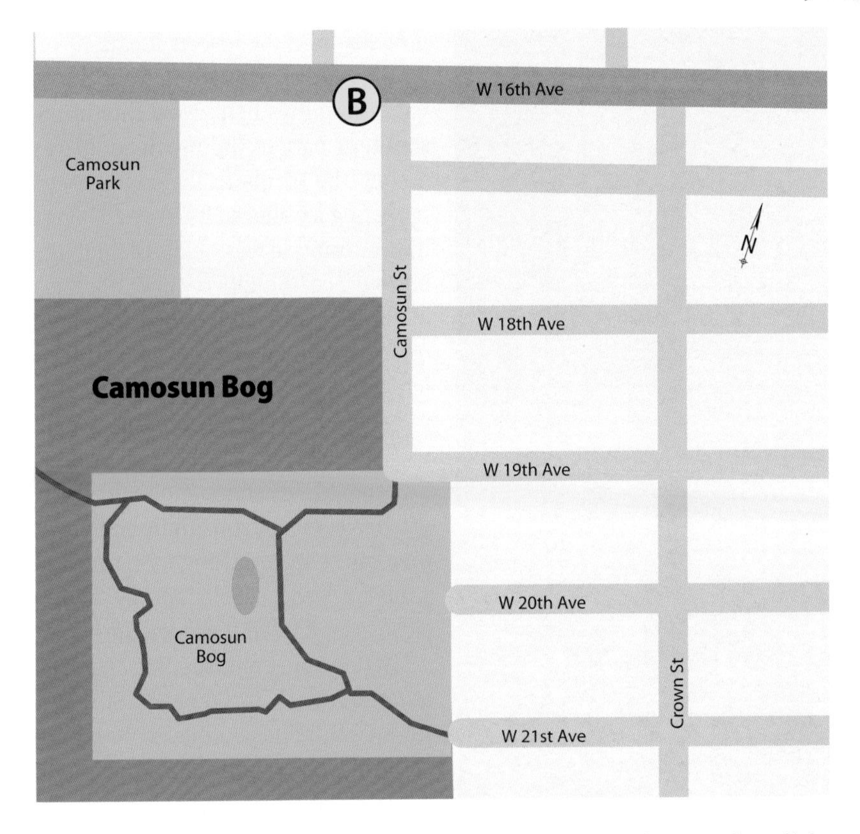

to bogs. The trees with needles in pairs are shore pines. They need sunlight and do not grow in the surrounding forest.

In May the bog shrubs come into flower. The bright pink flowers of swamp laurel come first, followed by the white blooms of Labrador tea. Swamp laurel leaves are thick and shiny, and the undersides have a grey waxy coating. Labrador tea leaves have rusty wool underneath. These features retard evaporation. Although this is a wetland, the cold acidic conditions make it difficult for plants to take up water; proximity to sea water creates somewhat comparable conditions.

The success of the restoration project is indicated by the health of the sphagnum moss.
James Holkko

Growing in the sphagnum moss carpet is one of the bog's special jewels, the sundew. The sundew is an insect-eating plant. Its red, spoon-shaped leaves are covered by sticky hairs. These hairs contain digestive juices as well as insect attractants and act as the sundew's external stomach. Bogs are not just cold and acidic, they are also nutrient-poor, and their few minerals are usually captured by the sphagnum mosses. The sundew gets the nitrogen it needs to build its

Camosun Bog, destroyed by local development, was restored by volunteers. *James Holkko*

proteins from the insects it eats.

Cloudberry, an 11,000-year survivor, also grows here. Now rare in the southern part of the province, it was among the plants to the south of the retreating ice sheets. Its leaves, shaped like currant leaves, closely hug the bog surface. Cloudberry and other bog plants probably grew along the edges of an ancient lake and expanded their territories when the bog replaced it.

A colony of yellow pond-lilies occupies the bog pond, which is bordered by a margin of sedges and rushes. The extensive area of sphagnum mosses at their most magnificent forms a third zone outward. The walkway allows close access to all these features.

At one time Camosun Bog extended as far south as King Edward (25th) Ave. An urban drainage project constructed about 80 years ago caused the site to gradually dry out and permitted the surrounding forest to invade it. But for the restoration project, Camosun Bog would have eventually been lost.

Because Camosun Bog creates an opening in the otherwise continuous coniferous forest, it attracts songbirds, so this is also a site for birders.

Visit any time of year, but the flowers are best during May or early June.

Nearby Locations

- Pacific Spirit Park, adjoining the bog, has 50 kilometres (31 miles) of popular walking and cycling trails

Some Alerts

- slippery boardwalk when wet or frosty
- stay on the trails, as the bog is very fragile

More Information

Camosun Bog: www.naturalhistory.bc.ca/CamosunBog
Metro Vancouver Regional Parks West Area Office: 604-224-5739

Musqueam Park

by Paul Harris Jones

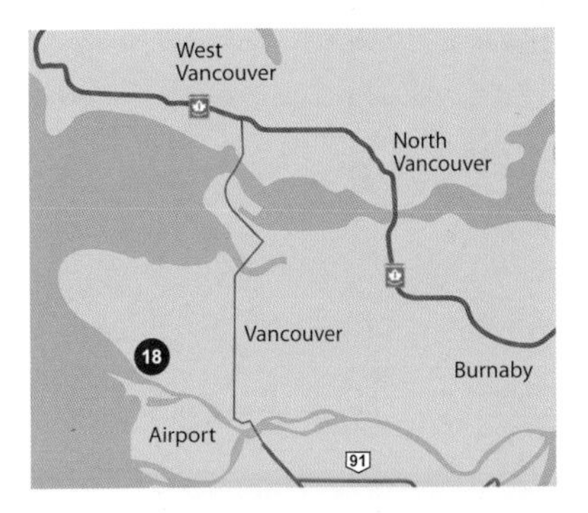

A salmon stream amid forest and meadows

Location

Musqueam Park is in southwest Vancouver at W 41st Ave. and Crown St.

Transit Information

The #41 Crown/UBC bus travels along W 41st Ave. The closest stop is at W 41st Ave. and Crown St.

For up-to-date information, contact TransLink at www.translink.ca or 604-953-3333.

Introduction

Musqueam Park, 22.5 hectares (56 acres) in size, was originally part of the Point Grey municipality before it amalgamated with the City of Vancouver in 1929. It appears in Park Board records for the first time in 1930. It lies just south of W 41st Ave. and is bordered by the Musqueam First Nations lands on the west and southwest and Alma St. on the east. Crown St. runs through the centre of the park, providing access to the First Nations lands.

Musqueam (Tin Can) Creek flows through the park, then through the First Nations lands and into the North Arm of the Fraser River opposite Iona

A shaded glen on the east side of Musqueam Park makes a good place for a picnic.
Paul Harris Jones

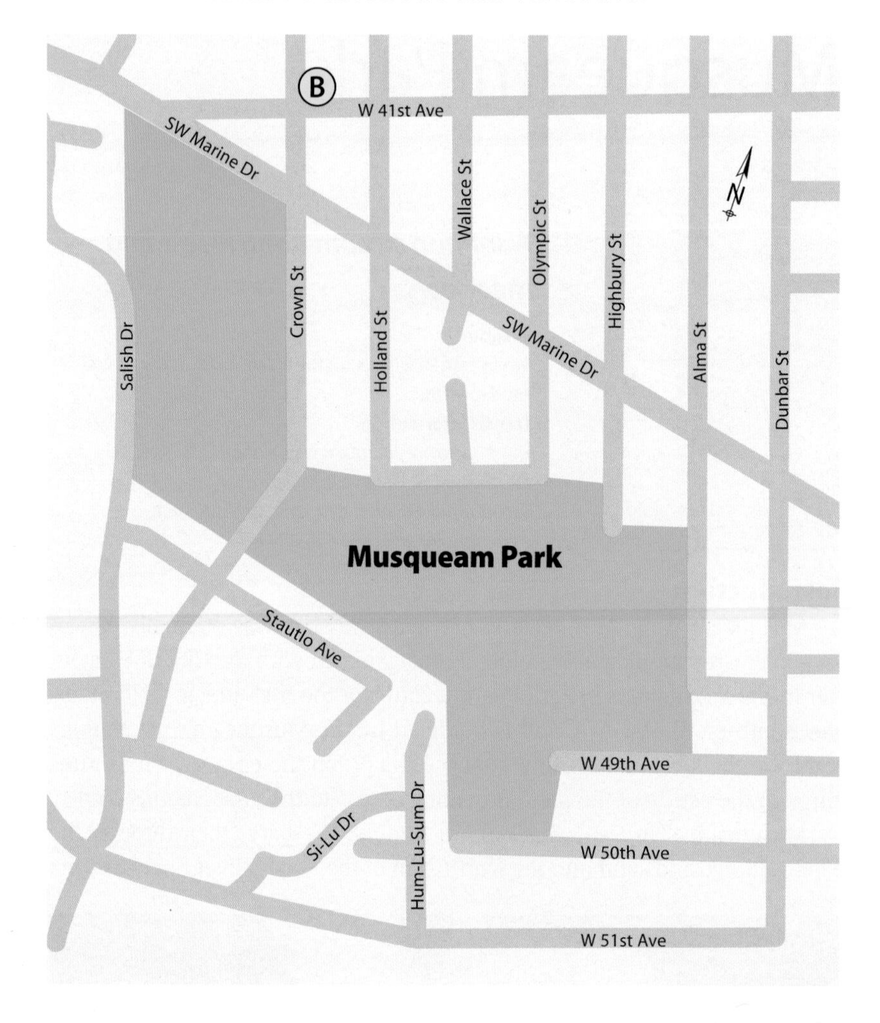

Island and the Sea Island Conservation Area. The creek is a salmon stream, and efforts to rehabilitate the waterway are now underway.

Natural History Visit

From the bus stop, walk to Musqueam Park on the south side of W 41st Ave. The park is a heavily treed creekside corridor lying between Pacific Spirit Park to the northwest and the riparian zones that fringe the North Arm of the Fraser River to the south. The park has grassy edges and a fine second-growth forest of Douglas-fir, western hemlock, western redcedar, bigleaf and vine maple and the occasional large grand fir. At present the forest is more than a hundred years old. You can see evidence of early logging in the stumps that remain; some have slots for springboards. Ground cover is mostly a tangle of sword fern, Oregon grape, salal, ocean spray and snowberry.

There are woods on either side of Musqueam Creek as well as an open

A brown creeper spirals up a tree seeking spiders and insects. Its back resembles bark.
Mark Wynja

area at the east side, which accommodates two soccer fields. Several trails, suitable for horseback riders and walkers, wind through the woods. Grassed areas also provide attractive places for picnics and recreation.

The park is the year-round home of brown creepers, pileated woodpeckers, red-breasted nuthatches and a host of other cavity nesters. In spring you can sometimes see American dippers and great blue herons along the creek's banks. In fall salmon enter the lower reaches of the creek.

The best time to visit Musqueam Park is in the summer when the trees are at their leafy best. You will hear American goldfinches, pine siskins and the liquid notes of Swainson's thrushes that inhabit the park.

Nearby Locations

- Pacific Spirit Park lies a short distance to the north; horse and pedestrian paths link the two parks
- the Southlands River Trail on the North Arm of the Fraser River is to the south; a path down the west side of Musqueam Park that continues west of the Point Grey Golf Course leads to it

Some Alerts

- horses on equestrian paths
- do not enter First Nations lands without special permission from the First Nations office; access is via Crown St.

More Information

Vancouver Park Board Recreation: 604-257-8400 or http://vancouver.ca/parkfinder_wa

Southlands

by David Cook

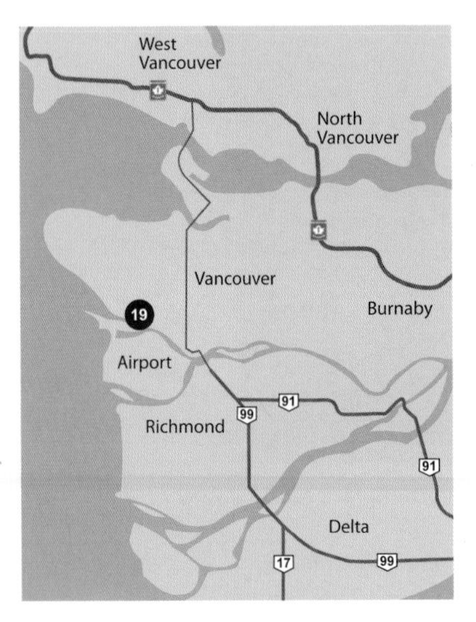

Equestrian rural setting beside the Fraser River

Location

Southlands area is in southwest Vancouver at Blenheim St. and Celtic Ave.

Transit Information

Bring your bicycle for the 1.4-kilometre (0.9-mile) ride to complete your journey; remember a bike lock.

From the Metrotown SkyTrain Station, board the #49 Dunbar Loop/UBC bus and alight at the Blenheim St. and SW Marine Dr. stop.

For up-to-date information, contact TransLink at www.translink.ca or 604-953-3333.

From the bus stop, cycle south down Blenheim St. to the Fraser River. The Southlands River Trail starts on your right. It's a pleasant ride past fields and equestrian stables.

Introduction

Southlands is a semi-rural neighbourhood at the foot of Blenheim St. in the Point Grey area of Vancouver. It follows part of the north shore of the

Lyngby's sedge is an important plant because of its slow, steady release of nutrients.
June M. Ryder

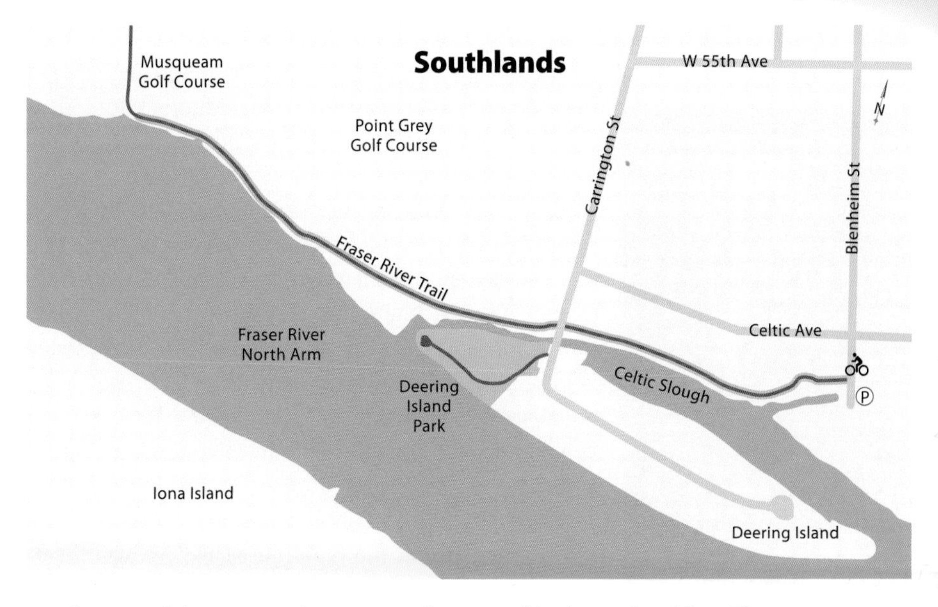

North Arm of the Fraser River among horse paddocks and stables. The area is part of the Fraser River flood plain and is still zoned for agricultural use.

The River Trail—a wide pathway for pedestrians, cyclists and horses—extends along the North Arm of the Fraser River, starting at the foot of Blenheim St. and extending about one kilometre (0.6 mile) west. The trail passes some houses, and beyond Carrington St., continues along the south side of the Point Grey Golf Course to the edge of the Musqueam Golf Course. From there the path continues northward away from the river to Musqueam Park. There are plans to extend this River Trail in future to connect the riverside greenway with other Metro Vancouver trails.

Southlands also includes the 0.74-hectare (1.8-acre) Deering Island Park, owned and operated by the City of Vancouver. You can access it from the River Trail at Carrington St. by heading south across the bridge and turning right. The park encompasses the western tip of Deering Island with its tidal marsh, planted in 1989. The park is an excellent spot for picnicking, watching the river traffic and birding. A rustic bench and shelter at the west end of the park provide some protection.

Natural History Visit

At the eastern end of the River Trail near Blenheim St. you will see an attractive row of Lombardy poplars. Wild chervil, belonging to the parsley and carrot family and looking rather like cow-parsnip, is an introduced plant that has taken over large areas bordering the trail. Himalayan blackberry along the Point Grey Golf Course section of the River Trail provides a tasty harvest in late summer and offer excellent bird habitat.

Celtic Slough separates Deering Island from the mainland and is a good location for birding. Nest boxes for swallows have been placed on the banks of the slough. Great blue herons and the occasional green heron can be seen fishing, and migratory birds including raptors pass through. Look for a bald eagle's nest in a tree at the foot of Blenheim.

Swallow nest boxes stand above the invasive purple loosestrife on Celtic Slough.
June M. Ryder

A healthy tidal salt marsh dominated by Lyngby's sedge lies off the western tip of Deering Island; you can access it by a small gravel trail from the River Trail. Lyngby's sedge, high in protein when young, is prime forage for geese during spring migration. This sedge is important for producing detritus, a food source for organisms upon which juvenile salmon feed. In July you can see the juvenile salmon migrating out to sea. You may be lucky enough to see them jumping, flopping and finning, usually during the early part of the run, particularly at the high-tide slack. As well, ever-curious harbour seals swim in the Fraser River.

Looking southwest from Deering Island Park, you will have unobstructed views of Iona Island in Richmond, and on a clear day, more distant views of the mountains on Vancouver Island and the Gulf Islands. This view can provide an inspiring display during some evening sunsets.

Visit year-round, but especially in spring for the eulachon run and from summer to fall for the sockeye and pink salmon runs, when the gulls and bald eagles circle for fish. There are dragonflies in late summer.

Nearby Locations

- Musqueam Park and Pacific Spirit Park are within cycling distance of the west end of the River Trail
- the River Trail continues for 1 kilometre (0.6 mile) from the east end along the south edge of McCleery Golf Course; cycle along Celtic Ave. to the foot of Balaclava St. where the trail resumes

Some Alerts

- horses on the trails
- wayward golf balls near the Point Grey Golf Course

More Information

Vancouver Park Board Recreation: 604-257-8400 or http://vancouver.ca/parkfinder_wa/
Dunbar Residents Association: 604-222-9824 or www.dunbar-vancouver.org
Southlands UEL Trail Riders: www.southlandsueltrailriders.com

Jericho Beach Park

by Daphne Solecki

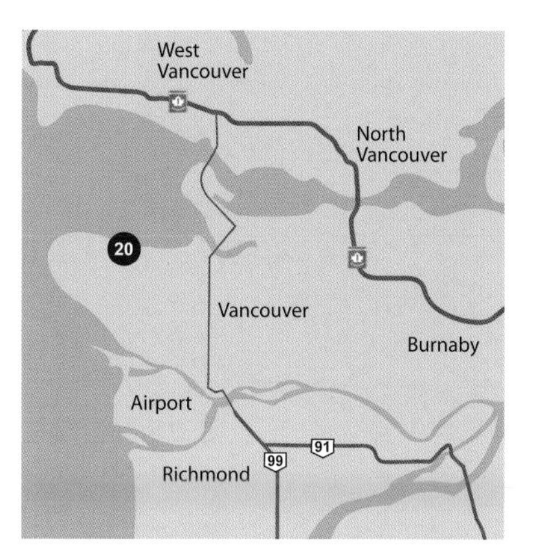

Sandy beaches, saltwater bay, freshwater ponds, woodland and meadow

Location

Jericho Beach Park is in northwest Vancouver at Point Grey Rd. and Wallace St.

Transit Information

The #04 UBC bus travels along W 4th Ave. and stops in two places alongside the park, at W 4th Ave. and Dieppe Lane and W 4th Ave. in the 4100 block.

For up-to-date information, contact TransLink at www.translink.ca or 604-953-3333.

Introduction

Jericho Beach Park lies between W 4th Ave. and Burrard Inlet, bounded by Wallace St. to the east and Discovery St. to the west. After Stanley Park, Jericho Beach Park at 54 hectares (133 acres) has the most varied habitat of any Vancouver city park and the greatest number of birds seen. The park also has an interesting history. "Jericho" is a shortened form of "Jerry's Cove," named after Jeremiah Rogers, who started logging the virgin forests of the area in the 1860s. A few stumps are still visible in the park.

Raspberry-shaped salmonberries, which ripen early, may be red or orange.
Dawn Hanna

After logging ended, Jericho was a major recreational area where people came by boat to picnic. Then the area was leased to the Jericho Golf and Country Club, and the ornamental trees were planted. In 1921 the federal government took over the land and built a concrete airstrip; its surviving remnant is known today as the "marginal wharf" and is now due for demolition. Barracks were constructed on the upland area. Today the Jericho Sailing Club and the Jericho Hostel both occupy parts of the old military base that existed between 1920 and 1971. In the 1970s the land reverted to the city and became the park as we see it today.

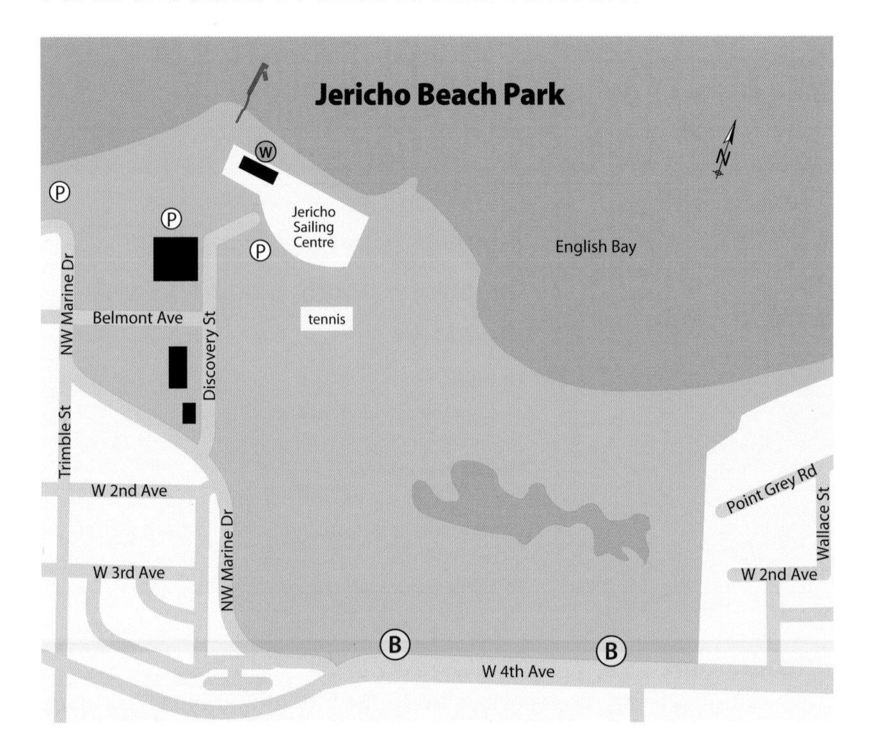

Natural History Visit

The park provides a mix of woodland, rough meadow, freshwater marsh and ponds, scrub, flat grassy areas, sandy foreshore and a saltwater bay.

For birders the best time of year starts in late September, when the birds return from the northern areas where they breed to overwinter in the park; they leave again in April and May. Spring migration brings many different birds through the area. At least 180 species have been found in the park, with 20 species known to breed in the park, including mallards, willow flycatchers, American robins, red-winged blackbirds, spotted towhees and song and white-crowned sparrows. Barn swallows make their nests under the wooden bridge.

The red-winged blackbird also has yellow margins on its epaulets.
Mark Habdas

In April, as most of the birds overwintering leave, the park begins to blossom with an amazing variety of trees, shrubs and flowers. Some are native, some introduced: alder, maple, cottonwood, willow, hawthorn, Nootka rose, Saskatoon, lupine, daisy and tansy. A great deal of work has been done in recent years to reduce invasive species and reintroduce native species. The results of this work are now evident; the park is really beautiful in spring and early summer and again when autumn colours the trees.

In early summer you can look over lupines and ponds to Stanley Park in the distance. *Dawn Hanna*

Another regular visitor to the park is the beaver. Almost every year a beaver, having been swept around Point Grey by the Fraser River, finds its way to the first freshwater site, the ponds in Jericho Beach Park. There it starts work on building a lodge, sometimes raising young. There is an ongoing battle between beaver and park staff, as the beaver tries to cut down trees and the staff tries to protect them.

The park is roughly divided into two halves: the northern recreational area with beaches, large lawns and picnic tables; and the southern portion south of the ponds and up the hill. This is the more natural area and more rewarding to the naturalist.

Many paths run east-west along the beach and through the park, so it is easy to zigzag back and forth across the park several times, with each route leading through somewhat different habitat. From everywhere there are spectacular views of English Bay, the city and the North Shore mountains.

Visit year-round.

Nearby Locations

- Locarno Beach, Spanish Banks, Pacific Spirit Regional Park and UBC campus lie west along the foreshore

Some Alerts

- in winter, wet trails across the upper part of the hill will soak ordinary sneakers

More Information

Vancouver Park Board Recreation: 604-257-8400 or http://vancouver.ca/parkfinder_wa

Point Grey Foreshore

by David Cook

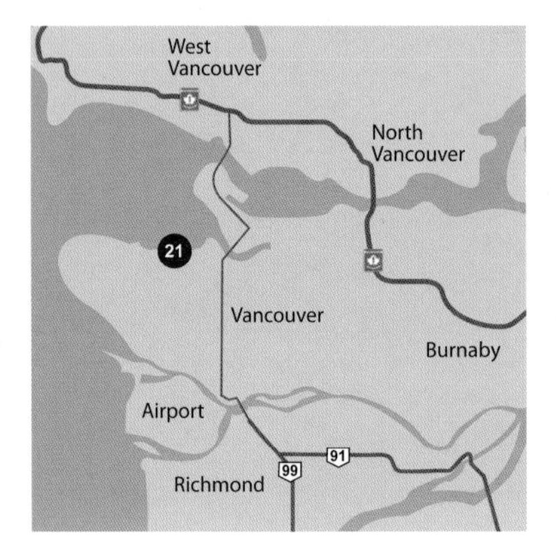

Intertidal biology and geology: from kelp forest to sandstone cliffs

Location

Point Grey Foreshore, in northwest Vancouver, runs parallel to Point Grey Rd. between Alma St. and Balsam St.

Transit Information

The #4 UBC bus travels along W 4th Ave. and stops at Balsam St. and Alma St., with many stops in between.

The #22 MacDonald/Knight bus stops at Cornwall Ave. and Balsam St.

For up-to-date information, contact TransLink at www.translink.ca or 604-953-3333.

Introduction

This 2-kilometre (1.2-mile) foreshore runs parallel to Point Grey Rd. between Balsam St. to the east and Hastings Mill Park at Alma St. to the west. There are access points to the beach at the foot of Balsam, Trafalgar, MacDonald, Bayswater, Balaclava, Waterloo and Dunbar streets. There is a pathway above the beach between Balsam St. and Trafalgar St. At some of the entrances there are maps and interpretive boards.

This shoreline strip is neither a park nor a reserve. Take care not to walk

A great blue heron's skill and patience are rewarded by its catch, a starry flounder.
James Holkko

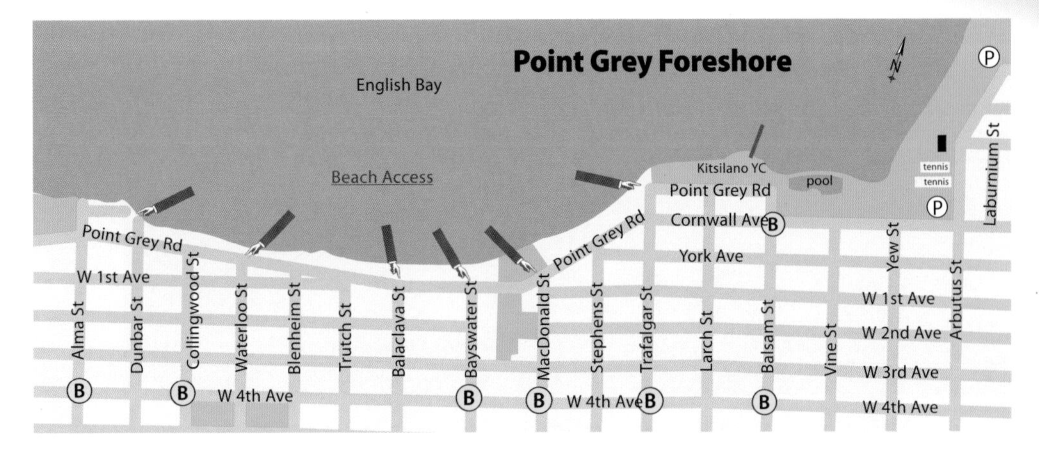

on marine life, and if you turn over rocks, replace them carefully without crushing the numerous shore crabs that seek refuge beneath them.

Natural History Visit

This is an excellent location to observe intertidal sea life on rocky beaches and on sand and mud flats when the tide is low. You can identify the main life zones and their dominant species. In the spray zone there are periwinkles and lichens; in the high-tide zone there are barnacles, limpets and rockweed; in the mid-tide zone there are mussels, sea stars and whelks and in the low-tide zone there is kelp. You also can find examples of green, brown and red seaweed. When the tide is low, much of the intertidal life lies hidden; shore crabs hide beneath rocks, and clams burrow in the mud.

Fish eat green isopods, found in mussel beds and seaweed or under rocks.
James Holkko

As you walk along the beach, you can see many outcroppings of sandstone. The sandstone—which includes some thin beds of siltstone, claystone and fossiliferous coal—was deposited about 50 million years ago as part of the delta of a river that drained from the mountains to the north. Faint diagonal layers in the sandstone, known as cross-beds, indicate the direction of the currents that laid down the sandstone long ago. Note that the originally flat layers of sandstone have been tilted up about 10° to the north. This is due to the rising of the Coast Mountains to the north and the sinking of the Georgia Depression to the south, two processes still taking place today.

At no fewer than three locations along the beach, dark and erosion-resistant basaltic dikes cut vertically through the sandstone. They form slightly raised ridges more or less at right angles to the beach. They were probably intruded into the sandstone 34 to 31 million years ago.

On a windy day it's exhilarating to walk along the foreshore and enjoy the fresh air.
James Holkko

The rounded knobs that protrude from the sandstone are concretions that formed where the sandstone was cemented more strongly. With weathering and wave erosion, they eventually fall out as large round boulders. However, many of the cobbles and boulders that lie on the beach are not sandstone but various types of granitic, volcanic and metamorphic rock. These were left after waves eroded the overlying glacial sediments that can still be seen in the sea cliffs of Point Grey to the west.

About 50 metres (164 feet) to the east of the Volunteer Park steps, a broad elevated section of clean sandstone bedrock protrudes from the cliff face. Broken clamshells litter the top of the rock where crows and gulls have dropped and smashed them from a considerable height. Some may still have clam flesh inside. A large variety of both resident and migrant species of seabirds, waterfowl and shorebirds visit the Point Grey foreshore. The attraction is the diversity of intertidal life, both living and dead, along the mud flats and rocky shores.

When the tide is high, access to the beach is limited, though the beach below the Trafalgar St. and Balsam St. path is usually accessible. When the tide is low, you can walk the full length of the beach.

Nearby Locations

- Kitsilano Beach to the east provides many recreational facilities
- Hastings Mill Park, Jericho Park Beach, salmon enhancement of Spanish Banks Creek and Pacific Spirit Regional Park lie to the west

Some Alerts

- when the tide is out, the beach is slippery, muddy and rough from rocks and cobbles; wear footwear that grips well
- watch the tides

More Information

Tide charts for Point Grey: www.waterlevels.gc.ca

Stanley Park: West

by Catherine Aitchison

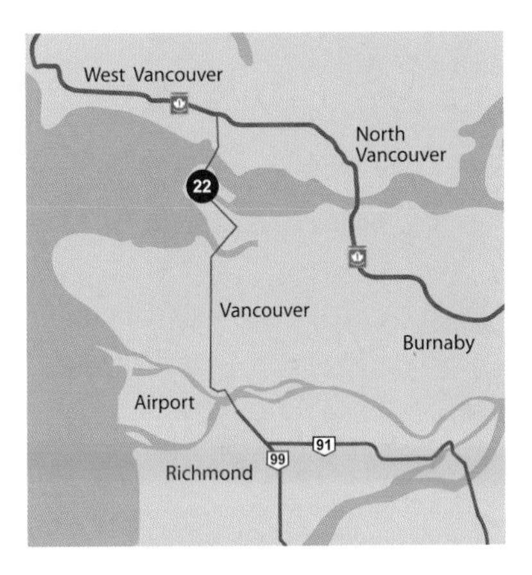

Sandy beaches, birds on the lagoon, wildlife in the forests and marshes

Location

Stanley Park is in northwest Vancouver at the west end of W Georgia St.

Transit Information

Take the #19 Stanley Park bus to the Lost Lagoon and Causeway stop, or wait until the final stop at the Stanley Park Loop. In summer you can connect there with the free Stanley Park shuttle bus, which circles the park and stops at designated places.

For up-to-date information, contact TransLink at www.translink.ca or 604-953-3333.

Introduction

Stanley Park is one of the most famous urban parks in North America. Tucked between the high-rise towers of the West End and the salt water of English Bay and Coal Harbour, just minutes from downtown Vancouver, it is enjoyed by millions of tourists and local residents.

Only two years after the City of Vancouver's incorporation, the city officially opened Stanley Park in 1888. At 405 hectares (1,000 acres), it is one of the largest municipal parks in North America. With a large variety of wildlife, flower gardens, a pitch-and-putt golf course, the Vancouver Aquarium, a cricket pitch, picnic areas, beaches and several children's playgrounds, it offers something for everyone.

Trees of many kinds grow in a tranquil meadow between Lost Lagoon and Second Beach. *Steve Britten*

Magnificent views of the North Shore mountains, the harbour and English Bay are features of the encircling Seawall, which has walking and bike-rollerblade paths. Maps of the park are available at any concession stand in the park.

Natural History Visit

Probably the most visited location in the park is Lost Lagoon, easily accessed from Georgia St. and the West End. You can enjoy a circular walk

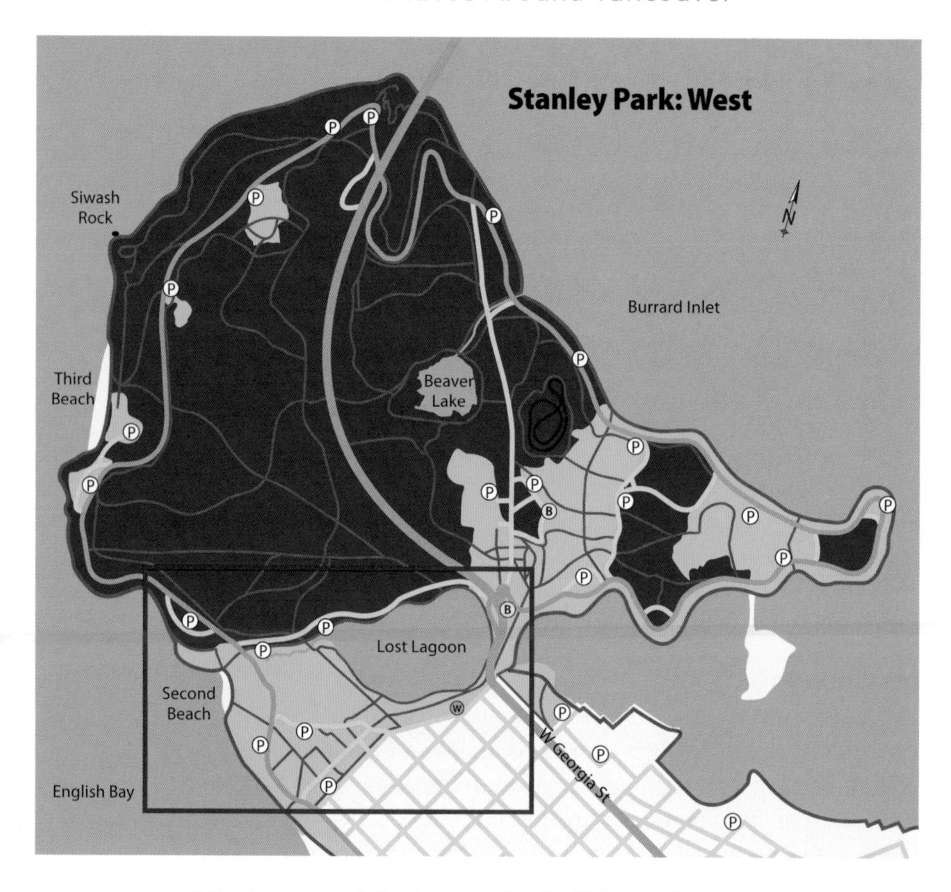

around the lagoon and the interpretive facilities at the Nature House of the Stanley Park Ecology Society, housed in the old boathouse. Walking and bike-rollerblade paths that connect with the Seawall pass close by the lagoon and the Nature House. A native plant demonstration garden lies just above the Nature House, and the rhododendron garden is to the west near the pitch-and-putt golf course.

The Barrow's goldeneyes with a white facial crescent are males; the others are females.
Mark Habdas

There is something to see in every season, but the best time of year for bird watching is from mid-September to mid-March, when the flocks of wintering seabirds return from their breeding grounds. Lost Lagoon often hosts large numbers of overwintering ducks including lesser scaups, common goldeneyes and buffleheads. As well, you can see saltwater species such as surf scoters, Barrow's goldeneyes, harlequin ducks, pelagic cormorants and common loons on the salt water near Second Beach.

A large and unusually urban colony of great blue herons is located near the Park Board office at the end of Beach Ave. There are currently more than 170 nests, and over 200 young now hatch here each spring. Signs beneath the colony explain the breeding cycle of the herons.

There is plenty of other wildlife in and around Lost Lagoon. Evidence of the resident beaver's tree-cutting activities is obvious along the water's edge. Also sharing the lagoon are mink and a family of river otters. Raccoons are numerous, and the occasional striped skunk puts in an appearance along the paths. Douglas squirrels, a native species, as well as eastern gray squirrels are often seen, especially near the stone bridge. In the lagoon itself there are large numbers of huge carp and many turtles, which can be seen warming themselves on any available log on a sunny day. These turtles are all red-eared sliders, not native to Canada.

Indian-plum is a harbinger of spring. It's one of the first shrubs to bloom. *Wayne Weber*

The man-made marsh in the north corner of the lagoon contains a mix of native plants such as salmonberry, salal, bulrush and cattail. It provides wonderful habitat for frogs, birds and insects such as butterflies and dragonflies. The marsh was created to purify rainwater runoff from the causeway road.

The heated Second Beach swimming pool, open in the summer months, is staffed by lifeguards, as are the beaches. English Bay beach to the south is

A gentle stream flows from Lost Lagoon in Stanley Park to English Bay. *Steve Britten*

Above: Two great blue herons greet each other, probably noisily, at the heron colony. *Mark Habdas*

Left: Red elderberry is an excellent food for birds.
Al and Jude Grass

within easy walking distance of Second Beach. Third Beach is farther north along the Seawall from Second Beach.

Visit year-round. The best birding is from mid-September to mid-March.

Nearby Locations

- the east side of Stanley Park—including Beaver Lake, Lumberman's Arch and the Rose Garden—is within walking distance
- the Seawall surrounds the park

Some Alerts

- watch for bicycles when you cross any of the bike-rollerblade paths

More Information

Stanley Park: http://vancouver.ca/parks/parks/stanley/index.htm
Vancouver Park Board Recreation: 604-257-8400 or http://vancouver.ca/parkfinder_wa
Stanley Park Ecology Society programs: 604-257-6908 or www.stanleyparkecology.ca/programs/
Wilderness on the Doorstep: Discovering Nature in Stanley Park, Nature Vancouver (VNHS) publication, Alison Parkinson (ed.), Harbour Publishing, 2006.
Stanley Park Shuttle: 604-257-8400 or www.city.vancouver.bc.ca/parks/parks/stanley/shuttle.htm

Stanley Park: East

by Robyn Worcester

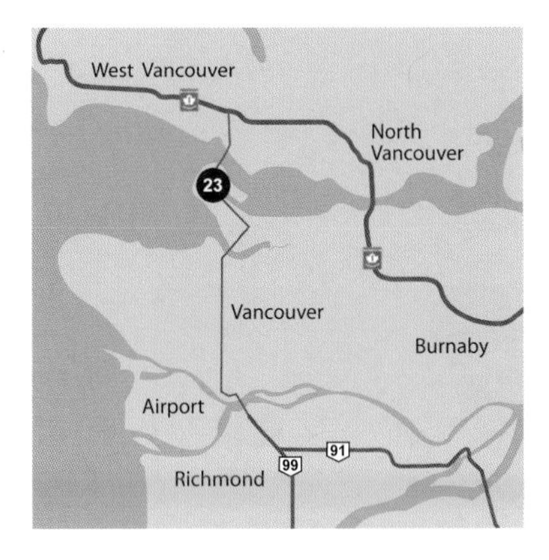

Colourful rose garden, cool forest walks and lakeside wetlands

Location

Stanley Park is in northwest Vancouver at the west end of W Georgia St.

Transit Information

Take the #19 Stanley Park bus to the final stop at the Stanley Park Loop. In summer you can connect there with the free Stanley Park shuttle bus, which circles the park and stops at designated places.

For up-to-date information, contact TransLink at www.translink.ca or 604-953-3333.

Introduction

Stanley Park serves as a natural and recreational area for over eight million visitors every year. The east side of the park provides a variety of experiences thanks to its forests, wetlands, historical sites and entertainment opportunities.

Natural History Visit

At the bus loop, walk southeast past the historic Dining Pavilion and Malkin Bowl to the Stanley Park Rose Garden. The Rose Garden began with a dare taken on by the Kiwanis community service organization in 1920. Many people doubted that roses would ever grow in Vancouver's wet, moist climate, but they were proven wrong, and the garden currently features over 3,500 individual plants. Walk across Pipeline Rd. and through the rose arches toward the forest; you will find the Shakespeare Garden nestled against the Park Board buildings on the right side of the path. These beautiful but non-native trees were planted as a cultural nod to the works of Shakespeare that mention them.

Wood ducks are cavity-nesting birds. Duck boxes are installed around Beaver Lake. *Robyn Worcester*

As you continue west across the grass and turn right along South Creek Trail, you will begin to see the effects of the massive windstorm that hit

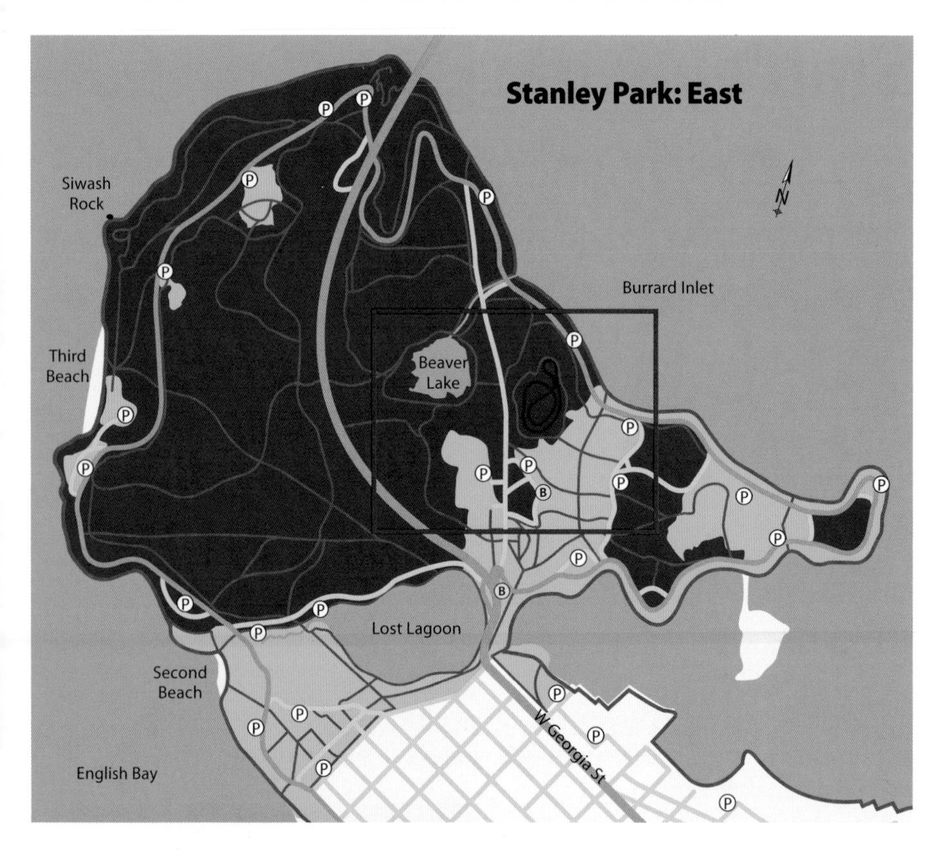

Bullfrogs were introduced to the Lower Mainland in the 1930s or 1940s as a food source. *Robyn Worcester*

Stanley Park in December 2006. This previously dark and mature section of forest is now brighter and more open; hundreds of trees were flattened by the storm. Although many of the fallen trees have been removed to reduce fire hazard, some were left behind to provide critical habitat for wildlife and to replenish the forest soil with their decaying nutrients. Opening up the forest canopy is bringing an increase in light-loving species. More deciduous plants and berry-producing shrubs grow here and attract a greater diversity of forest birds and other animals. Dead trees, standing or fallen, provide feeding, nesting and den sites for birds and small mammals and are essential for the park's terrestrial salamanders.

At the end of this trail you will reach Beaver Lake, one of Vancouver's few remaining natural wetlands and one of the most scenic areas of Stanley

A western white pine (left) and a tree of heaven (right) near the Rose Garden. *Robyn Worcester*

Park. Some of the signs that you have reached the wetlands are the many skunk cabbage plants and deciduous trees you'll spot along the trail. Wetlands are environmentally sensitive areas that provide homes for some of the park's threatened species. As you walk to your right around the lake, you might observe frogs, songbirds, waterfowl, hunting herons and even the occasional river otter.

As you leave Beaver Lake at the northeast corner, on Beaver Lake Trail or Ravine Trail, keep your eyes open for the roosting barred owls that nest in this area. Both of these cool, moist trails run parallel to Beaver Creek, one of Vancouver's last remaining salmon streams. Head directly east across Pipeline Rd. and take Tunnel Trail. Here you can see evidence of Stanley Park's logging past; massive stumps and fallen giants are scattered in the forest, left over from logging in the mid-1800s. Almost all of Stanley Park's historic trails were once skid roads used to haul logs out of the forest.

At the east end of Tunnel Trail you will reach Lumberman's Arch, an area of great historical significance. Hidden under the grassy mounds are shell middens—First Nations garbage dumps and sometimes burial heaps—from a longstanding village called Xway-Xway. The village existed for at least 500 years, likely as a communal gathering place for Coast Salish groups.

Beaver Lake was called Ahka-chu, meaning "little lake," by First Nations people. *Robyn Worcester*

This open grassy area, a favourite for picnics, is close to the water park, concession stands and a small beach. Walk back past the Vancouver Aquarium, playground, petting zoo and children's train to the bus loop.

Visit year-round. Spring and fall are the best times for birding in the forest and Beaver Lake. The gardens are at their best in spring and summer. The outdoor amenities such as the water park and concessions are open in summer.

Nearby Locations

- the west side of Stanley Park—including Lost Lagoon, Second Beach and Third Beach—is within walking distance
- the Seawall surrounds the park

Some Alerts

- it is best to have a companion on forest trails for personal safety
- do not walk on forest trails during high winds

More Information

Stanley Park: http://vancouver.ca/parks/parks/stanley/index.htm
Vancouver Park Board Recreation: 604-257-8400 or http://vancouver.ca/parkfinder_wa
Stanley Park Ecology Society programs: 604-257-6908 or http://www.stanleyparkecology.ca/programs/
Wilderness on the Doorstep: Discovering Nature in Stanley Park, Nature Vancouver (VNHS) publication, Alison Parkinson (ed.), Harbour Publishing, 2006.
Stanley Park Shuttle: 604-257-8400 or www.city.vancouver.bc.ca/parks/parks/stanley/shuttle.htm

Stanley Park Seawall

by June M. Ryder

Marine life, forests and the rocks that underlie Vancouver

Location

Stanley Park is in northwest Vancouver at the west end of W Georgia St.

Transit Information

Take the #19 Stanley Park bus to the final stop at the Stanley Park Loop. In summer you can connect there with the free Stanley Park shuttle bus, which circles the park and stops at designated places.

For up-to-date information, contact TransLink at www.translink.ca or 604-953-3333.

Introduction

Stanley Park, which has been described as a lush evergreen oasis and a natural gem, lies in the heart of the Vancouver urban region. The park, logged prior to its establishment in 1887, consists primarily of mature second-growth forest. However, it also includes manicured gardens, an aquarium and recreational facilities such as tennis courts, beaches and the Seawall. The Seawall, consisting of a walkway in both directions and a one-way bicycle path for counter-clockwise travel only, extends for 9 kilometres (5.6 miles) around the entire marine shoreline of Stanley Park. Pathways around Lost Lagoon enable you to complete the 10-kilometre (6.2-mile) circuit of the park.

Basalt columns are prominent in the high cliff below the Prospect Point lookout. *June M. Ryder*

During a walk along the Stanley Park Seawall, you will pass mostly natural areas where wildlife abounds, both inland and on the shore. You can also see the Lions Gate Bridge close-up from underneath. Most distant views include the southernmost peaks of the Coast Mountains, the urban high-rises of downtown Vancouver and the waterscapes and ships of English Bay and Burrard Inlet's inner harbour.

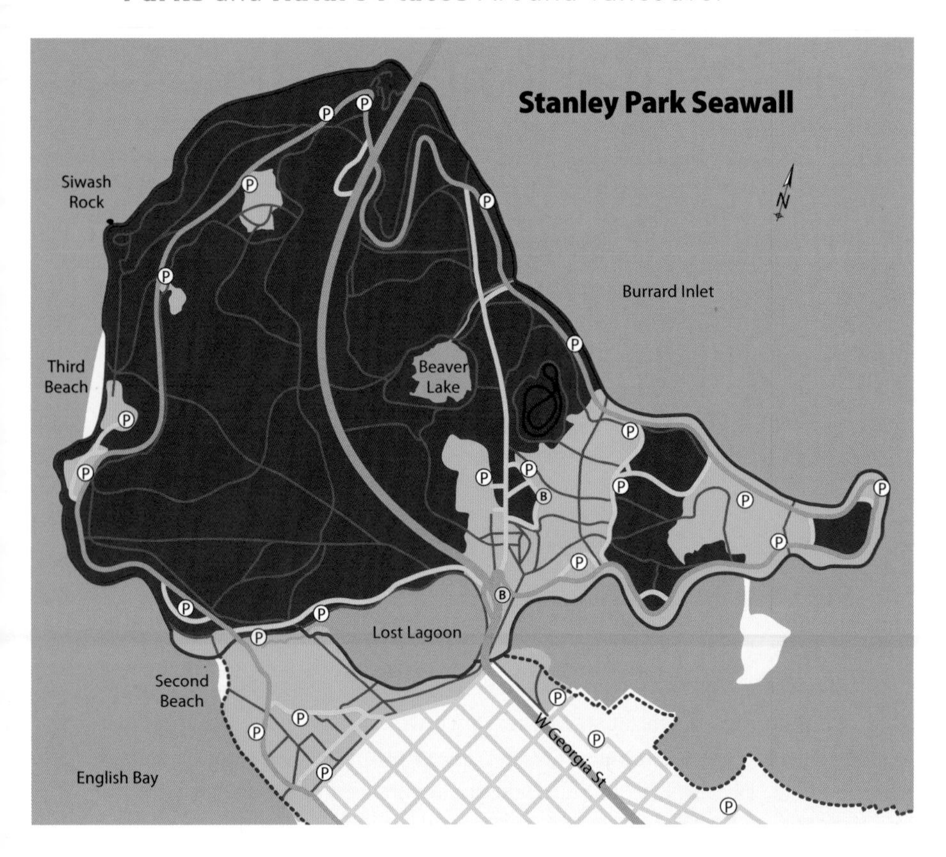

The tall forests of western redcedar and Douglas-fir that extend across much of the park adjoin the Seawall along the eastern Burrard Inlet shoreline and the western English Bay shore south of Ferguson Point. Most of the shoreline consists of bouldery beaches; Third Beach on English Bay has the best stretch of sand. Between Third Beach and the Lions Gate Bridge, the Seawall is flanked by steep, rocky cliffs, and rock outcrops extend seaward across the beaches. These geological features provide the most extensive and clearest view of the rocks that underlie Vancouver.

At Third Beach a basalt dike forms a low, steep-sided ridge across the bouldery foreshore. *June M. Ryder*

Natural History Visit

If you are a strong walker or a cyclist, you can complete an entire circuit of the park. If you prefer a shorter walk, in summer you can use the Shuttle Bus to and from the starting and finishing points. To see the geological features, walk the 3-kilometre (1.9-mile) stretch of Seawall along the rugged northwest section from Lions Gate Bridge to the south end of Third Beach. To reach the Seawall near Lions

A Seawall walk offers an excellent way to enjoy geology, birds, sea mammals and plants.
June M. Ryder

Gate Bridge, at Prospect Point, follow the steep downhill Eldon Trail from just north of the concession building.

On this section of the Seawall, examine a clean rock and see that the sandstone is made up of tiny sand grains cemented together. Now look carefully at a moderately distant cliff face, and you may be able to see the thick layers, called beds, in which the original sediments were deposited between 70 and 50 million years ago. On the foreshore, if the tide is low, you can see rock layers in the mounds and low ridges of bedrock. Also note that the layers incline very gently to the south, showing how the rocks were tilted slightly when slowly heaved up above sea level. Look for tiny pockets of black coal along the breaks between the sandstone layers.

About 32 million years ago lava, which is molten rock, was injected into cracks in the sandstone. In two places along the Seawall, at Prospect Point and near Siwash Rock, this lava formed vertical sheets of dark basalt bounded by margins of baked, partly melted, sandstone. The basalt and baked sandstone are harder and more resistant to erosion than the normal sandstone and tend to form the steepest cliff segments and jagged outcrops. Basalt dikes are clearly visible at Prospect Point, where rock columns that are typical of basalt are visible high in the cliffs. Siwash Rock is a sea stack

Squat black turnstones feed in the seaweed along rocky tidal shores. *Virginia Hayes*

that has survived erosion because it consists of hard basalt. At low tide on the rocky foreshore between Siwash Rock and Third Beach, you can see one or more dikes. They are narrow ridges and peninsulas with vertical sides.

The Seawall is well visited, so for a quiet walk, avoid weekends and holidays when the walkway and cycle path can be crowded. For land birds, early mornings are the best observing time, especially during spring and early summer. Look for seabirds in fall, winter and early spring.

Nearby Locations

- the rest of Stanley Park is within walking distance; the Seawall bicycle and walking path extends around the city waterfront for many kilometres, from the Canada Place cruise ship terminal all the way to the Maritime Museum in Kitsilano

Some Alerts

- slippery rock outcrops on the foreshore and bouldery beaches
- slopes above the Seawall may be unstable, especially during heavy or prolonged rainfall; never attempt to climb up these slopes
- during stormy weather, large waves can splash up over the Seawall

More Information

Stanley Park: http://vancouver.ca/parks/parks/stanley/index.htm

Vancouver Park Board Recreation: 604-257-8400 or http://vancouver.ca/parkfinder_wa

Stanley Park Ecology Society programs: 604-257-6908 or www.stanleyparkecology.ca/programs/

Wilderness on the Doorstep: Discovering Nature in Stanley Park, Nature Vancouver (VNHS) publication, Alison Parkinson (ed.), Harbour Publishing, 2006.

Stanley Park Shuttle: 604-257-8400 or www.city.vancouver.bc.ca/parks/parks/stanley/shuttle.htm

VanDusen Botanical Garden

by Michael Le Geyt

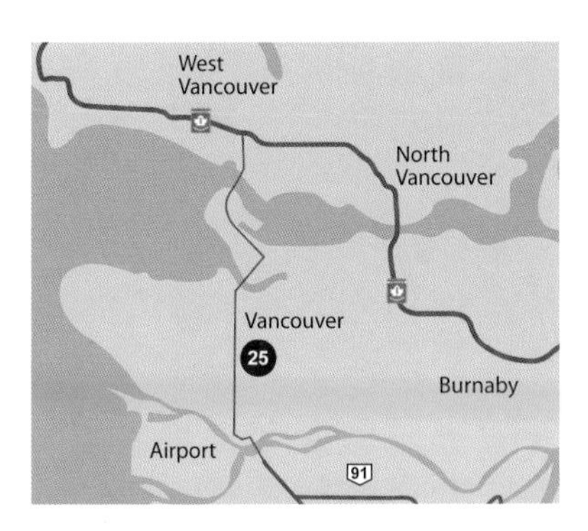

A living museum of plants from around the world

Location

VanDusen Botanical Garden is in south Vancouver at Oak St. and W 37th Ave.

Transit Information

Take the #17 Oak bus and alight at the Oak St. and W 37th Ave. stop.

For up-to-date information, contact TransLink at www.translink.ca or 604-953-3333.

Introduction

The VanDusen Botanical Garden is operated by the Vancouver Park Board and the VanDusen Botanical Garden Association. It is a spectacular 22-hectare (54-acre) reserve in the heart of Vancouver. Thousands of plants from around the world are displayed in verdant rolling terrain that includes a sinuous watercourse of lakes, ponds and waterfalls.

March and April are the best months to view the garden's stunning magnolia blooms. *Michael Le Geyt*

The plant collections are exhibited by geographical region, for example, the Sino-Himalayan Garden, Western North America Garden and Southern Hemisphere Garden; and by species, for example, oaks and maples; and by special interest, for example, the Canadian Heritage Garden and Maze.

Plants bloom throughout the year, even in January when fragrant witch hazels perfume the air. In spring camellias, rhododendrons and magnolias burst forth, followed by laburnums, azaleas and fabulous Himalayan blue poppies. In early summer the rose gardens are a delight, while the Perennial Garden blooms all summer long. In autumn the fall leaf colours can be spectacular, especially the Japanese maples and the Eastern North America collection. In winter the bark

VanDusen Botanical Garden

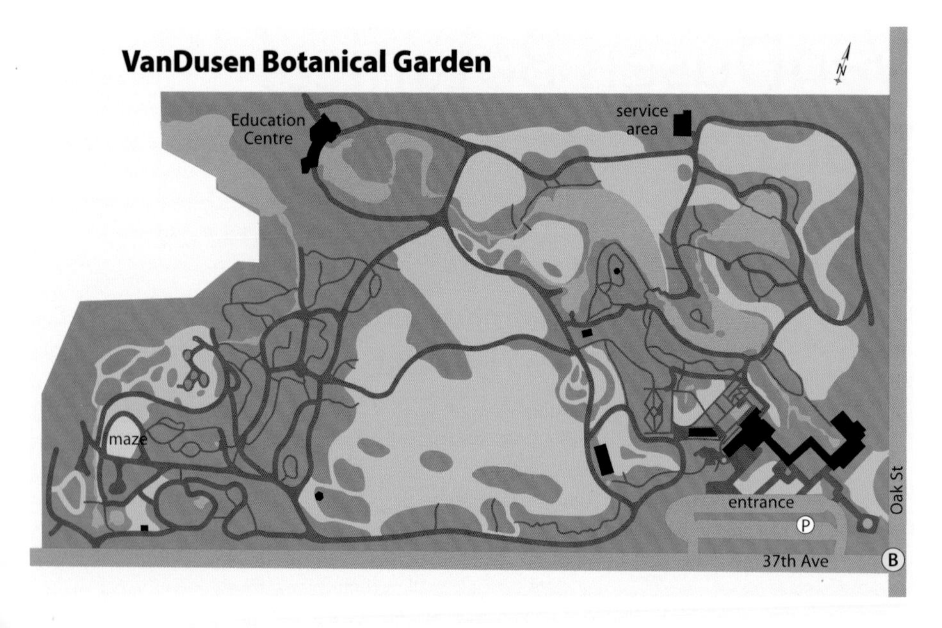

and branching structure of deciduous trees are fully revealed, and the hollies display their spectrum of berry colours.

There is an admission fee for visiting the garden.

Natural History Visit

The garden entrance lies at the intersection of W 37th Ave. and Oak St. Because of the garden's large size, a free visitor's guide outlines tours of varying length, from 20 minutes to 2 hours. This guide also contains an

Finding the centre of the Elizabethan Maze is a popular challenge for children. *Peggy Heath*

In the latter half of May, the Laburnum Walk becomes a long golden archway. *Nancy Wong*

excellent map giving the location of the principal plant collections. You can enjoy the garden according to your interests and stamina.

The areas closest to the garden entrance are intensively cultivated, while those in the farther reaches tend to be less developed. Interpretive signs are located throughout the garden. Take the time to read these; they contain a wealth of fascinating information about the plants and their history, uses, medicinal properties and so forth.

Watch for interesting bird life throughout the garden but especially in the less developed sections where feeding opportunities and shelter are better. You may see waterfowl paddling on the lakes and ponds, ravens croaking high in the Douglas-firs and songbirds foraging underneath the shrubbery. In woodland glades there may be raptors in winter and even the occasional owl roosting in a dense conifer. Bird watching is particularly good during

Top: Japanese maples often turn fiery red in autumn. *Michael Le Geyt*

Bottom: A red-eared slider has hauled out to bask in warm sunlight on a rock near water. *Michael Le Geyt*

the spring and fall migrations. At this time a knowledgeable volunteer leads a regular monthly bird walk.

In the less developed areas of the garden, look for decaying nurse logs that nourish a host of young plants and provide food and shelter for beetles, insects and small mammals. Turtles, frogs and carp inhabit the lakes while iridescent dragonflies swoop over their surfaces in pursuit of insect prey. The garden maintains extensive hives of honeybees; you can purchase their delicious honey in the garden shop.

The main walking routes through the garden are asphalt, but in places the pavement is uneven because of uplifting tree roots. As well, surfaces can be slippery in rainy weather. It is permissible to walk on the lawns, but they can become quite soggy during the winter months. Visitors are encouraged to explore the secondary trails that wander through the garden, but these are less maintained.

A botanical garden changes constantly throughout the seasons, which makes VanDusen Garden an excellent destination for repeat visits. Plants are in bloom every month of the year but peak during spring and summer.

Nearby Locations

- Queen Elizabeth Park and Bloedel Conservatory lie about 1 kilometre (0.6 mile) east; the W 37th Ave. bikeway leads directly from VanDusen Garden to Queen Elizabeth Park

Some Alerts

- feeding bread to the fish or waterfowl is discouraged; it is a hazard to wildlife
- picking flowers or stealing cuttings is strictly forbidden; both are hazardous to the conservation of the plant collections

More Information

VanDusen Botanical Garden: 604-878-9274 or www.vandusengarden.org
VanDusen Botanical Garden: http://vancouver.ca/parks/parks/vandusen/index.htm

Queen Elizabeth Park

by Alex Downie

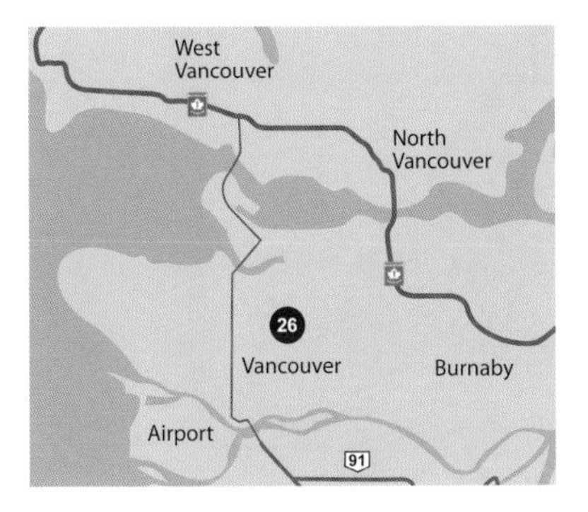

Superior garden plantings at Vancouver City's highest point

Location

Queen Elizabeth Park is in south Vancouver at Cambie St. and W 33rd Ave.

Transit Information

Take the #15 Cambie bus and alight at the W 33rd Ave. and Cambie St. stop.

For up-to-date information, contact TransLink at www.translink.ca or 604-953-3333.

Introduction

This beautifully maintained 52-hectare (128-acre) park is the highest point in the City of Vancouver at 167 metres (548 feet) above sea level. Known as Little Mountain, the site was logged by 1890. Miners moved in to quarry basalt used to pave the city's first streets. The City of Vancouver bought the site with its abandoned quarries for parkland in 1927.

In 1940 the park's name was changed from Little Mountain to Queen Elizabeth Park in honour of the wife of King George VI; the monarchs had visited our city the previous year. An arboretum was started on the north

The Plaza on the top of Little Mountain is adorned with red tulip blooms in spring.
Alex Downie

Over the Small Quarry Garden, you can see downtown Vancouver and the North Shore mountains. *Alex Downie*

side of the park in 1948, followed by landscaping of the larger of two rock quarries in 1953. The smaller quarry was transformed in 1961. Many features were added in the 1960s, including an 18-hole pitch-and-putt golf course, lawn bowling club and rose garden and culminating in the construction of the Bloedel Conservatory.

The park receives nearly six million visitors a year who marvel at its brilliantly coloured, artistically designed garden plantings with meticulously tended displays. The park is wonderful to visit, but be aware that some paths are steep and make walking difficult for inactive or disabled people.

Natural History Visit

From the bus stop, walk east into the park along W 33rd Ave. Turn right at the ring road (Park Dr.) and head east for five minutes to the Rose Garden on your left.

The Rose Garden was built in 1967 to commemorate Canada's Centennial.

There are over 100 varieties of roses showcased in formal beds with companion plantings to extend the floral season beyond the peak rose bloom time of May to October. Walk uphill to the rock wall, where you'll see the crown-like layout of the garden.

Follow the path uphill past the Lawn Bowling Club to reach the summit of the park. Proceed west through the parking lot toward the Plaza and Bloedel Conservatory dome. This 1.2-hectare (3-acre) plaza and parking lot are built entirely atop Vancouver's main water reservoir! The redeveloped plaza was opened in 2007 and features an impressive fountain with a dancing waters theme and Henry Moore's imposing sculpture *Knife Edge – Two Piece,* donated in 1969.

Descend the broad steps next to the Bloedel Conservatory to the eastern lookout. Here you'll see the bronze figures of *The Photo Session* sculpture by J. Seward Johnson Jr. Take in the view and look down into the jewel-like

Azalea blooms in various colours create a brilliant display in spring. *Alex Downie*

You can view the seasonal plantings in the Large Quarry Garden close-up or from above.
Alex Downie

Small Quarry Garden. To your right is the restaurant, where Bill Clinton and Boris Yeltsin dined in 1993. Walk back toward the Bloedel Conservatory, then head west for a panoramic view of the Large Quarry Garden, renowned for its spring and summer floral displays.

Cross the waterfall bridge and turn right to descend into the manicured landscape of the Large Quarry Garden, a favourite with wedding parties during the warmer months. Highlights include sweeping displays of spring bulbs and summer flowering annuals. Check out the massive leaves of the Chilean rhubarb near the pond. At the eastern end of the garden you'll see the arching canes of the Chinese timber bamboo, which thrives in our West Coast climate.

Continue downhill past the bamboo to enter the arboretum. This area features native and exotic conifers including western redcedar, Douglas-fir, Sitka spruce, coast redwood and the massive Wellingtonia, which has thick fire-resistant bark. Resident Cooper's hawks make their home here, and bald eagles frequent the taller trees in this area.

Turn left when you reach Park Dr. and follow the road around to W 33rd Ave. where you began this tour. Along the way you'll see plantings of African cedars and larches and an extensive collection of oaks. If you're lucky, you might spot a coyote galloping among the trees!

Queen Elizabeth Park is worth a visit at any time of year. Best times for floral display are mid-March through mid-October. The Japanese cherry trees are in peak bloom from late March through early May. Deciduous trees are cloaked in fall colours starting mid-October.

A Cooper's hawk has a long tail and short rounded wings that allow it to hunt among trees. *Peter M. Candido*

Nearby Locations

- the Bloedel Conservatory is on-site
- VanDusen Botanical Garden is several blocks west

Some Alerts

- lookouts high above the Quarry Gardens
- do not climb slippery rock walls above cliff faces
- sharp spray nozzles and possible broken glass in the Plaza fountain
- undrinkable water in all watercourses and fountains
- thorny brambles along forest trails
- highly poisonous mushrooms, especially red-capped fly agaric in the fall

More Information

Queen Elizabeth Gardens: http://vancouver.ca/parks/parks/queenelizabeth/
Vancouver Park Board Recreation: 604-257-8400 or
http://vancouver.ca/parkfinder_wa

Bloedel Conservatory

by Alex Downie

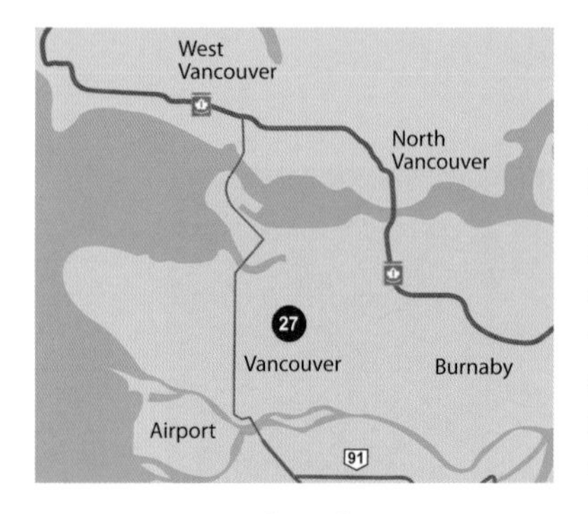

Year-round displays of rainforest, subtropical and desert plants

Location

Bloedel Conservatory is in Queen Elizabeth Park, in south Vancouver. It's at Cambie St. and W 33rd Ave.

Transit Information

Take the #15 Cambie bus and alight at the W 33rd Ave. and Cambie St. stop.

For up-to-date information, contact TransLink at www.translink.ca or 604-953-3333.

Introduction

The Bloedel Conservatory is atop Queen Elizabeth Park at the highest point within the city, 167 metres (548 feet) above sea level. It is the second-largest single-span conservatory in North America. Built in 1969, it is named for timber magnate Prentice Bloedel, who paid $1.25 million for its construction. The dazzling triodetic dome is 43 metres (141 feet) in diameter and 23 metres (75 feet) high.

The Bloedel Conservatory features three simulated climate zones—rainforest, subtropical and desert—containing over 500 species of plants from around the world. Dazzling displays of seasonal flowers, colourful koi fish

On a rainy day, the weather is always perfect inside the Bloedel Conservatory. *Alex Downie*

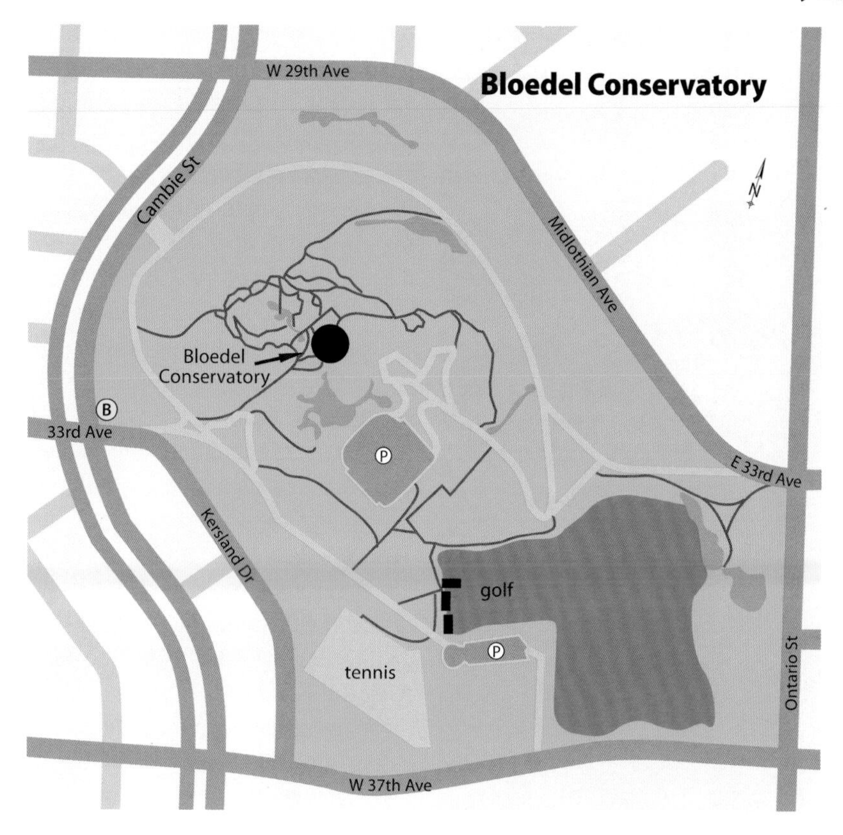

and over 100 species of free-flying tropical birds and parrots complete the scene. In December the Conservatory is dressed in holiday finery, with hundreds of multi-coloured poinsettias, amaryllises, tender narcissi and twinkling lights.

A modest admission fee is charged.

Green-winged macaws are native to the northern forests of South America. *Alex Downie*

Natural History Visit

From the bus stop, walk east into Queen Elizabeth Park along 33rd Ave. Cross the ring road (Park Dr.) and head up to the top of the hill. At the entrance to the Bloedel Conservatory, pick up a self-guided tour brochure. This describes the main points of interest.

Walking clockwise, take in the towering palms, including the clustering fishtail palm from Thailand. Cross the bamboo bridge into the rain forest, where you'll see tree ferns, lobster-claw gingers and giant banana trees. Nearby you can study a pair of green-winged macaws. Look up into the tree canopy to see vining philodendrons and colourful bromeliads clinging to the trees. Around the corner is a charismatic Moluccan cockatoo who loves to perform for kids!

Next you'll enter the subtropical zone, where you'll see a giant banyan tree with rope-like aerial roots. Look for showy tropical flowers such as Hawaiian hibiscus, bougainvillea and lantana, among others that thrive here. You may see several parrots on perches in this area, including an African gray parrot, a pygmy macaw from Venezuela, an Amazon parrot and a blue-and-gold macaw.

Colourful koi fish, exotic birds and lush vegetation are all at the rainforest pond. *Alex Downie*

You're now entering the desert zone. Towering Peruvian candelabra cactus and yucca trees with huge flared trunks dominate the scene. Cacti and succulent plants adorn the rocky landscape. Here you can see Mexican agaves, a source of fibre for waterproof ropes and the basis of alcoholic drinks like tequila. Sit on the bench across from the bird feeder; this is the best place to view the many species of finches and fruit-eating birds that make their home here. Noteworthy birds include African splendid starlings, Vietnamese thrushes, Japanese waxwings and touracos from Sierra Leone.

Visit year-round. It is a wonderful place to escape our sometimes dreary winter weather! It is a good venue for an outing with inactive or disabled people.

Nearby Locations

- the Bloedel Conservatory is located within Queen Elizabeth Park
- VanDusen Botanical Garden is several blocks west

Some Alerts

- parrots can inflict painful bites; keep a safe distance
- cactus plants are spiny
- stones bordering the path can be slippery

More Information

Bloedel Conservatory: 604-257-8570 or
http://vancouver.ca/parks/parks/bloedel/index.htm

Hastings Park Sanctuary

by Pat Miller

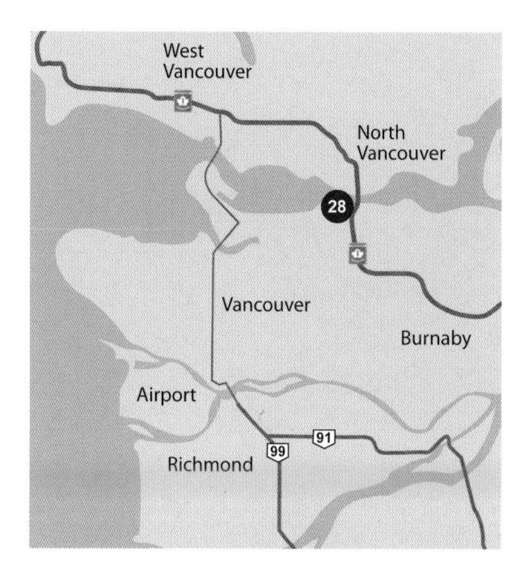

Amazing recent reclamation of a wetland habitat

Location

Hastings Park Sanctuary is in northeast Vancouver in the PNE Grounds at E Hastings St. and Renfrew St.

Transit Information

The #135 SFU bus and the #10 Hastings bus both travel along E Hastings St. Alight at the Renfrew St. and E Hastings St. stop.

Alternatively, from the 29th Ave. SkyTrain Station, take the #16 Arbutus bus to the Renfrew St. and E Hastings St. stop.

For up-to-date information, contact TransLink at www.translink.ca or 604-953-3333.

Introduction

In 1996, following many years of lobbying by the Hastings Sunrise community, Vancouver City Council and Park Board approved a plan to restore Hastings Park to public green space. Asphalt and several buildings were demolished on the site of the Pacific National Exhibition (PNE) and replaced by a formal Italian garden, a children's playground, a skate park and the Sanctuary, a 4-hectare (9.9-acre) wetland consisting of two beautiful ponds surrounded by lush plantings of native West Coast vegetation.

The black rump and white wing patch of this shy dabbling duck identify it as a gadwall. *Les Leighton*

Since its opening in 1999 the wetland at the heart of the Sanctuary has matured, and the site has become East Vancouver's green jewel, a refuge for the area's human residents as well as a diversity of wildlife. The Hastings Park Conservancy, a community stewardship group that advocates for continued regreening and sponsors monthly nature walks in the Sanctuary, has recorded more than 100 bird species in the park. One goal is to daylight Hastings Creek all the way through New Brighton Park to Burrard Inlet and restore salmon to the stream.

The Sanctuary provides habitat for migrating birds and for nesting residents such as red-winged blackbirds, bushtits and spotted towhees. Bald eagles nest nearby and often soar overhead.

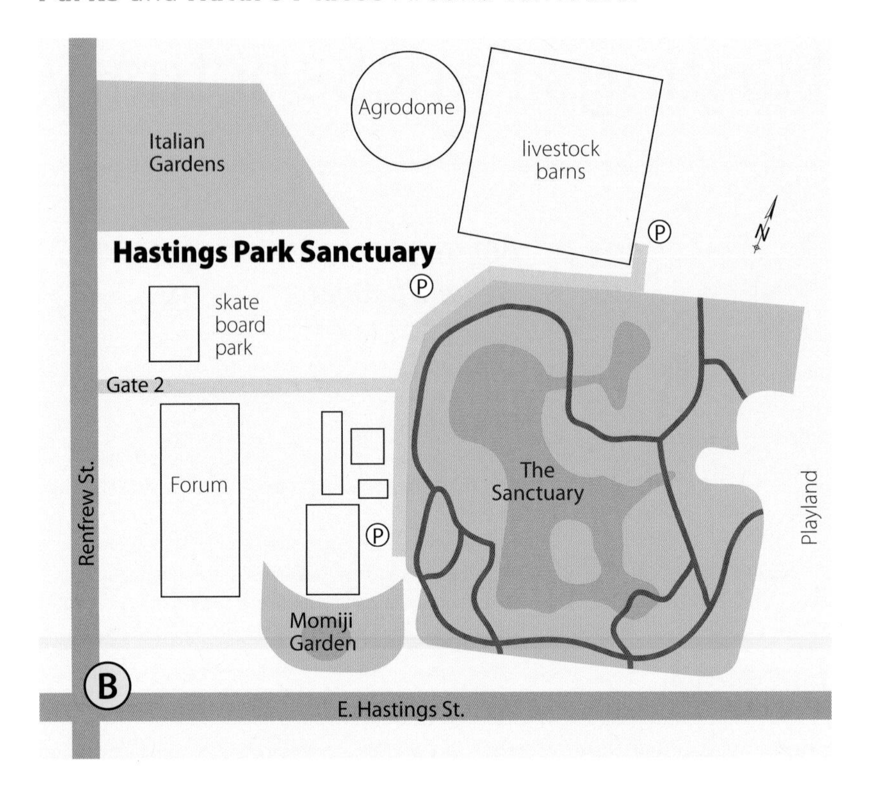

Natural History Visit

Enter the park from Renfrew St. using Gate 2. Follow the path around past the red livestock barns to the Sanctuary on your right. Gravel paths linked by a series of three bridges wind through the Sanctuary.

Beneath the first bridge a short section of stream, fed by surface runoff and stormwater, connects the upper and lower ponds. On the larger upper

Visitors on the boardwalk may observe sparrows, chickadees and kinglets in the willows.
Les Leighton

Trees and cattails provide habitat for red-winged blackbirds, rails and coots.
Les Leighton

pond you may glimpse a pied-billed grebe as it dives into the water in pursuit of small fish and aquatic insects. Mallard ducks are year-round residents; common and hooded mergansers, ring-necked ducks, buffleheads and scaups visit from fall through spring. Keep an eye out for a hawk; there's usually at least one nearby, hidden among the leaves of a large cottonwood or perched on a power pole. At dusk on a summer evening, little brown bats swoop out over the still water in pursuit of their insect prey. An occasional coyote may visit, skulking after small mammals or enjoying a feast of berries in season.

The stone terrace benches are a great place to sit for a rest and look out over the upper pond. Several large plane trees and tulip trees offer welcome shade in summer. You can see many species of songbirds such as finches, kinglets, chickadees and robins flitting through the treetops high above.

Beyond the stone terraces and the second bridge, take the lower path to the floating bridge. In spring listen for the musical call of a male red-winged blackbird: *konk-la-reee!* You may spot a nest in the cattails; watch for a drab brown female blackbird returning with a mouthful of grubs to feed her hungry babies.

Follow the path back around to the west side of the Sanctuary to another seating area, a series of wide steps leading down to the water. Look for schools of bright orange goldfish; the introduced species attracts a variety

Jewelweed or touch-me-not seed pods explode when tapped, scattering the seeds. *Les Leighton*

of interesting predators. From spring through fall, great blue herons and green herons stalk the pond shallows, while ospreys hunt from above, diving steeply down to seize a prize fish in their talons. Late in the year when temperatures decline, these fish disappear into deep water to overwinter.

Visit from dawn to dusk any time. Note that during the PNE, from mid-August to Labour Day, the Sanctuary is accessible only with admission to the exhibition.

At ponds, spot the male mallard with his glossy green head and red-brown chest. *Les Leighton*

Nearby Locations

- the PNE Playland amusement park, a skate park, a basket ball court, a bocce court, a children's play area, Il Giardino Italiano, Momiji Garden and the Hastings Park Horse Race track are on-site
- New Brighton Park is to the north
- Hastings Community Centre, with tennis courts and water park, is to the south

Some Alerts

- footbridges may be slippery in winter
- please do not release goldfish or other aquatic pets in the ponds
- please do not feed ducks

More Information

Hastings Park Conservancy: www.hastingspark.ca
Hastings Park: 604-257-8400 or http://vancouver.ca/parkfinder_wa/index.cfm?fuseaction=FAC.ParkDetails&park_id=72

Renfrew Ravine Park

by Val and Anny Schaefer

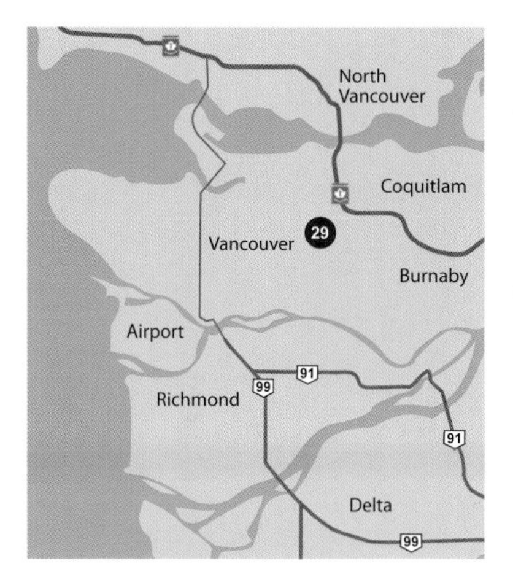

One of Vancouver's few remaining streams

Location

Renfrew Ravine Park is in northeast Vancouver opposite the 29th Ave. SkyTrain Station at E 29th Ave. and Kaslo St.

Transit Information

The 29th Ave. SkyTrain Station is at the south end of the ravine.

Alternatively, the #16 29th Ave./Arbutus bus stops at both Boyd Diversion and E 22nd Ave. near the north end of the ravine and the 29th Ave. SkyTrain Station at the south end of the ravine.

For up-to-date information, contact TransLink at www.translink.ca or 604-953-3333.

Introduction

Renfrew Ravine at 4 hectares (9.9 acres) contains Still Creek, one of the few open streams that remain in Vancouver, which used to have hundreds of streams. Although the creek is now underground for much of its length, it is still visible in Renfrew Ravine Park between the 29th Ave. SkyTrain

Even in summer, Still Creek has a healthy flow of water. *Val and Anny Schaefer*

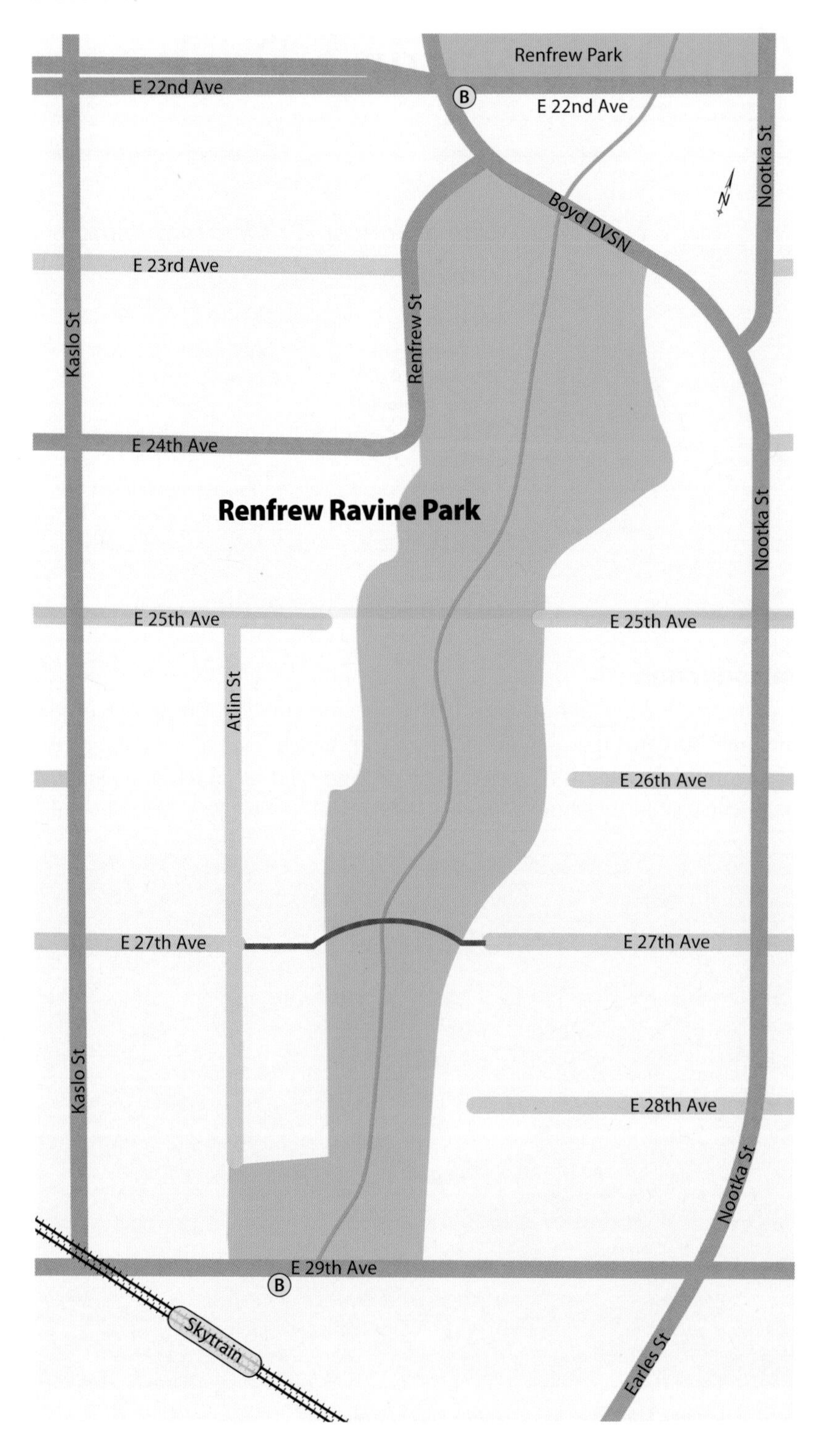
Renfrew Park
E 22nd Ave
B
E 22nd Ave
Nootka St
Boyd DVSN
N
E 23rd Ave
Kaslo St
Renfrew St
E 24th Ave
Renfrew Ravine Park
Nootka St
E 25th Ave
E 25th Ave
Atlin St
E 26th Ave
E 27th Ave
E 27th Ave
Kaslo St
E 28th Ave
Nootka St
E 29th Ave
B
Skytrain
Earles St

Raccoons use their hand-like paws to fish. *Steve Britten*

Station and 22nd Ave. at the Boyd Diversion (near Renfrew St.). The creek continues to be visible in adjacent Renfrew Park across 22nd Ave., another lovely park to visit.

The headwaters of Still Creek are in a small lake in Central Park next to Metrotown town centre in Burnaby. Downstream from the Renfrew area, Still Creek flows eastward to Burnaby Lake. Still Creek, Burnaby Lake, Deer Lake and the Brunette River together make up the Brunette River drainage basin, which is the largest urban watershed within the Vancouver and Burnaby region. Ultimately these waters empty into the Fraser River at Sapperton in New Westminster, home of the first European settlement in the area.

In 1997 the community completed an inspiring neighbourhood greenway through the ravine that features park-like areas, native plants and interpretive signage. Public art includes mosaics, sculptures, stonework and a labyrinth based on a medieval design at Chartres Cathedral in France.

In recent years Still Creek Stewardship Society has been responsible for the protection, rehabilitation and enhancement of Renfrew Ravine. Currently the society, along with Vancouver Park Board, is developing a master plan for Renfrew Ravine Park. Still Creek Stewardship Society holds a Moon Festival in the fall.

Natural History Visit

From the 29th Ave. SkyTrain Station, cross 29th Ave. and find the entrance

Top: Tiny bushtits travel in flocks for protection, landing as a swarm on food supplies.
Mark Habdas

Bottom: The trailhead tempts a visit to one of Vancouver's few remaining open streams.
Val and Anny Schaefer

to Renfrew Ravine Park. The trail follows the bank of the ravine down the east side. The ravine has a small forest of bigleaf maple (including some very large trees), red alder, black cottonwood, Douglas-fir and western redcedar. Dull Oregon grape, salal, sword fern, bracken fern and lady fern cover the forest floor. Vine maple, red elderberry and salmonberry are the common shrubs. There are large patches of Himalayan blackberry at many places along the forest edge.

Renfrew Ravine, a small haven for wildlife, is a good place to watch birds. Spotted towhees, song sparrows and winter wrens find refuge here. Warblers, chickadees, bushtits, kinglets, juncos and other birds travel through here in flocks, feeding on the rich supplies of insects and berries. Douglas squirrels live here. As well, coyotes and raccoons hide in the forest or travel through on their way to other parts of the city.

The plants in the ravine can best be seen from March to October. In summer numerous dragonflies hover over open grassy areas.

Nearby Locations

- Renfrew Park adjoins Renfrew Ravine Park
- Central Park is a short SkyTrain ride away

Some Alerts

- dirt trails are slippery when wet
- dangerous steep slopes off the ravine trail
- water is not safe for human consumption or for wading

More Information

Vancouver Park Board Recreation: 604-257-8400 or http://vancouver.ca/parkfinder_wa
Renfrew Park Community Centre: 604-257-8393 or http://vancouver.ca/parks/cc/renfrew/website/index.html
Renfrew Ravine Moon Festival www.moonfestival.net/

Everett Crowley Park

by Margo A. Longland

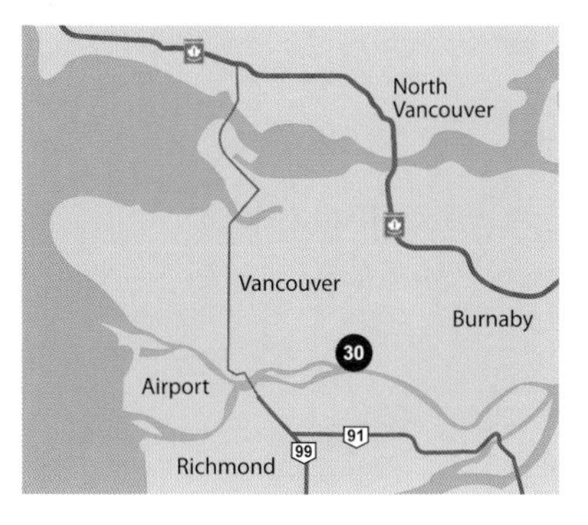

Deciduous forest regeneration at a recently restored landfill

Location

Everett Crowley Park is in southeast Vancouver at Kerr St. and E 63rd Ave.

Transit Information

At the 29th Ave. SkyTrain Station, board the #26 Joyce Station bus and alight at the Kerr St. and Rosemont Ave. stop. For up-to-date information, contact TransLink at www.translink.ca or 604-953-3333.

Introduction

Everett Crowley Park is a green and tranquil oasis in the city for nature and nature lovers alike. As the City of Vancouver's third-largest municipal park at 40 hectares (99 acres), Everett Crowley plays an essential role in supporting resident and migrating wildlife, particularly birds. Everett Crowley's deciduous woodland—primarily of red alder, bigleaf maple and black cottonwood—makes it unlike most other large parks in the area, which tend to be dominated by dense coniferous forest. The park also features extensive areas of low shrubs, mainly blackberry, as well as open field habitat and a small wetland.

A male goldfinch's bright breeding plumage is conspicuous in spring and summer. *Margo A. Longland*

The site is named for Everett Crowley, a long-time local resident, former Park Board commissioner and founder of nearby Avalon Dairy, currently Vancouver's only working dairy. Interestingly the park is the former site of the City of Vancouver landfill and consequently provides many opportunities to observe the ongoing process of natural regeneration and active restoration by city and community volunteers. Visitors should allow time to take in the variety of sites and habitats in the park.

Natural History Visit

From the bus stop, head south down Kerr St. to the parking lot on the east side of the road. Three trails begin at the parking lot. Avoid the wide, packed gravel trail on the west side of the parking lot by the wooden kiosk. Instead

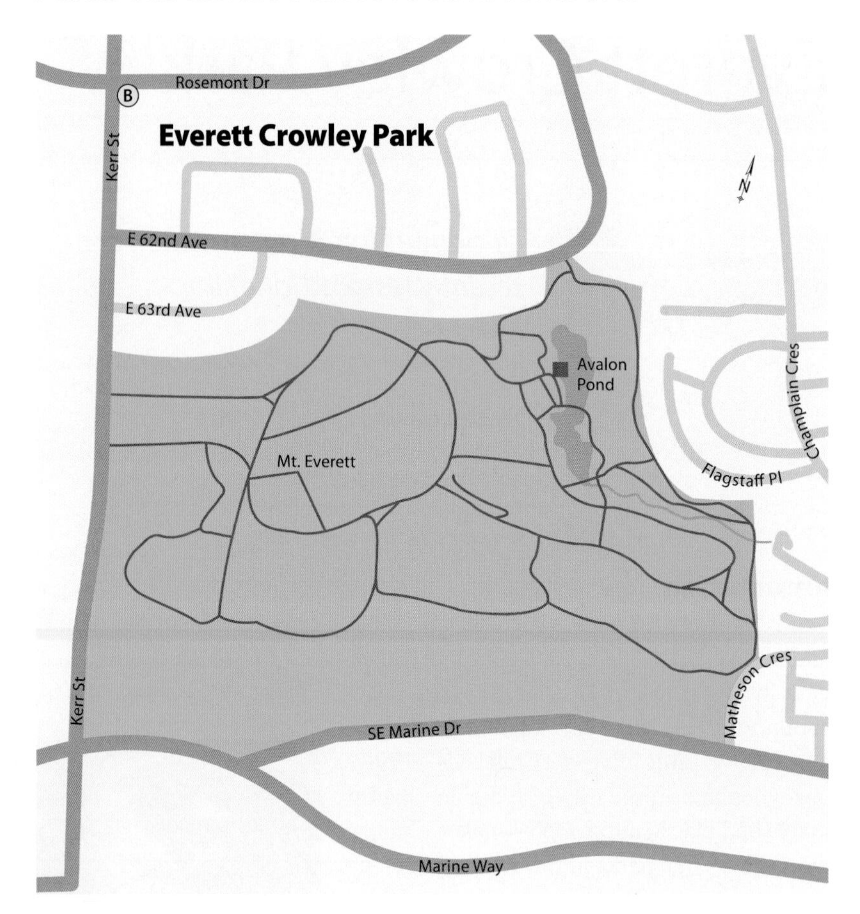

Bigleaf maple buds burst open into clusters of greenish yellow flowers.
Margo A. Longland

begin on one of the other two trails, which start at the north and south ends of the parking lot and pass through mature mixed forest. There are many native shrubs in the eastern side of the park including salal, red huckleberry, snowberry and wild rose.

Avalon Pond, in the northeast corner, is an on-leash area for dogs. Dogs must not be allowed to disturb the wetland area. In the spring and summer look for dragonflies, mallard ducklings and swallows. On a summer's evening, you can enjoy a treefrog chorus and see many bats circling overhead. In spring and fall you may see a variety of waterfowl. Avalon Pond is also a good place to see and hear the four species of woodpeckers known to use the park: northern flicker, downy woodpecker, hairy woodpecker and pileated woodpecker.

South of the lake, Kinross Creek has a pleasant creekside trail and is a good place for birding in the winter and spring. Woodpeckers, varied

Hardy deciduous trees and blackberry bushes have colonized the Kinross Creek area. *Margo A. Longland*

thrushes, Swainson's thrushes and winter wrens are frequently visible.

Lookout Trail, running across the park, provides attractive views of Richmond cranberry fields, the Fraser River, and on a clear day, Mount Baker to the southeast. Here in the winter and spring you can spot birds of prey including bald eagles, red-tailed hawks and Cooper's hawks. In the spring migrating warblers frequent the trees and shrubs on the south slope.

Memorial Grove is planted with native plants and shrubs in honour of a founding park volunteer. Here you can contemplate the spirit of volunteerism described in Margaret Mead's quote on the granite stone at the back of the grove. In spring look for beautiful dark blue camas, red-flowering currant, wild rose, red columbine and coastal strawberry. In summer visitors often see cedar waxwings and black-headed grosbeaks.

The Steam Vents and field habitat area on the southeast side of the park was the last part to be closed to landfill activity. As a result there are more signs of recent disturbance: trees are younger and there are extensive areas

Avalon Pond provides habitat for frogs, waterfowl, herons, woodpeckers and bats.
Margo A. Longland

of Himalayan blackberry and Japanese knotweed, two non-native plants that excel in colonizing disturbed sites. In addition, due to the ongoing decomposition process in the underlying landfill, steam vents occur in various locations.

Everett Crowley has something to offer in every season, but spring is a favourite with many locals since the air takes on a wonderful sweet smell and birdsong is everywhere.

Nearby Locations

- Fraserview Perimeter Trail around Fraserview Golf Course is across Kerr St.; its extensive natural areas include many old coniferous trees hosting birds that do not frequent Everett Crowley Park
- Burnaby Fraser Foreshore Park is to the south

Some Alerts

- coyotes
- some steep trails
- boardwalks around Avalon Pond are slippery when wet

More Information

Vancouver Park Board Recreation: 604-257-8400 or
http://vancouver.ca/parkfinder_wa
Everett Crowley Park Committee: 604-718-6575 www.vcn.bc.ca/ecpc/index.html

burnaby city

Previous page: Visiting Burnaby Lake at sunrise can be a magical experience.
Michael Wheatley

Top: A Nootka rose has larger and showier scented flowers than other native roses.
Bill Kinkaid

Central Park

by Bill Kinkaid

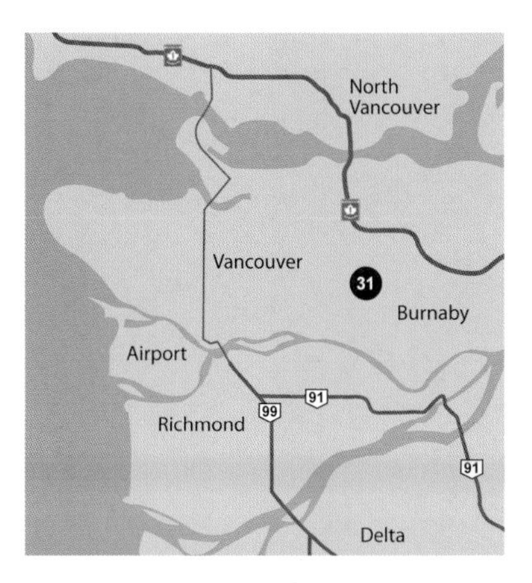

Dense deciduous and coniferous forest, wetland and ponds

Location

Central Park is on the west side of Burnaby at Kingsway and Boundary Rd.

Transit Information

The #19 Stanley Park/Metrotown bus travels along Kingsway. Alight at any stop between Kingsway and Boundary Rd. and Kingsway and Patterson Ave.

Alternatively, the Patterson SkyTrain Station is at the north-east corner of the park.

For up-to-date information, contact TransLink at www.translink.ca or 604-953-3333.

Introduction

This 90-hectare (222-acre) multi-use City of Burnaby park is in the most densely populated part of Burnaby. While there is intensive recreational usage—including Swangard Stadium, tennis courts, ball diamonds, pitch-and-putt golf and an outdoor swimming pool—there are also large natural areas with a network of trails to be explored.

In 1860, under the direction of Colonel R.C. Moody of the Royal Engineers, the False Creek Trail was built to connect the then-capital of British Columbia, New Westminster, to Vancouver. The trail was needed to expedite the movement of troops to defend the harbour in the event of an American invasion. In 1863 the area of highest land was recognized as a forest reserve to provide timber for the Royal Navy and was established as a city park in 1891.

Pacific ninebark is a common shrub, inconspicuous except when in flower.
Bill Kinkaid

The wife of David Oppenheimer, the mayor of Vancouver at the time, was from New York, and the park was named Central Park in her honour. The False Creek Trail, which was known as Westminster Rd. at the Vancouver end, is now Kingsway. In the early 20th century, the Central Park interurban line from Vancouver to New Westminster ran through the northeast corner of the park, and the SkyTrain line now follows the old right-of-way.

Natural History Visit

The park is mostly flat but is on the high land between the Fraser River to the south and the Deer Lake-Burnaby Lake drainage system to the north. The Upper and Lower lakes, which are really just ponds, form the core of the park; these drain through long-buried underground creeks, emerging as Still Creek at Renfrew Ravine.

The ponds themselves are home largely to mallards and glaucous-winged gulls as well as introduced bullfrogs, red-eared slider turtles and several large koi. Several interesting riparian and wetland plants can be found along the creek between the ponds.

Most of the park was logged in the late 19th century, but a large part of it—especially the east central area—has regrown as dense mixed deciduous and coniferous forest, providing a serene oasis from the nearby hustle. There is a large variety of non-native species, especially on the edges. Highlights include a number of large oak trees near the parking lot on Boundary Rd. and one yew tree among Douglas-firs south of the bandstand and just south of the stadium in the northwest corner of the park.

Many birds use the area year-round, primarily forest species such as sparrows, towhees and finches. In spring and summer there are warblers and vireos. Common ravens, not so common in urban areas, are resident in the park. Smaller mammals are common, though most are seldom seen apart from introduced gray squirrels and native Douglas squirrels. Both seem equally comfortable with the human presence in the park.

Visiting Central Park is pleasant year-round. Botanizing is best in fall and summer, and birding is best in spring and early summer. If you seek peace and quiet, avoid the park on busy summer weekends and during soccer matches at Swangard Stadium, although the woods on the east side are usually relatively tranquil.

Above: A quiet and pleasant rock garden surrounds a stream running out of the busy Upper Lake. *Bill Kinkaid*

Top: ***A picturesque bridge crosses the creek at the east end of the Lower Lake.*** *Bill Kinkaid*

Nearby Locations

- Byrne Creek Ravine Park is a short SkyTrain ride away
- the BC Parkway walking and cycling route intermittently follows the SkyTrain route between New Westminster and downtown Vancouver

Some Alerts

- cyclists
- stray golf balls near the pitch-and-putt area

More Information

City of Burnaby Parks: 604-294-7450 or www.burnaby.ca/cityhall/departments/departments_parks

Burnaby Fraser Foreshore Park

by Bill Kinkaid

Riverside dike walk near a recently restored wetland

Location

Burnaby Fraser Foreshore Park is in southwest Burnaby at Byrne Rd. and Fraser Park Dr.

Transit Information

The #116 Metrotown Station/Edmonds Station bus runs along North Fraser Way. The North Fraser Way and Glenlyon Parkway stop is the most convenient.

For up-to-date information, contact TransLink at www.translink.ca or 604-953-3333.

Introduction

This City of Burnaby park runs along the North Arm of the Fraser River from Boundary Rd. at the west to Terminus Park in the east, near Metro Vancouver's incinerator. It extends approximately 5 kilometres (3.1 miles) along the riverbank. The park's core activity centre is at the bottom of Byrne

A row of cottonwoods lining the river makes a scenic backdrop for the open grassy meadow. *Bill Kinkaid*

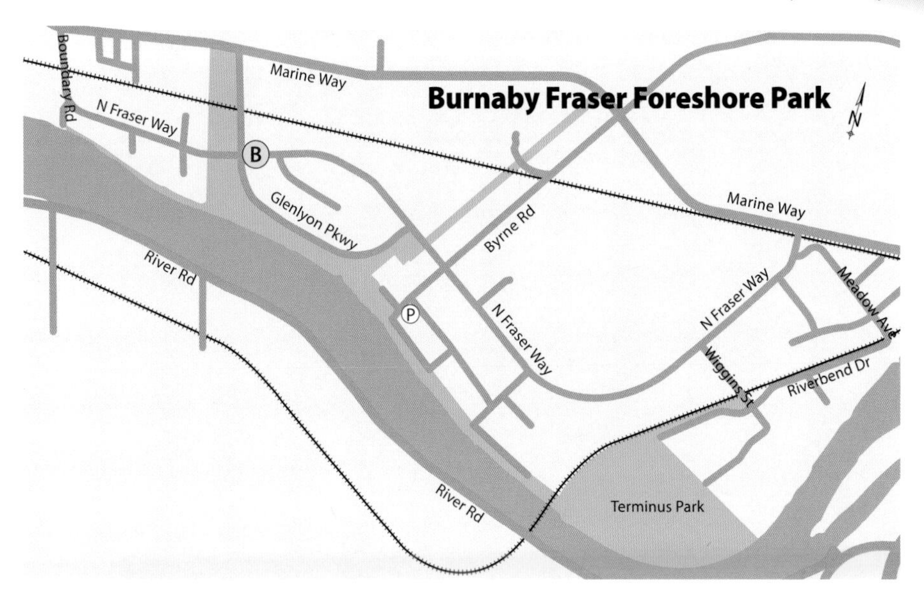

Rd. The Fraser is a working river, and walking the dike provides an excellent opportunity to see tugboats, barges and other river activity.

Natural History Visit

The focus of this park is the dike along the north side of the Fraser River. The typical foreshore and riparian woods are dominated by black cottonwood and red alder with an understory of salmonberry and snowberry. As well, there are many other shrubs and trees, both native and introduced. Chickadees, juncos and sparrows are typical winter birds, with warblers and vireos in spring and summer.

A Savannah sparrow, recognizable by its yellow eye stripe, sings among the blackberries. *Mark Habdas*

This is a newer park, and most of the area has only been developed within the past few decades. Industrial activities in neighbouring areas and the ensuing environmental damage have necessitated a fair amount of environmental regeneration.

Terminus Park, at the east end of the Burnaby Fraser Foreshore Park, includes varied restored wetland, alder woods and grassland habitat, much of it off-limits to the public. Migrant bird highlights in the various habitats include Savannah sparrows in the meadow, common yellowthroats in

Skunk cabbage grows in wetter and shadier parts of the alder woods. *Bill Kinkaid*

the marsh areas and Swainson's thrushes and olive-sided flycatchers in the woods. As well, a number of backwater sloughs and ponds have been created to provide off-channel salmon spawning habitat.

Visiting Burnaby Foreshore Park is pleasant year-round. Botanizing is best in fall and summer, and birding is best in spring and early summer.

Nearby Locations

- Byrne Creek Ravine Park is within walking distance to the east

Some Alerts

- heavy truck traffic on weekdays on access routes
- do not venture off the dike, especially onto mud flats at low tide
- stay off all railway tracks and railway bridges

More Information

City of Burnaby Parks: 604-294-7450 or
www.burnaby.ca/cityhall/departments/departments_parks

Byrne Creek Ravine Park

by Val and Anny Schaefer

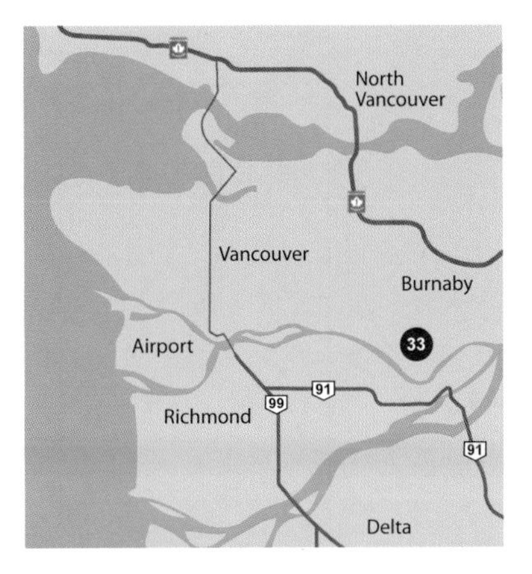

Restored salmon stream amidst large big leaf maples and conifers

Location

Byrne Creek Ravine Park is in south Burnaby at Marine Dr. and Southridge Dr.

Transit Information

The Edmonds SkyTrain Station is at the north end of the park.

Alternatively, for the south end of the park, from 22nd St. Station, take the #100 Airport Station bus to the Marine Dr. and Southridge Dr. stop.

For up-to-date information, contact TransLink at www.translink.ca or 604-953-3333.

Introduction

Byrne Creek Ravine extends 1 kilometre (0.6 mile) downhill from Edmonds St. and Griffiths Dr. to Marine Dr. and Southridge Dr. Byrne Creek Ravine is one of six large ravines along Burnaby's south slope that were formed by erosion along the edges of the Burrard Peninsula. This peninsula—where large parts of the cities of Vancouver, Burnaby and Coquitlam are located—is an upland underlain by glacial till, outwash and marine sediments.

Byrne Creek continues on to the Fraser River flood plain for another kilometre (0.6 mile) before draining into the Fraser River itself. Salmon and cutthroat trout were caught here just a few decades ago. Several large storm drains channel water into the creek from as far away as Kingsway to the north.

The horns on the great horned owl, the region's largest resident owl, are feather tufts. *Wayne Weber*

In 1987 the Vancouver Angling and Game Association (VAGA), under the leadership of Ken Glover, performed restoration with local schools. They removed garbage from the creek, marked storm drains to emphasize the impact of runoff on water quality and stocked the creek with salmon fry.

When a toxic spill killed 5,000 fish in 1998, concerned community

members joined with VAGA to form the Byrne Creek Streamkeepers. This organization has been restoring habitat, monitoring local conditions and educating the public since 1999.

Natural History Visit

The main trail extends from Edmonds SkyTrain Station along the top of the ravine through Ron McLean Park and then down alongside the creek at the south end of the park, ultimately emerging at Marine Dr. near Southridge Dr. At Ron McLean Park, a side trail that begins behind the lacrosse cage goes down to the creek and extends another 100 metres (328 feet) alongside the water.

Bitter cherry fruit is popular with songbirds such as robins and cedar waxwings. *Wayne Weber*

Even on a hot summer day Byrne Creek Ravine is a cool, quiet oasis in the city. The twittering of juncos and chickadees and the soothing sound of rushing water block out noisy traffic on nearby Southridge Dr. Vine maples arch over the trail, and especially during the wetter months of the year, mosses and licorice ferns sprout from the trunks of bigleaf maples. Sword ferns decorate the slopes of the ravine. Massive cedar trees stand sentry, and snags and stumps provide fascinating sculptures for visitors to discover.

The ravine is a rich ecosystem. The plant communities reflect the dramatic changes in soil moisture created by the steep slopes. A mature community of bigleaf maples follows the creek. Salmonberry, red elderberry and vine maple provide excellent habitat for birds and cover the banks of the creek to shelter salmon. Skunk cabbage and horsetail are common at the mouth of the ravine.

The drier slopes of the ravine have large Douglas-fir, western redcedar and western hemlock. Protected from the wind by the ravine, these trees have grown to great heights. Beneath the trees, sword ferns and lady ferns screen the forest floor. Along the edge at the top of the ravine are red alder, paper birch and bitter cherry. The ground cover includes Oregon grape and salal.

The ravine attracts many animals. The undersides of stones in the creek support clinging invertebrates such as stonefly nymphs. The insects and berries in the ravine provide food for a wide range of birds including warblers, thrushes, woodpeckers, cedar waxwings, chickadees and even great blue herons. The tall trees are used by red-tailed hawks, bald eagles and great horned owls. Mammals such as coyotes and raccoons hunt in the ravine or use it as a wildlife corridor while travelling to various parts of the city.

Visit year-round. From mid-October to the end of December, you can see adult returning salmon; chum return first, and coho appear toward mid-November.

A staircase invites you to walk through the cool ferns beside Byrne Creek. *Val and Anny Schaefer*

Nearby Locations

- Ron McLean Park and John Matthews Creek Ravine Park are nearby

Some Alerts

- dirt sections of the trail are slippery during the rainy season
- gaps in the railings along the switchbacks down to the creek from Ron McLean Park
- stay off the steep ravine slope

More Information

Byrne Creek Streamkeepers: http://www.byrnecreek.org
City of Burnaby Parks: 604-294-7450 or
www.burnaby.ca/cityhall/departments/departments_parks

Deer Lake Park

by George Clulow

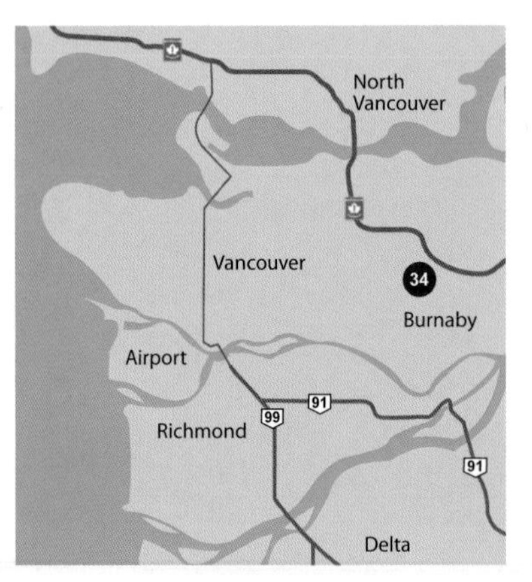

Lakeside trails, meadows, dense forest and an arts complex

Location

Deer Lake Park is in central Burnaby at Canada Way and Sperling Ave.

Transit Information

From the Metrotown or Lougheed Town Centre SkyTrain Station, take the #110 Metrotown Station/Lougheed Station bus and alight at the Burnaby City Hall stop. Alternatively, from Metrotown Station, take the #144 SFU bus to Canada Way/Sperling Ave.

For up-to-date information, contact TransLink at www.translink.ca or 604-953-3333.

Introduction

There are places in Deer Lake Park where it's easy to believe that you've left the city far behind and to imagine yourself in some distant natural setting. A beautiful lake, old farm fields, glimpses of the North Shore mountains and forests make the park the perfect setting for a family outing intended to provide some encounters with nature.

Barn swallows feed on the abundant insects that hatch in the lake. *Mark Habdas*

Deer Lake in the City of Burnaby covers just over 200 hectares (494 acres). It's a diverse place, with wilder natural habitats dominating the western two-thirds of the park. The northern and eastern portions contain galleries, studios, a theatre, a village museum and formal gardens, among other people-centred activities. Plenty of trails make most of the park easily accessible. For the slightly more adventurous, smaller hidden trails offer escape to some of the more isolated sections of the park. If it's nature you're looking for, head west to explore a bounty of surprises the park offers.

Natural History Visit

The bus takes you right to the park and the art gallery, theatre, museum and studios. It is easy to find your way down to Deer Lake and the many trails and boardwalks.

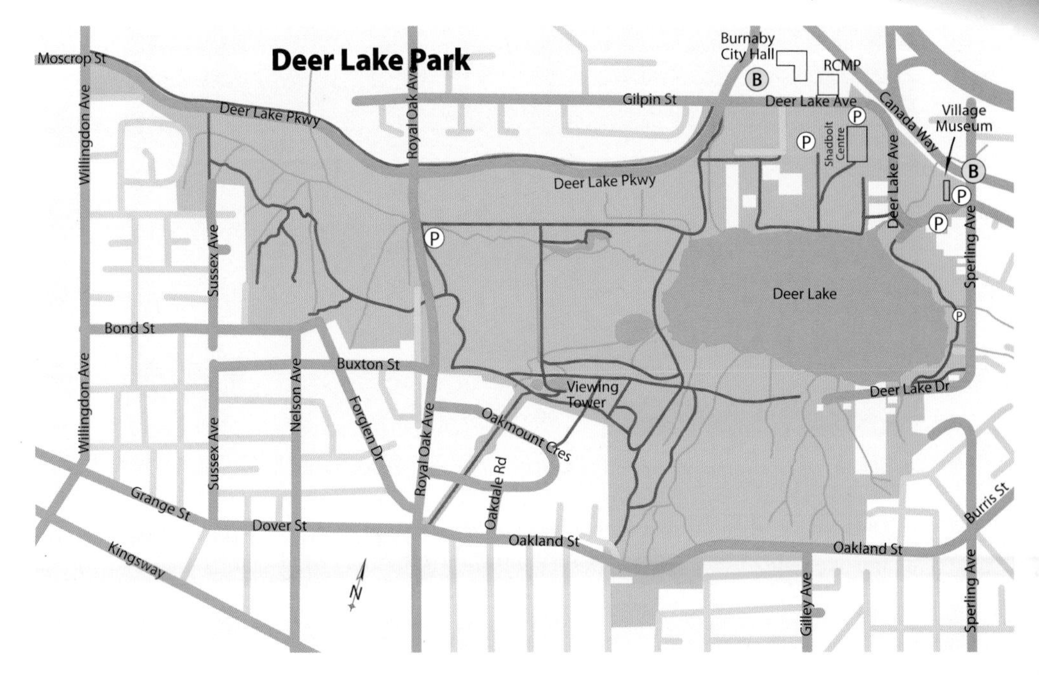

Beavers, bats, birds, butterflies, hawks, herons, forests and fields: the park has something for all ages and interests. The lake itself is a haven for waterbirds, and the lakeside trails are great places to observe wildlife. Turtles sun themselves on logs, while great blue herons stalk fish and frogs in the shallows. In summer ospreys are common. Their spectacular dives into the lake after fish are a highlight for a patient observer. Swallows are numerous here, too, particularly in the spring, when you can easily see up to five species—tree, violet-green, barn, cliff and northern rough-winged swallows—swooping over the lake.

Three totem poles created during a Year 2000 community clay sculpture project.
Rosemary Taylor

The old field meadows between Royal Oak Ave. and the west end of the lake are home to thousands of Townsend's voles. Such a food source makes the meadows a favourite hunting ground for resident red-tailed hawks. Kestrels may also be seen here in migration. Northern harriers, too, have discovered the meadows' food bounty and have nested here since 2004. If dogs are kept leashed, there's a good chance the hawks will continue to nest here. As you walk the meadow paths, keep a lookout for the beautiful and harmless

Deciduous trees, swamp vegetation and water lilies adorn Deer Lake. *Rosemary Taylor*

garter snakes sunning themselves trailside. Common yellowthroats abound in the wet meadows, their *witchety-witchety* calls declaring claims to territory. Savannah sparrows make their reedy calls, and song sparrows and spotted towhees sing from the hedgerows. In the forests listen for the *kek-kek kekking* of Cooper's hawks, which nest in several locations in the park. At dusk listen for great horned or barred owls hooting from the forest.

A kestrel, a small falcon, waits to hover over its prey of mice, small birds or grasshoppers. *Mark Habdas*

Deer Lake is a year-round park where each season offers much for a family interested in observing nature. Winter birds are varied, and good numbers of ducks are present on the lake. Forest birds are numerous all year, many of them resident species. Some birds are seasonal, such as varied thrushes in winter and black-headed grosbeaks in summer. Spring migration brings a great variety of birds to the park's fields and forests. Dragonflies are a summer feature, and at dusk you can find beavers at work building their lodges and dams around the lake. A really lucky observer may see a river otter, a rare visitor to the park.

Nearby Locations

- Burnaby Lake is a 20-minute walk north along Kensington Ave.

Some Alerts

- coyotes
- trails with steep stretches in the southeast section; only confident hikers should attempt these

More Information

City of Burnaby Parks: 604-294-7450 or
www.burnaby.ca/cityhall/departments/departments_parks

Burnaby Lake Regional Park

by George Clulow

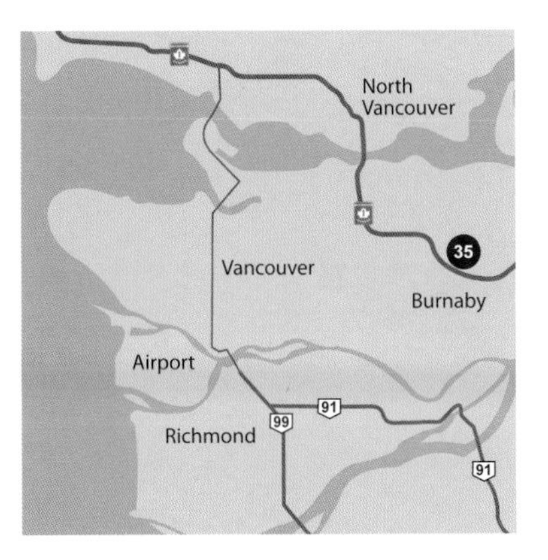

Blackbirds to beavers, coots to cattails, nature here is close-up

Location

Burnaby Lake Regional Park is in central Burnaby at the south end of Piper Ave. off Lougheed Hwy.

Transit Information

From the Metrotown Station or Lougheed Town Centre SkyTrain Station, take the #110 Metrotown Station/Lougheed Station bus and alight at the Government Rd. and Piper Ave. stop.

For up-to-date information, contact TransLink at www.translink.ca or 604-953-3333.

Introduction

An active Burnaby Lake Park Association of committed volunteers and a Nature House open many weekends make Burnaby Lake a fabulous park to visit. On weekends volunteers are often available to explain the park's bountiful wildlife. As well, special events throughout the year are geared to families. The park offers many opportunities to observe nature at close hand.

Burnaby Lake Regional Park is a park of approximately 300 hectares (741 acres) operated by Metro Vancouver. It centres on the long, marshy lake that occupies a large portion of the park. Metro Vancouver runs many summer programs here that focus on the aquatic environments and animals of the lake. Visitors will likely first focus on the lake, too, before exploring the forest habitats that are also full of interesting wildlife in all seasons.

Fireweed stabilizes disturbed land. Its nectar produces excellent honey. *Michael Wheatley*

Natural History Visit

From the bus stop, walk south down Piper Ave., cross Winston St. and pass Warner Loat Park on your left. Cross the railroad tracks, and soon you'll find the Nature House on your right. Just beyond it, Piper Spit juts out into the lake.

Spotting a bald eagle is always exciting whether it is perched or soaring overhead. *Michael Wheatley*

The spit provides some of the easiest wildlife viewing in the whole park. Exotically plumaged wood ducks are common here, and you can observe them at close range. Many large nest boxes have been erected in this area to help these cavity-nesting birds. Depending on the season, a number of other ducks—including mallards, gadwalls, northern shovelers and green-winged, cinnamon and blue-winged teals—are easily seen. Very secretive Virginia rails sometimes abandon their usual reedy cover here and provide an uncommon sighting.

At the end of the spit be sure to take a good look at the large beaver lodge. Look across to the far side of the lake to see nesting bald eagles. To the east a large number of tree swallow boxes have been erected on wooden stakes. You may enjoy watching the swallows that swoop over the lake to forage for flying insects and return to their nests to feed their young.

If you return to the base of the spit, you can head east or west to explore some of the forested habitats of the park. The main trail circles the lake entirely—approximately 10 kilometres (6.2 miles)—and many runners use this popular circuit. As you head east, you can walk through some interesting forest on quieter loop trails such as Conifer and Spruce Loop trails. After approximately 1.5 kilometres (0.9 mile), you will come to the Cariboo Dam that controls the lake outlet into the Brunette River. Forest birds abound here in all seasons. In spring look for migrating yellow-rumped warblers and breeding black-throated gray warblers. Cedar waxwings and willow flycatchers are often seen where shrubby areas border the lake. Western tanagers, red-eyed vireos and Swainson's thrushes are found in the more forested areas.

A visit to Burnaby Lake is enjoyable in all seasons.

Nearby Locations

- Warner Loat Park, a small park with large trees, is on your way from the bus stop
- Deer Lake is a 20-minute walk south along Kensington Ave. from the west end of the park

Some Alerts

- extremely deep mud on the lake margin; access the lakeshore using designated trails

More Information

Metro Vancouver Regional Parks:
www.metrovancouver.org/services/parks_lscr/regionalparks/Pages/default.aspx
Metro Vancouver Regional Parks West Area Office: 604-224-5739

Snow-topped mountains and reflections in the still lake create a place of serenity.
Mark Habdas

Burnaby Mountain Conservation Area

by George Clulow

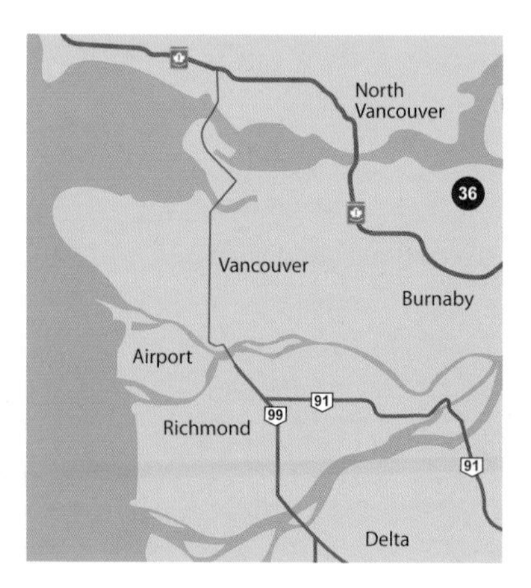

Stunning views, forested trails and spectacular spring bird migration

Location

Burnaby Mountain Conservation Area is in northeast Burnaby. It's at the north end of Centennial Way off Burnaby Mountain Parkway.

Transit Information

Take any of these buses to SFU: #135 SFU bus, #144 SFU bus or #145 SFU bus. Alight at the University Dr. West and West Campus Rd. stop, just past the Shell station behind the university.

For up-to-date information, contact TransLink at www.translink.ca or 604-953-3333.

Introduction

Stunning views of the Lower Mainland, along with forests and trails to explore in every season, make Burnaby Mountain Conservation Area one

The fjord of Indian Arm is one of the spectacular views from Burnaby Mountain.
Rosemary Taylor

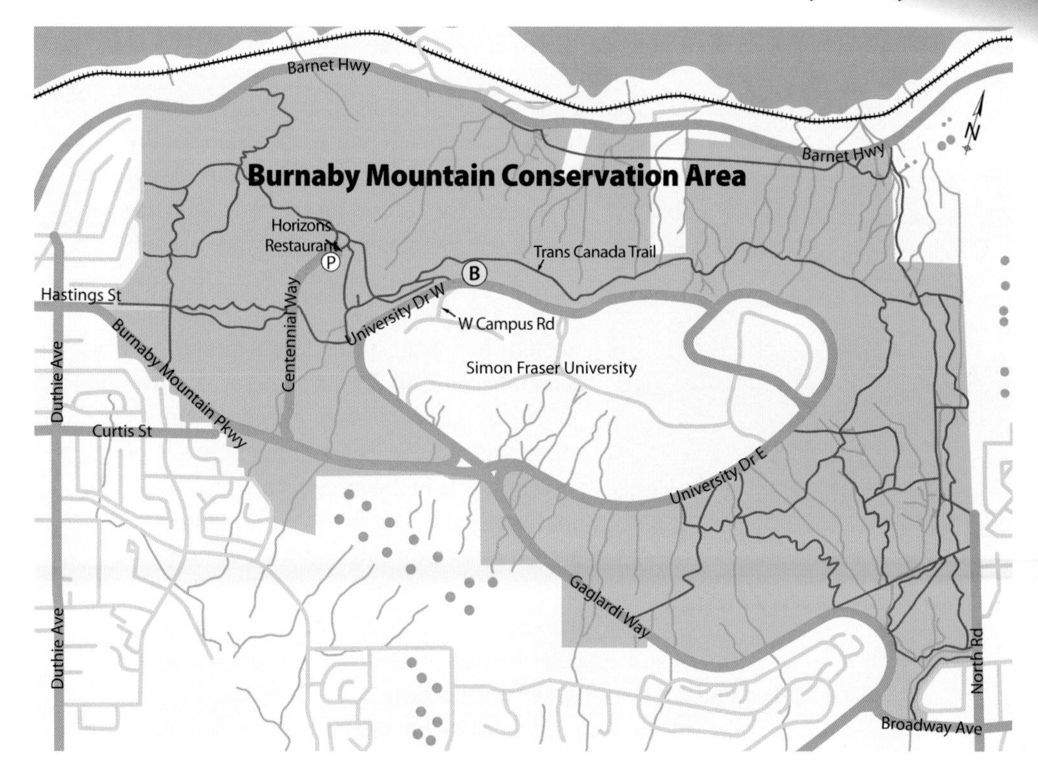

of the more spectacular but lesser-known Lower Mainland parks. It offers impressive viewpoints. As you look north across the inlet, the fjord of Indian Arm cuts a dramatic slash through the towering wall of the Coast Mountains. Views of Vancouver to the west and the Gulf Islands to the south impress out-of-towners and locals alike.

This 575-hectare (1,420-acre) City of Burnaby park has extensive areas of mixed forest, largely second-growth. It is a wonderful place for the family to enjoy nature by easy walking or more strenuous trails. The forests change through the seasons, and spring bird migration is particularly notable. The east-west Trans Canada Trail bisects the park.

Natural History Visit

From the bus stop, take the trail behind the bus shelter that enters the forest heading west. Follow this trail downhill, bearing right to reach the parking area. Below Horizons Restaurant, multiple trails radiate in many directions.

Walk up the slope through the gardens to the fence that traces the mountain's north rim. Standing on the same 50- to 60-million-year old sandstone that makes up the Gulf Islands, you can take in the vistas up Indian Arm and along the North Shore mountains. To the west you can see downtown Vancouver, Stanley Park and the West Vancouver shoreline. The Fraser River delta, Gulf Islands and San Juan Islands spread out to the south and southwest.

After you absorb the magnificent scenery, it's time to explore. The Trans Canada Trail is fairly easy walking. Note that much of the north slope of the mountain has dangerous cliffs and is closed to access. The forests on the mountain are mixed, with occasional dense stands of conifers. Look for bigleaf maple, red alder, vine maple, Douglas-fir, western redcedar and western hemlock. In the forest understory, salmonberry abounds; its early spring flowers are a particular favourite with rufous hummingbirds. Trees are in many stages of their life cycle in the forests, and dead snags are heavily used by cavity-nesting birds. In particular look for huge pileated woodpeckers, northern flickers, downy and hairy woodpeckers and red-breasted sapsuckers. Red-breasted nuthatches are common, as are black-capped and chestnut-backed chickadees.

The hovering rufous hummingbird's orange-red throat feathers shine in the sunlight.
Virginia Hayes

In April and May, during the early morning hours after an overnight rain, migrating wood warblers and flycatchers often "fall out" here in truly spectacular numbers. Local bird watchers are usually on hand for these events and will happily point out what to look for.

Burnaby Mountain Park is good to visit in all seasons, but if birds are a particular interest, April and May can be spectacular. In summer the forests are shady refuges, and in fall they are more colourful as bigleaf maples turn yellow and vine maples turn red. In winter the forests open up to the warming rays of the sun. In any season you can expect to find low cloud or fog making the experience more ethereal.

Nearby Locations

- none within walking distance

Some Alerts

- coyotes
- strictly respect the posted No Entry areas on the mountain's north side; tragically, two young men died here in 2006 when they took an informal trail off the north side of the mountain and fell to their deaths
- mountain bikers frequent the south slope of the park below the ring road

More Information

City of Burnaby Parks: 604-294-7450 or www.burnaby.ca/cityhall/departments/departments_parks

Barnet Marine Park

by Louise Irwin

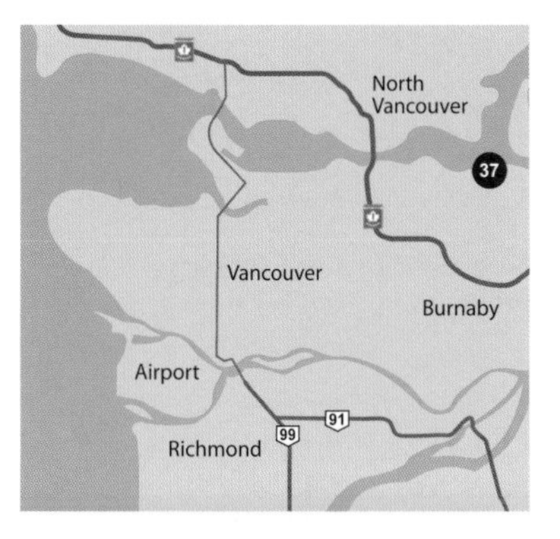

Marine and plant life, trails and historical artefacts

Location

Barnet Marine Park is in northeast Burnaby on Barnet Hwy. just east of Texaco Dr.

Transit Information

The #160 Vancouver/Port Coquitlam Station bus travels along Barnet Rd. Alight at the Barnet Rd. and 8300 block stop at the main entrance to the park on its east side. For up-to-date information, contact TransLink at www.translink.ca or 604-953-3333.

Introduction

Barnet Marine Park, Burnaby City's only ocean-access park, is included in the Burnaby Mountain Conservation Area. The park is a narrow, flat strip of land on the shoreline, presently about 3 kilometres (1.9 miles) long. It is sandwiched between Barnet Rd. and Burrard Inlet with the CPR rail line running parallel in between. The park landscape was created 10,000 to 13,000 years ago by a prehistoric landslide from the cliffs above on the north side of Burnaby Mountain. Historically interesting as well as a nature lover's delight, the park offers rain forest, views of the North Shore mountains and the entrance to Indian Arm, a sandy beach and rocky areas for exploring marine life.

Almost transparent, the lion's mane is a red jellyfish that stings. Admire but do not touch!
Steve Britten

The company sawmill village of Barnet was established in 1899, and there are still a few remains of the original settlement. A metal plaque affixed to the ruins of the mill's sawdust burner at the water's edge gives a brief history of the mill. A few rotting pilings from the log greenchain still stand in the water, and a remnant of the concrete planing mill is nearby. The only remaining original village house stands on the hill above, and the village row house foundations are in the woods near the parking lot.

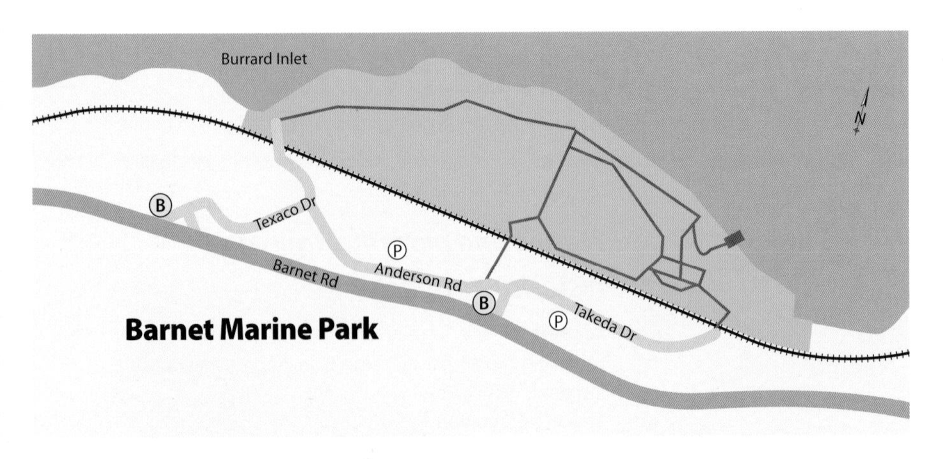

Natural History Visit

From the crosswalk by the bus stop on Barnet Rd., follow the park road downhill. At the parking lot, you will see two main access trails over the rail line to the shore. Either proceed to the left and go down the wheelchair-accessible overhead walkway or take the road to the right. You will find a trail opposite the parking lot.

At the grassy picnic area there are maps, picnic tables and other amenities. Beside the small sandy

Burns Point lighthouse is a landmark for both walkers and boaters on Burrard Inlet. *Steve Britten*

Cottonwoods along the trail emit a spicy aroma when their sticky buds swell in spring.
Steve Britten

beach is a public pier for fishing, catching crabs or observing beautiful views, boat traffic and marine bird life.

Walk to the left, west along the shore, to the few historic relics and the wooded areas where you might see or hear a variety of bird species such as thrushes, warblers and woodpeckers. The original old-growth trees are long gone, replaced by a mixture of deciduous species such as bigleaf maples and red alders as well as a few coniferous second-growth hemlocks. Native shrubs are plentiful and include salmonberry, red elderberry and Indian-plum as well as numerous invasive plants and non-native trees. Along the shoreline trail at low tide there are barnacle-coated rocky beaches and a few tide pools worth exploring after a scramble down the bank.

Beyond the former Texaco pier pilings and a grassed-in area, the present trail continues for about 1 kilometre (0.6 mile). In the wet area between the railway fence and the shore, native plants thrive: miner's-lettuce, fringecup, piggy-back plant, large-leaved avens, sword fern and shrubby red-osier dogwood. The shoreline trail soon peters out at another small, sandy undeveloped beach area. Future plans include the westward extension of this trail.

When you return to the central amenities area, a short walk along the sandy beach to the right (east) will lead you to a much drier area with a greater diversity of native plant life. Above the shoreline is a profusion of Nootka rose, silverweed, hardhack and cow-parsnip. Currently the park ends at the General Chemical plant fence opposite the Burns Point light-

Top: Across the inlet, Cates Park lies to the northwest. *Steve Britten*

Bottom: After pollination, western trillium blooms turn pink and become less alluring to insects. *Wayne Weber*

house across the inlet.

Burnaby City's future development plans include a bicycle and pedestrian overpass at the western end of the park to connect with the foreshore trail, a Heritage Display Centre and information plaques along the walk. The eastern end of the park may be extended along the foreshore to connect with Rocky Point Park in Port Moody.

Visit at any time of year. In winter you can see overwintering birds. In spring, especially in the later part of April, you may see songbirds and early spring flowers, perhaps a trillium or two. In May and June look for birds and also later-blooming flowers, deciduous trees and shrubs leafing out. During July and August the park is crowded on sunny days as families enjoy the safe beach and picnicking, swimming, bird life and exploring the many short rough trails, history and marine life. In fall you can enjoy the drier trails and all other activities.

Nearby Locations

- Port Moody Shoreline Park is a bus ride east from the park
- the Burnaby Mountain trails are nearby; for an active hike, cross the Barnet Rd. crosswalk and continue up through the overflow parking lot for at least 2 kilometres (1.2 miles) to a multi-use trail that takes you up the mountain

Some Alerts

- the CPR railway main line is fenced the length of the park, with gates at the two road crossings; whistles warn when trains approach

More Information

City of Burnaby Parks: 604-294-7450 or www.burnaby.ca/cityhall/departments/departments_parks

In the Shadow by the Sea: Recollections of Burnaby's Barnet Village, Harry Pride and Jim Wolf (eds.), published by the City of Burnaby in 2004; you can purchase it at Burnaby City Hall.

east of vancouver

Previous page: Belcarra Regional Park is one of many nature places east of Vancouver.
James Holkko

Top: The Golden Ears mountains are visible across the Fraser River from Sapperton Landing. *Mark Habdas*

Belcarra Regional Park

by David Cook

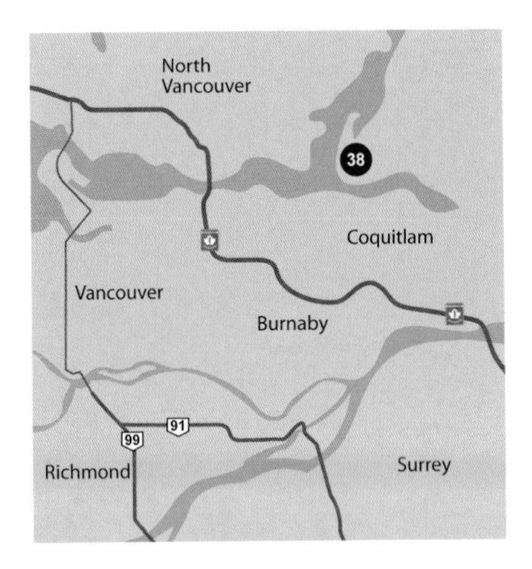

Rain forest, rocky headland, beach and wetland flanking a fjord

Location

Belcarra Regional Park is in Belcarra at the west end of Bedwell Bay Rd. off 1st Ave. in Port Moody.

Transit Information

From Port Moody Station, take the #C26 Belcarra bus. Alight at the Belcarra Bay Rd. and Midden Rd. stop for Belcarra Picnic Area.

Alternatively, in summer only, from Port Moody Station, take the #C25 White Pine Beach bus to White Pine Beach.

For up-to-date information, contact TransLink at www.translink.ca or 604-953-3333.

Introduction

This 1,085-hectare (2,680-acre) Metro Vancouver park, nearly three times the size of Stanley Park, covers the greater part of a peninsula west of Ioco. The park's 9 kilometres (5.6 miles) of rocky, pebbly and sandy beaches border Burrard Inlet near the outlet of the Indian Arm fjord. The highest points within the park are 550 metres (1,804 feet) on Buntzen Ridge in the north and 275 metres (902 feet) at Admiralty Height in the southwest.

The park has two main swimming and picnicking areas. Belcarra Picnic Area is on Burrard Inlet, and White Pine Beach is on freshwater Sasamat Lake. Both locations have excellent facilities and are accessible by public transit.

Slender haircaps cover and protect the haircap moss's lidded spore cases. *James Holkko*

Archaeological studies in the Belcarra picnic area show that during at least the last 1,000 years the site was occupied by Coast Salish people. The main village was Tum-tumay-whueten. There are midden sites at the Takaya Tours canoe rental hut, along Ferguson Point Trail and in exposed banks above Belcarra Bay beach.

Natural History Visit

The park area's history of varied use and disturbances has resulted in multi-aged forest stands at various stages of succession. Western hemlock is the dominant tree.

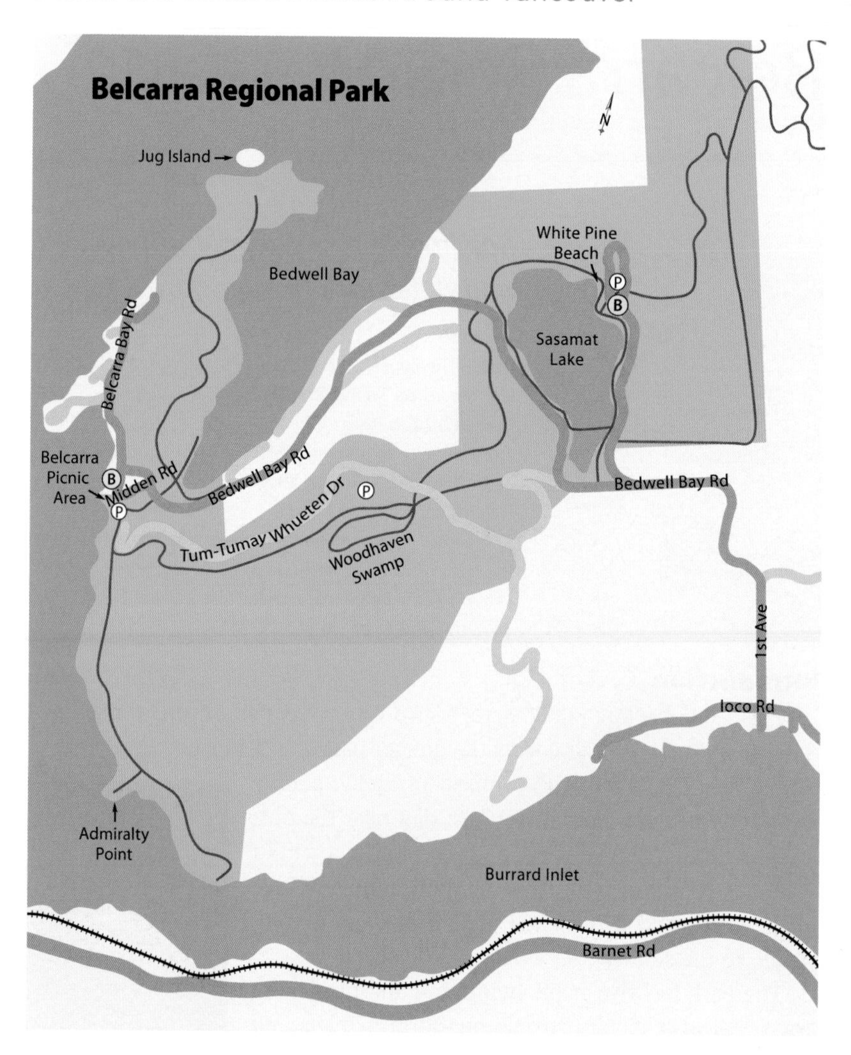

Areas of deciduous forest and areas of well-developed understory provide the greatest variety of habitat for birds and therefore the greatest diversity of bird species. In the mature coniferous forest, birds are limited to the seed- and insect-eating species such as woodpeckers, chickadees and winter wrens. Sooty grouse can be heard throughout the forested areas. You can see an old-growth Douglas-fir, once used as a nest tree by bald eagles, at the west end of Admiralty Point peninsula and an osprey's nest on the hydro tower near Woodhaven Swamp. Woodhaven Swamp is a man-made wetland site with a well-maintained 2.5-kilometre (1.6-mile) loop trail and interpretive signage. The south end of Sasamat Lake is also wetland.

For divers and snorkellers there are a number of good locations; the most popular is Whiskey Cove, where visitors can see rockfish, sunflower stars, orange and white plumose anemones and nudibranchs. Two harbour seal

Insect-eating round-leaved sundews thrive in the sunshine along a log in the swamp. *James Holkko*

haul-outs are visible on rocks at the northern end of the Bedwell Bay peninsula. When the tide is low, Bedwell Bay empties and reveals species characteristic of tidal flats, and there are significant intertidal areas along the shore from the Belcarra Picnic Area to Admiralty Point.

The rounded granite mound was smoothed and scratched by rocks in an overriding glacier. *James Holkko*

Dungeness and red rock crabs inhabit the eelgrass beds of Bedwell Bay and the subtidal zone off Belcarra Beach. Take care not to crush intertidal life. Overturn rocks as little as possible and return rocks to their original position without crushing the organisms beneath. The intertidal areas and mud flats provide important winter habitat for migrating birds, waterfowl and shorebirds.

The park is underlain by granite rocks that are about 10 million years old. South of the picnic area you can see a large, glacially rounded, smoothed and striated bluff of granitic bedrock used by gulls and crows for smashing clams. Jug Island is a glacially carved beehive dome of

Coral fungi are common in the coniferous forest. There are many colourful species.
James Holkko

coastal granitic rocks; it lies just offshore north of the Bedwell Bay peninsula in Indian Arm. The handle of the rock that gave Jug Island its name eroded away many years ago.

The best time to visit depends on your interests. Flowering plants and migratory birds are abundant from spring to fall. July, August and September are the best diving months. Snow can be expected at the higher elevations during winter.

Nearby Locations

- Buntzen Lake Recreation Area and Indian Arm Provincial Park to the northeast are both accessible by trails

Some Alerts

- many rough, steep trails require hiking boots
- intertidal forays call for waterproof footwear
- red jellyfish may be a hazard to divers in the fall

More Information

Metro Vancouver Regional Parks:
www.metrovancouver.org/services/parks_lscr/regionalparks/Pages/default.aspx
Metro Vancouver Regional Parks Central Area Office: 604-520-6442

Buntzen Lake Recreation Area

by Niall Williams

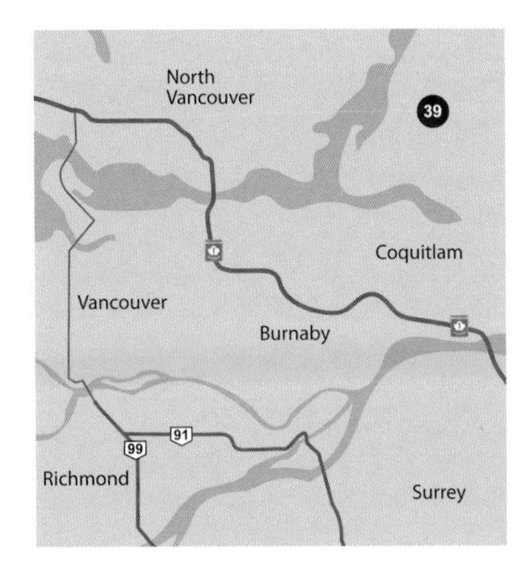

Lake Beautiful, where recreation and hydropower coexist

Location

Buntzen Lake Recreation Area is in Anmore at the north end of Sunnyside Rd. off 1st Ave. in Port Moody.

Transit Information

From Port Moody Station, board the #C26 Belcarra bus. During summer weekends and holidays the bus travels to South Beach at Buntzen Lake. At other times, alight at the final bus stop near the entrance gate and walk 1.8 kilometres (1.1 miles) to South Beach.

For up-to-date information, contact TransLink at www.translink.ca or 604-953-3333.

Introduction

Known as Trout Lake and later as Lake Beautiful, Buntzen Lake is now named after Johannes Buntzen, manager of the British Columbia Electric Railway (BCER) and Vancouver Power Company. This is the Lake Beautiful of the First Nations legend of the flood told by Pauline Johnson, the place where the giant canoe took off to escape the deluge.

Canada goldenrod usually has many small insects, especially beetles, feeding on it.
Niall Williams

In 1903 the Vancouver Power Company initiated the Buntzen hydroelectric project to provide the first hydroelectric power to Vancouver. The project involved raising the level of the dam on Coquitlam Lake and excavating a 3.6-kilometre (2.2-mile) tunnel to carry water from Coquitlam Lake to the northern end of Buntzen Lake. This raised the elevation of Buntzen Lake—previously two small lakes—by about 10 metres (33 feet).

Located just north of Ioco, approximately 30 kilometres (18.6 miles) from

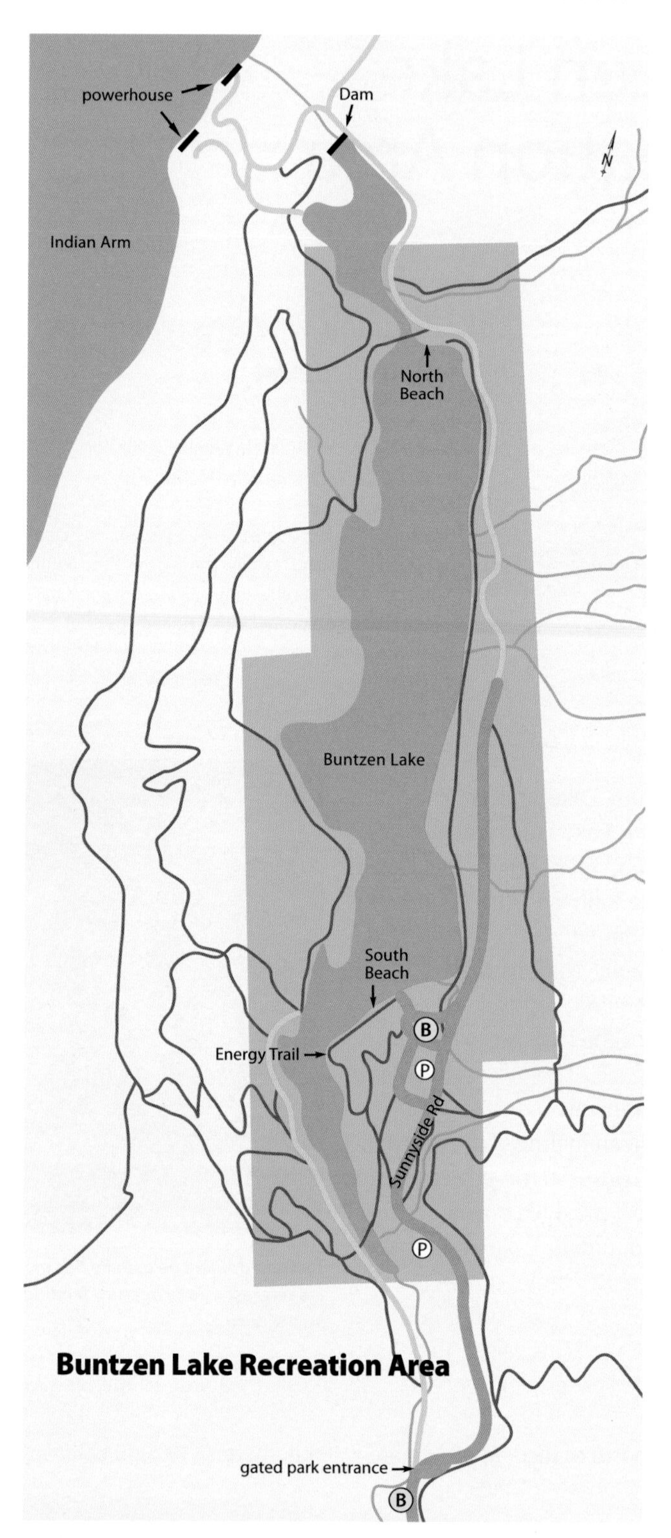
powerhouse
Dam
N
Indian Arm
North Beach
Buntzen Lake
South Beach
B
Energy Trail
P
Sunnyside Rd
P
Buntzen Lake Recreation Area
gated park entrance
B

Vancouver, Buntzen Lake is 4.8 kilometres (3 miles) long and 151 hectares (373 acres) in area. It is surrounded by mostly steep rocky terrain. Now BC Hydro operates the lake and the 182 hectares (450 acres) surrounding it as a free, day-use recreational area.

There are two main beaches. South Beach is near the parking lots in the area most visited. The other beach is near the much quieter northern end, accessible by a hike along the trails or gravel road. Many long, steep hiking trails through the lakeside forests have amazing panoramic views from the higher elevations. Maps are available from the kiosks around the recreation area. This hiking should only be undertaken by experienced and fit hikers; check the information provided by the park.

Natural History Visit

The Energy Trail near South Beach is a 1-kilometre (0.6-mile) loop that passes through a variety of forest landscapes and past attractive views of Buntzen Lake. It has interpretive signs and is suitable for children. A side trail leads to a floating boardwalk across a shallow arm of the lake. This is an excellent place for close-up views of the fish, aquatic insects and wetland plants associated with these shallows. All over the lake there are partially submerged tree stumps.

The lake supports at least 11 fish species. Cutthroat trout to 1 kilogram (2.2 pounds) and rainbow trout to half a kilogram (1.1

At the floating bridge, stumps and shallow water form good plant and animal habitat.
Niall Williams

pounds) are the dominant species. Kokanee are thought to be a remnant population that entered from Coquitlam Lake through the connecting tunnel.

Deer and black bears are a common sight, especially along the power lines, roads and other open areas. Eagle Ridge to the east parallels the lake, and true to its name, is often a good place to see eagles at the higher elevations.

Blue common California aster adds a splash of colour among white and yellow flowers.
Niall Williams

Many of the lower-elevation trails pass through second-growth western hemlock forests under which deer ferns, western sword ferns and liquorice ferns dominate the fern communities. Salal, salmonberry, Oregon grape, twinberry, Indian-plum, thimbleberry and devil's club grow where conditions are right for them. Numerous types of mushrooms, lichens, algae and ferns abound along the trails.

The park, popular with visitors from spring through fall, is especially busy on hot summer days.

Nearby Locations

- Sasamat Lake in Belcarra Regional Park is nearby to the southwest
- Indian Arm Provincial Park adjoins the park to the southwest

Some Alerts

- bears and coyotes
- steep rocky terrain, especially near the powerhouses beside Burrard Inlet
- no lifeguards
- Buntzen Lake is dangerously cold because of its greatest depth to 65 metres (213 feet) and average depth of 30 metres (98 feet)
- the lake floor drops off rapidly in many areas
- allow plenty of time when hiking longer trails
- leave before the gate is locked for the night

More Information

Buntzen Lake Warden's office: 604-469-9679
BC Hydro, Buntzen Lake:
www.bchydro.com/recreation/mainland/mainland1208.html
Power plant history: www.powerpioneers.com/BC_Hydro_History/1860-1929/Stories/history1860-1929_11070301.aspx
Indian Arm Provincial Park: www.bcparks.ca
Canoe rentals at the Anmore Store on Sunnyside Rd.: 604-469-9928

Sapperton Landing Park

by Kelly Sekhon

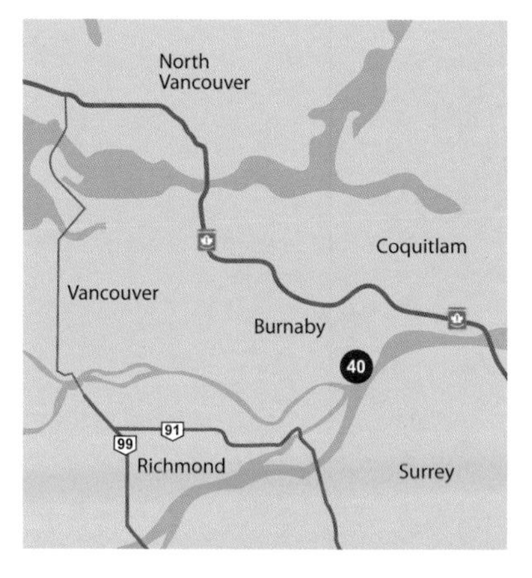

Scenic views from a riverside trail in a historic setting

Location

Sapperton Landing Park is on the east side of New Westminster at the foot of Cumberland St. off E Columbia St.

Transit Information

By SkyTrain, travel to the Sapperton Station near the park. Alternatively, from New Westminster Station, board the #112 Lougheed Station bus, or from Lougheed Station, board the #112 Edmonds Station bus. Both buses travel along E Columbia St.; alight at the E Columbia St. and Cumberland St. stop. For up-to-date information, contact TransLink at www.translink.ca or 604-953-3333.

Introduction

Sapperton Landing, at the confluence of the Brunette and Fraser rivers, was once a First Nations village landing place. In 1859 the Royal Engineers established themselves here with a mandate to keep law and order, develop transportation routes and survey the colony. By 1864 New Westminster was the capital of the colony of BC, and the first Legislative Assembly was conducted in the abandoned camp barracks. After BC had joined Canada, the nearby BC Penitentiary was opened there in 1878 and operated until 1980.

A curious harbour seal watches from the river. *Joan Lopez*

In 2001 the City of New Westminster, TransLink and Metro Vancouver collaborated to create the first regional park in New Westminster. Currently this 2.2-hectare (5.4-acre) linear waterfront park, extending from the foot of Cumberland St. to the junction of Columbia and Front St., shelters an abundance of vegetation and wildlife. It is easy to forget that you are only a few metres from a busy transportation corridor. There are plans for future extensions to the park in both directions: 3 kilometres (1.9 miles) east to Hume Park and 2.5 kilometres (1.6 miles) west to Westminster Quay.

This approximately 1-kilometre (0.6-mile) scenic walk provides beautiful views of the Fraser River, Golden Ears peaks and other mountains in the Fraser Valley. If you look upstream and downstream, you can see four

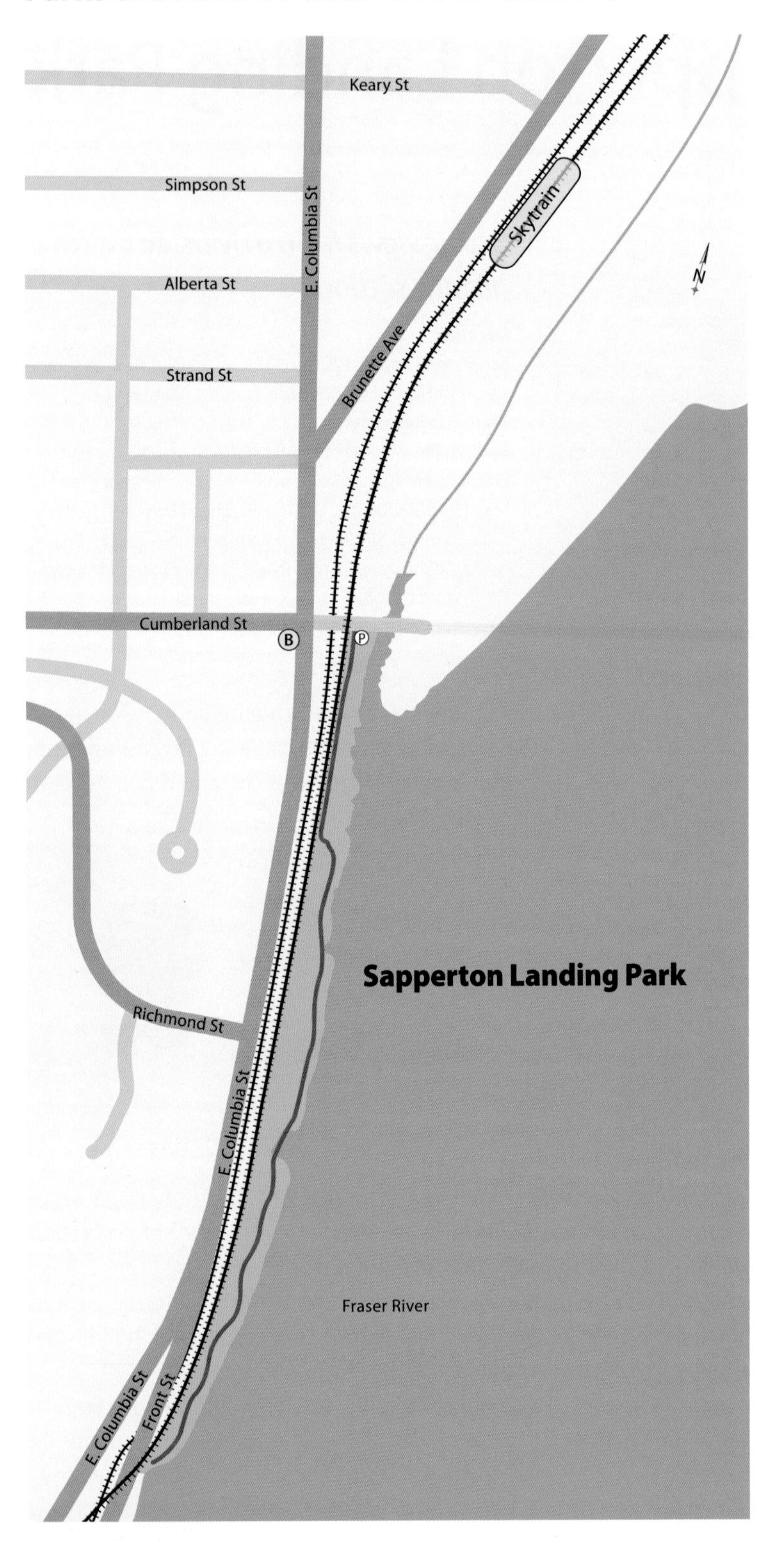
Keary St
Simpson St
Alberta St
Strand St
E. Columbia St
Brunette Ave
Skytrain
N
Cumberland St
B
P
Sapperton Landing Park
Richmond St
E. Columbia St
Fraser River
Front St
E. Columbia St

The Sapperton Landing trail winds alongside the Fraser River. *Mark Habdas*

Fraser River crossings. The Port Mann Bridge lies toward the mountains in the east. Close together to the west, you can see the low CN Rail bridge, the Pattullo Bridge roadway and the SkyTrain bridge high above. You may also see some interesting river traffic passing underneath.

The park has two separate paths, a paved access road at the back for cyclists and a gravel path by the water for walkers. Several viewpoints close to the river have wooden benches and can be used for fishing. A fishing pier is accessible from land or water, and there is also a picnic shelter.

A green heron, actually more blue than green, watches patiently for a fish. *Mark Habdas*

Natural History Visit

From the SkyTrain station, walk west along Keary St., cross E Columbia St. and turn left. Walk south along E Columbia St. to Cumberland St. and cross back to the east side of E Columbia St.; this route avoids a dangerous road crossing. The entrance to the park is across two railway tracks at the foot of Cumberland St. Alternatively, from the bus stop, just walk down Cumberland St.

The park has open grassy areas, hedgerows and riparian habitat along the river. Native trees such as red alders, bigleaf maples, black cottonwoods,

Across the Fraser River, often busy with boats, you can see Golden Ears mountains.
Mark Habdas

Pacific crab apples and a few ornamental trees provide a variety of habitats for birds. Hedgerows of red-osier dogwood, hardhack, thimbleberry, Pacific ninebark and tall Oregon grape support small birds including white-crowned and song sparrows, dark-eyed juncos and spotted towhees. There is a small slough, and from the wooden bridge at low tide you can see sedges and cattails, which are typical marsh vegetation.

Several nesting boxes attract cavity-nesting birds such as chickadees, swallows and woodpeckers. A green heron has been spotted near the entrance, and an American bittern and a Cooper's hawk also frequent the park. Pilings in the river provide good perching spots for double-crested cormorants, bald eagles and ospreys. An osprey's nest rests on one of the pilings. In early spring and summer this park is potentially a good spot for bird watching. You can often see harbour seals in the river, and starting in mid-March, during the eulachon run you may spot a California sea lion.

You can visit the park any time of the year; it will have something different to offer in each season.

Nearby Locations

- Westminster Quay is a short ride to the southwest by SkyTrain or bus
- Hume Park to the northeast is accessible from the Braid St. SkyTrain Station

Some Alerts

- coyotes
- fast-flowing river
- to ensure personal safety, avoid visiting alone in early morning or late evening

More Information

New Westminster Parks and Recreation: 604-527-4567 or www.nwpr.bc.ca

Shoreline Park, Port Moody

by Elaine Golds

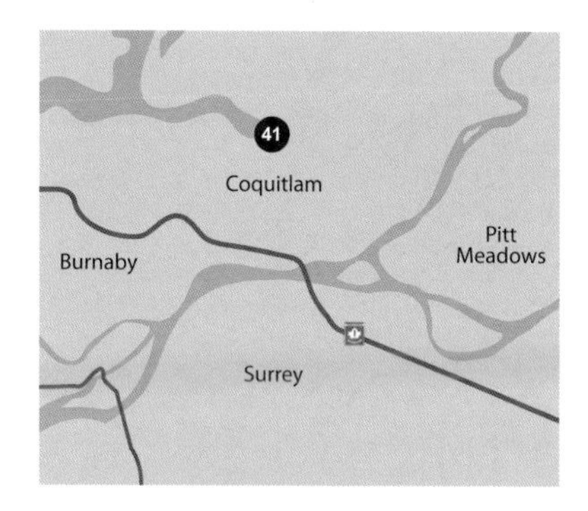

Forests, meadows, wetlands and seashore beaches

Location

Shoreline Park is in Port Moody at Ioco Rd. and Newport Dr.

Transit Information

From the Lougheed SkyTrain Station, take the #97 B-Line bus and alight at the Ioco Rd. and Newport Dr. stop at the entrance to the park.

For up-to-date information, contact TransLink at www.translink.ca or 604-953-3333.

Introduction

Shoreline Park in the City of Port Moody, a narrow U-shaped band of green surrounding the eastern end of Burrard Inlet, harbours an amazing diversity of wildlife within its 30 hectares (74 acres). Extending from Rocky Point Park at the south end to Old Orchard Park on the north shore, a 3-kilometre (1.9-mile) trail winding through Shoreline Park leads you through

A black bear strolls along the boardwalk over the intertidal marsh at Pigeon Cove.
Rick Saunier

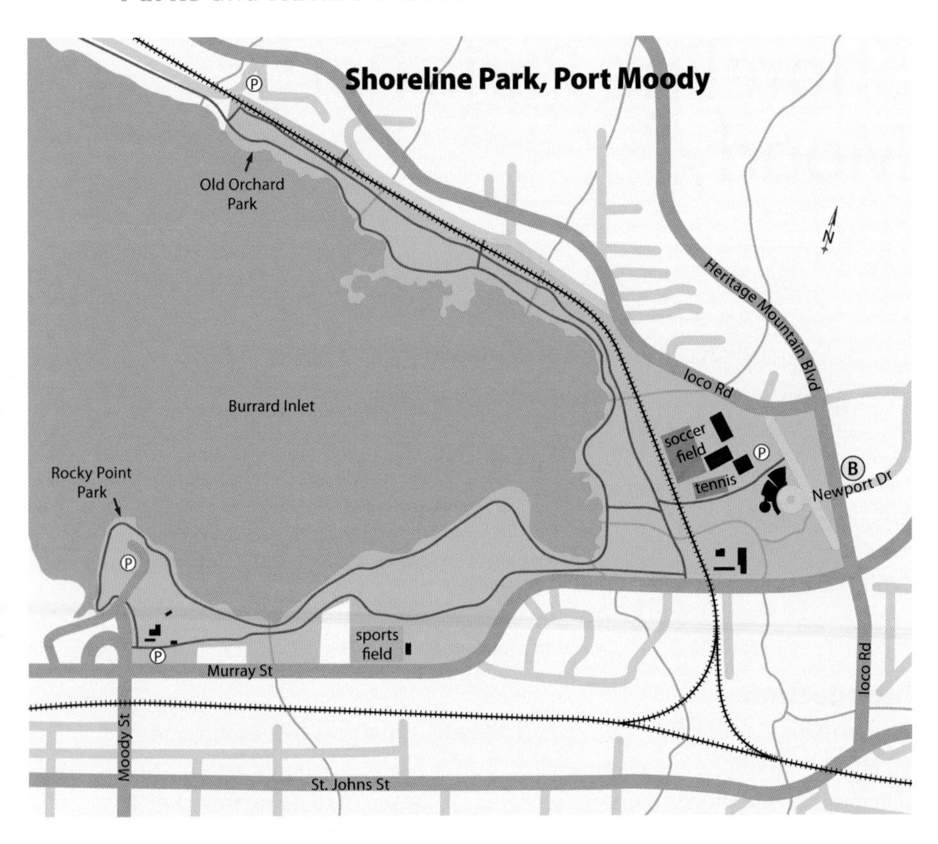

coniferous forests, open meadows, wetlands and mixed deciduous forests to a sandy beach. From several vantage points along the trail you will have excellent views of the North Shore mountains and open waters of Burrard Inlet.

The park surrounds 54 hectares (133 acres) of protected tidal mud flats. You can enjoy watching the ever-changing tides from the park. Viewing highlights include waterfowl and shorebirds in winter. In spring and summer, Rocky Point pier offers excellent views of nesting purple martins and ospreys. You can follow either the shoreline trail—a walking path that takes you on boardwalks over the mud flats—or the paved bike path that is popular with people pushing strollers or wheelchairs. You will see a number of interpretive signs along both routes.

Natural History Visit

From the bus stop, cross the street and walk through the civic building complex. The trail to the park starts on the north side of the skating arena between a soccer field and Noons Creek. You will reach the paved bike path first; just beyond it, the shoreline trail more closely follows the contours of the shoreline. Turn left for Rocky Point, turn right for Old Orchard Beach or go straight ahead for a stunning view of Burrard Inlet.

Near Noons Creek, water completely covers the mud flats at high tide. *Kiyoshi Takahashi*

The trail to Rocky Point leads through a copse of Pacific crab apple that becomes a bower of white blossoms in late spring. In summer songbirds and hummingbirds are drawn here by the profusion of Nootka rose, black twinberry and other shrubs. The black lily, a species more commonly found along the north coast of BC, also grows at the head of the inlet. After the boardwalk over Pigeon Cove, you will enter a shady coniferous forest with a number of viewing areas. Pigeon Cove is named for the band-tailed pigeons that come to the mud flats each spring. There they can eat the calcium-rich minerals to make a milk-like substance to feed to their young; they roost in the adjacent forest. At Rocky Point the pier end provides close views of a large colony of nesting purple martins, ospreys and eagles. Great blue herons often feed in the intertidal shallows.

The trail to Old Orchard Park will take you across Noons Creek, where you should see returning adult salmon every fall and occasional American dippers in winter. The deciduous forests here attract a variety of songbirds. Where the path opens to a small meadow, a series of created wetlands on the right provides nesting areas for red-winged blackbirds and habitat for amphibians. On the left a boardwalk leads to an inlet viewpoint, where the remnants of an old sawmill provide roosting areas for ducks. Just beyond, a side trail leads to a sawmill site that children like to explore at low tide. Soon the trail ends at Old Orchard Beach, where double-crested cormorants often perch on logs just offshore with wings spread for drying.

The head of Burrard Inlet attracts a number of dabblers including green-winged teals.
Mark Habdas

This is a popular park in a rapidly growing community. For enjoyment of wildlife, avoid busy times, especially on sunny days. A little rain enhances your experience of the natural features in this gem of a park.

Regardless of the season, there is always something interesting to see. Autumn is a time to view spawning salmon, while the winter months are best for waterfowl. Late spring blossoms at the head of the inlet are a photographer's delight.

Nearby Locations

- the Noons Creek Hatchery, where you can view spawning chum and coho salmon every fall, is a few metres upstream from the Noons Creek Bridge
- the Trans Canada Trail runs through Shoreline Park

Some Alerts

- bears
- slippery boardwalks during rainfall and especially in winter
- tidal mud flats are unstable and not safe for walking
- stay out of treed areas during strong windstorms

More Information

Shoreline Park: www.cityofportmoody.com/Recreation+and+Parks/Parks/Shoreline+Park+System+Trail.htm
The City of Port Moody: 604-469-4500
Heritage brochure and bird checklist available from City Hall-Library building.
Wildlife Inventory of the Shoreline Park: 1994 is available in the Port Moody Public Library.
Noons Creek Hatchery: 604-469-9106 or www.noonscreek.org

Como Lake Park

by Elizabeth Thunstrom

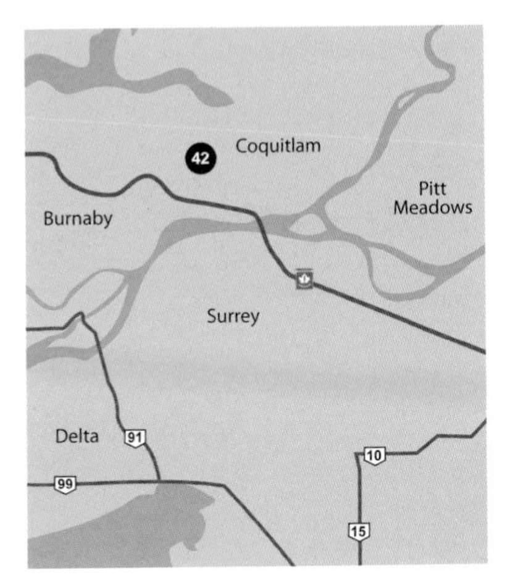

An unexpected urban oasis where ospreys fish in summer

Location

Como Lake Park is in central Coquitlam at Gatensbury St. and Grover Ave.

Transit Information

For the south entrance, from Lougheed Station, take the #151 Coquitlam Station bus along Foster Ave. and alight at the Foster Ave. and Gatensbury St. stop.

For the north entrance, from Lougheed Station, take the #156 Braid Station bus along Como Lake Ave. and alight at the Como Lake Ave. and Gatensbury St. stop.

For up-to-date information, contact TransLink at www.translink.ca or 604-953-3333.

Introduction

An unexpected urban oasis for migratory birds and home to a thriving wetland, Como Lake nestles in a developed residential area of central Coquitlam. Over 70 species of birds have been seen at the lake, including ospreys, loons, snow geese and nighthawks. Throughout the park non-native trees, similar to some of those found in the Riverview Arboretum, make interesting variations among the native vegetation.

Cattail, a marshland plant, provides nesting habitat and cover for many birds.
Rosemary Taylor

The park is designated a municipal sanctuary by the City of Coquitlam. It covers an area of 11 hectares (27 acres) around the 5-hectare (12-acre) lake that is the headwaters of Como Creek, which drains into the Fraser River. A small wetland and pond, created in 1998 at the north end of the lake, are surrounded by cottonwood and alder trees and various native shrubs. Grassy areas with clumps of trees buffer the lake from the nearby houses. Native plants along the inflow streams and lake edges are excellent habitat for small birds. The level 1-kilometre (0.6-mile) loop trail is easy walking for children and seniors.

Natural History Visit

The park is accessed from the south or north by way of Gatensbury St.

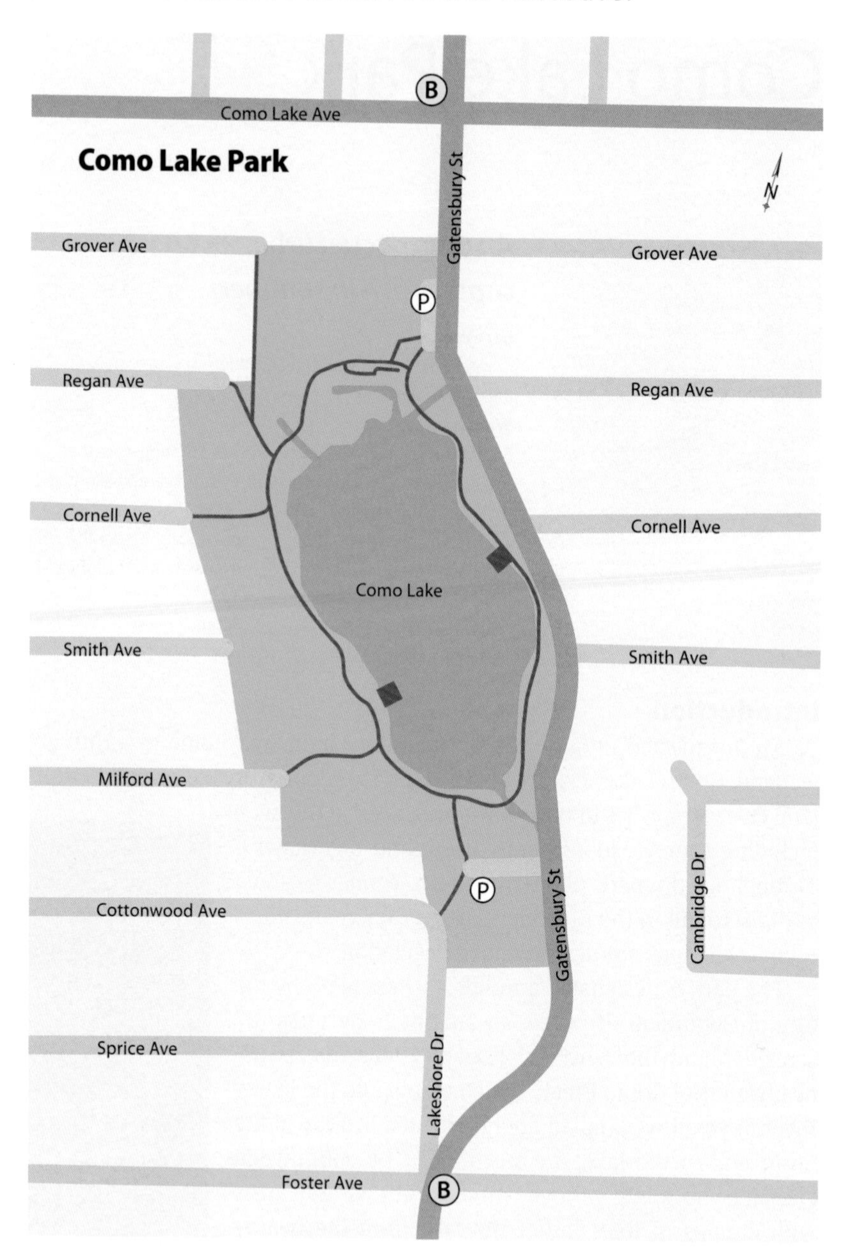

Visitors coming from the south can walk a short way north on Gatensbury St. and arrive at a grassy area with picnic tables and scattered trees. There is an excellent view toward the mountains and the extensive cattail beds, where red-winged blackbirds nest in spring. A small island provides safety for young geese and maybe a basking turtle. Herons sometimes rest on the island's willow tree. You can reach the west side of the lake over a small bridge. Canada geese congregate on the grassy open area, especially when moulting and flightless in July. Several families of goslings and ducklings hatch each year.

On both the east side and the west side of the lake, there is a dock for viewing and fishing. Along the lakeshore, the trees and shrubs are home to small songbirds that eat the numerous insects hatching from the water. You may spot a family of mallard ducks or pied-billed grebes, a belted kingfisher diving or shorebirds such as sandpipers.

The wetland is edged by Douglas-fir and pines as well as mature cottonwoods, which are a favoured roost for great blue herons and occasional bald eagles. Alder thickets screen the pond area where yellow native water lilies grow; this area is off-limits to visitors, but you can read about it in information boards on the raised viewpoint. Blackberries nearby provide food and cover for birds and coyotes.

The north entry to the loop trail from Gatensbury St. is near a grove of six sequoias that screen the road. From the bridge you may see raccoon tracks on the sandbar, trout hiding under the bank or ducks feeding in the small pond. Through the willows, look for the ospreys diving into the water. This

Como Lake is a place of natural tranquility within a residential area. *Mark Habdas*

is also a good spot for watching the sunset and the bats skipping across the water at dusk. Listen for a bullfrog's deep voice in the cattails.

Canada geese rest beside the lake. *Mark Habdas*

There is something to see at all seasons and times; even regular visitors will find new delights on each visit. The morning and evening hours are usually best for observing wildlife activity. There are great sunset views as well! Spring is the time to see migratory birds as well as cherry and dogwood blossoms. Summer showcases the ospreys, nighthawks, goslings and bats, while carp spawn in the shallows and water lilies thrive in the wetland. Fall brings many migratory ducks, geese and gulls. In winter the lake seldom freezes entirely and in windy weather is full of gulls and cormorants. Cormorants, amazingly organized fishers, drive trout into the creeks.

Nearby Locations

- Mundy Park is a bus ride away along Como Lake Rd.

Some Alerts

- coyotes
- Canada geese with young may be aggressive if approached
- trails can be muddy in wet weather and slippery if frosty or snowy
- water is not suitable for swimming or wading

More Information

City of Coquitlam: 604-927-3000 or www.coquitlam.ca/default.htm
Burke Mountain Naturalists: www.bmn.bc.ca
Como Watershed Group: www.vcn.bc.ca/cwg/

Mundy Park

by Judy Donaghey

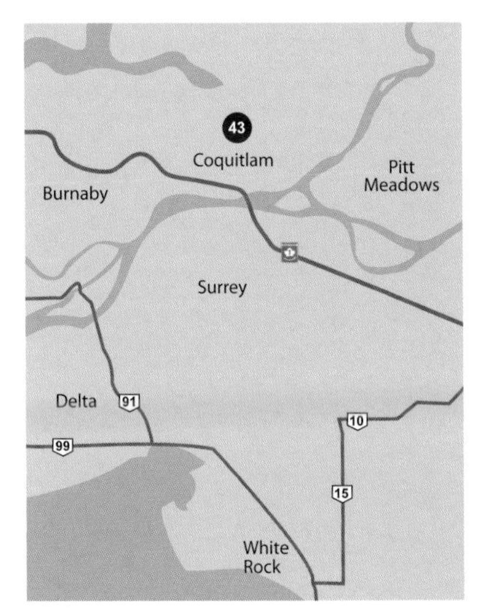

Extensive wilderness refuge with trails to lakes and creeks

Location

Mundy Park is in central Coquitlam at Hillcrest St. and Foster Ave.

Transit Information

For the west entrance on Hillcrest St., from either Lougheed SkyTrain Station or Coquitlam Station, take the #151 Lougheed Station/Coquitlam Station bus to the Foster Ave. and Linton St. stop.

Alternatively, for the east entrance on Mariner Way, from either Lougheed SkyTrain Station or Coquitlam Station, take the #152 Lougheed Station/Coquitlam Station bus to the Mariner Way and Chilko Dr. stop.

For up-to-date information, contact TransLink at www.translink.ca or 604-953-3333.

Introduction

Mundy Park's large forested portions, totalling 180 hectares (445 acres) including Riverview Forest, were dedicated in 1993 by popular referendum as Mundy Urban Forest Parkland to conserve and enhance native plants and animals. It provides second-growth forested bog habitat for a wide variety of native species. Mundy Park's sheer size makes it Coquitlam's dominant wilderness refuge. Its extensive 13.5-kilometre (8.4-mile) trail network winds through lush, pristine rain forest past two natural lakes, Mundy Lake to the west and Lost Lake to the east. On its west side the park also provides a range of recreational facilities.

Delicate blossoms of Hooker's fairybells are in pairs. They develop into red berries. *Wayne Weber*

The Mundy Park site was logged in the early 1900s, then subdivided and sold. Mr. Munday (note the different spelling) was one of the early owners before the lands reverted to the District of Coquitlam. In 1993, after a public referendum defeated a proposed golf course development by 84 percent, these forested lands were dedicated as urban forest parkland.

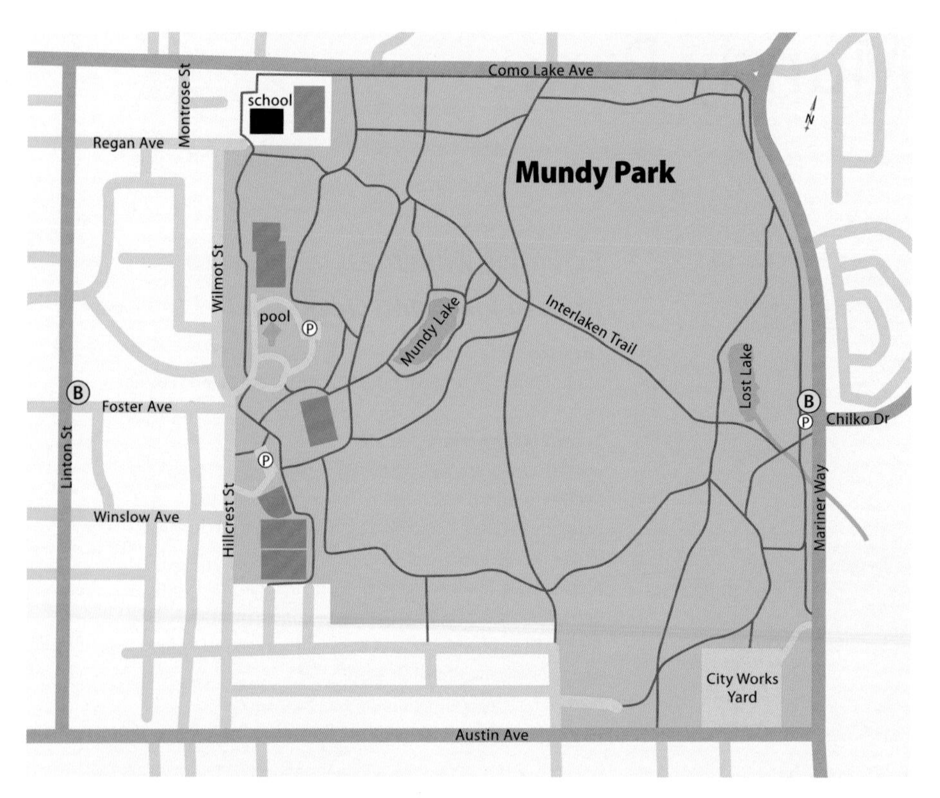

The peregrine falcon is a streamlined bird of prey with pointed wings and narrow tail. *Les Leighton*

Both Mundy Lake and Lost Lake and their outflow streams, Mundy Creek and Lost Creek, are suitable only for dependent park wildlife. Public swimming and fishing are not permitted. Be aware that this is a wildlife habitat that supports black bears with cubs, coyotes, raccoons and black-tailed deer, so proceed with caution.

A 2001 inventory revealed the presence of a red-listed (endangered) Pacific water shrew, blue-listed (vulnerable) red-legged frogs, a double-crested cormorant, a great blue heron and a peregrine falcon. At least nine amphibian species, three reptile species, 82 bird and 18 mammal species were noted in the inventory, though many others are known to be in the park.

Natural History Visit

You can enter the park either by the Hillcrest St. entrance on the west side, which leads in toward Mundy Lake, or by the Mariner Way entrance on the east side, which leads in toward Lost Lake.

Mundy Lake has white pond-lilies floating on its surface in summer months.
Rosemary Taylor

To reach the Hillcrest St. entrance from the bus stop, walk east on Foster Ave. a few blocks to Hillcrest St. Then turn right and continue half a block to the entrance.

From this entrance you can reach Mundy Lake by travelling east along the Perimeter Trail to the marked Mundy Lakeside Loop trail. Rare and fragile plants grow along the lakeside, including bog blueberry, cranberry, Nootka rose, cloudberry, Labrador tea, western bog laurel, king gentian, shore pine and the carnivorous sundew. You may see yellow and white pond-lilies in summer months with red huckleberry, Saskatoon, thimbleberry and trailing blackberry. Mock-orange, Hooker's fairybells, self-heal, enchanter's nightshade, western trillium, false lily-of-the-valley and Indian-pipe are among the many other delightful species that thrive here.

Alternatively, from the Mariner Way entrance, take the gravel trail into the park; on your right you will see Lost Lake as you pass by on the Interlaken Trail. Enjoy the view at the lake lookout. Unlike Mundy Lake, Lost Lake has no trails around it as there is very sensitive wildlife habitat at the head of Lost Creek.

The Interlaken Trail leads diagonally through the park and joins the two lakes. This was the main logging spine through the area when its old-growth forest was logged. Large numbers of old-growth stumps, some more than 1,000 years old, are visible near the northeast corner of the park and along the southern portions of the Waterline and Perimeter trails. Now they function as soil for new trees and shrubs and as nesting sites for birds and other animals.

A stag statue is naturally formed from a tree remnant. *Rosemary Taylor*

Birds in the park include ground-nesting species such as sparrows, winter wrens, hermit and Swainson's thrushes and spotted towhees. Other visitors include Cooper's and red-tailed hawks, bald eagles, ospreys, peregrine falcons and great horned, barred, northern saw-whet and northern pygmy-owls.

For best wildlife viewing, arrive at either first light or dusk when creatures are waking, feeding and retiring.

Nearby Locations

- Como Lake Park is about four blocks to the west

Some Alerts

- bears and coyotes
- nesting owls defend their territory during breeding season by chasing people short distances
- stay on the trails to protect habitat

More Information

City of Coquitlam: 604-927-3000 or www.coquitlam.ca/default.htm

Nature Trail Guidebook and a comprehensive Urban Forest Guidebook for Mundy Park, both generated by The Friends of Mundy Park Heritage Society: 604-933-6226 or 604-468-7946

Colony Farm Regional Park

by Larry Cowan

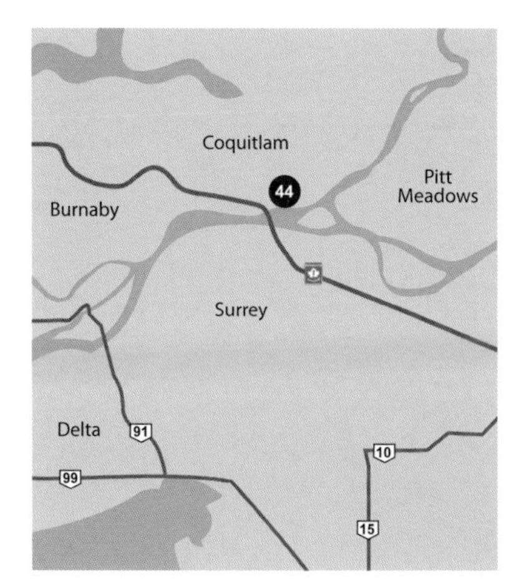

Nesting lazuli buntings, Bullock's orioles and black-headed grosbeaks

Location

Colony Farm Regional Park is on the east side of Coquitlam on Colony Farm Rd. off the Lougheed Hwy.

Transit Information

From the Braid St. SkyTrain Station, board the #159 Port Coquitlam bus to the Shaughnessy St. and Mary Hill Bypass stop opposite the southeast park access.

Return from the same location or from the west park entrance, boarding the #177 Braid St. bus at the Colony Farm Rd. and Cape Horn Ave. stop just west of Lougheed Hwy.

For up-to-date information, contact TransLink at www.translink.ca or 604-953-3333.

Introduction

Colony Farm Regional Park, on the border of Coquitlam and Port Coquitlam, has become a magnet for naturalists and hikers who enjoy its mix of forest, field and river landscapes. It preserves a country setting in an ever-sprawling urban landscape.

This 136-hectare (336-acre) Metro Vancouver park straddles the lower Coquitlam River at its confluence with the Fraser River. The Coquitlam River splits the park into two sections that are connected by the Millennium

Wildflowers bloom along dike edges. A female purplish copper butterfly nectars on tansy flowers. *Kiyoshi Takahashi*

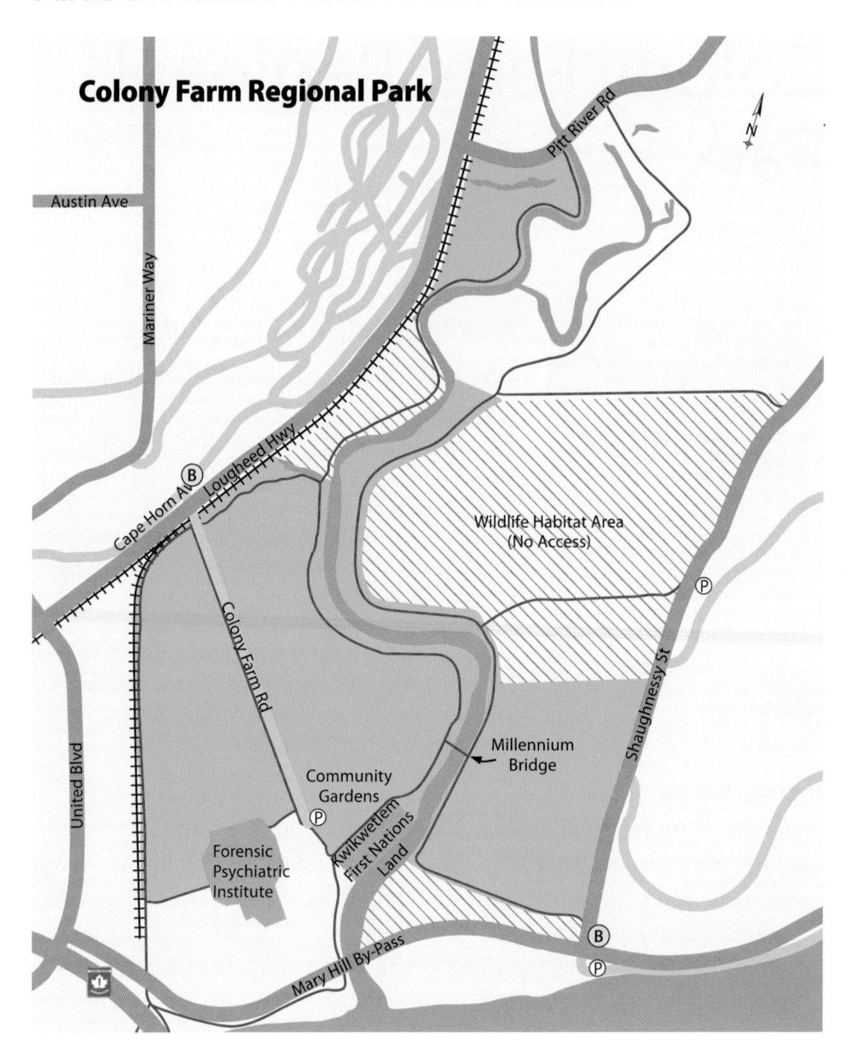

Bridge spanning the river. The flat land of the park is part of the Coquitlam River flood plain.

The park was created to save its old field habitat and associated wildlife. It now also contains a 2.8-hectare (6.9-acre) community garden for local residents to create some homegrown produce. Park facilities are located near the garden at the east end of Colony Farm Rd., a 10-minute walk from the Millennium Bridge.

The park supports many breeding birds such as lazuli buntings and eastern kingbirds through spring and summer. Many migrant species, including northern shrikes and red-tailed hawks, spend the fall and winter here. The Coquitlam River has runs of chum and coho salmon and winter-run steelhead, which pass through the park on their journey to the breeding redds farther upstream.

Natural History Visit

The park has a 9-kilometre (5.6-mile) field and dike-top trail system. All trails are flat, well maintained and for the most part open for nature viewing.

The main attraction for many naturalists is the abundant bird population at the park. Many people come to see the lazuli buntings that have a breeding population present from mid-May till the end of July. Close to 190 bird species have been observed at the park over the years, with more than a few rarities including an indigo bunting in 2007. Rufous hummingbirds, black-headed grosbeaks, Bullock's orioles, eastern kingbirds and green herons are a few of the other interesting summer resident breeding birds.

Winter brings another dimension to Colony Farm's appeal.
Kiyoshi Takahashi

The pond on the east side of the park has a good selection of overwintering waterfowl in fall and winter. Bitterns, soras and Virginia rails can also be seen occasionally at this pond. Most years pied-billed grebes have successfully bred in the pond area. In spring and summer it is not uncommon to see large flocks of tree, barn, cliff and northern rough-winged swallows actively feeding over the pond. You may see small Vaux's swifts at any time hunting for flying insects.

In summer the wooded areas along the southern boundary and along the Coquitlam River are home to many forest-dwelling birds such as yellow warblers, Swainson's thrushes, warbling vireos and Bullock's orioles. In winter you may see varied thrushes and golden-crowned kinglets.

The park has large open areas with natural grasses, fields and colourful wildflowers. You may spot its several resident coyotes hunting the fields for voles and other prey.

Top: The warbling vireo, with its long unhurried warbling call, is more often heard than seen. *Mark Habdas*

Left: A northern shrike, also called a butcher bird, often skewers its prey on barbs and thorns. *Mark Habdas*

Visit the park year-round. You may enjoy it best in spring when birds nest and wildflowers bloom. For bird watching, morning or evening is best. Winter brings overwintering species of birds such as hawks, shrikes and herons. Herons can be seen hunting for voles in the fields.

Nearby Locations

- the Riverview Lands are a short distant to the west of the park
- the 25-kilometre (15.5-mile) Traboulay PoCo Trail that encircles the City of Port Coquitlam passes through the park heading northeast

Some Alerts

- bears and coyotes

More Information

Metro Vancouver Regional Parks: www.metrovancouver.org/services/parks_lscr/regionalparks/Pages/default.aspx

Metro Vancouver Regional Parks Central Area Office: 604-520-6442

Colony Farm Park Association: www.parkpartners.ca/partners/colony%20farm/colony.htm

Traboulay PoCo Trail map: www.portcoquitlam.ca

Minnekhada Regional Park

by Rosemary Taylor

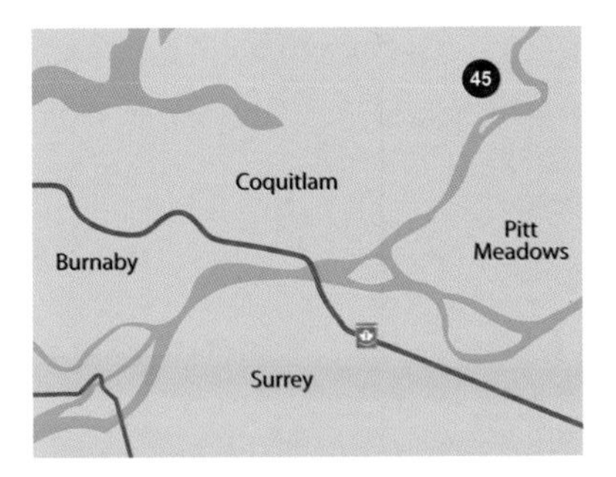

A cedar waxwing, with red waxy wing tips, is recognizable from its crest and black mask. *Virginia Hayes*

Misty marshes, beavers and bears, loons, lakes and lookouts

Location

Minnekhada Regional Park is in northeast Coquitlam on Quarry Rd. off Victoria Dr.

Transit Information

Bring your bicycle for the 2.7-kilometre (1.7-mile) ride to complete your journey; remember a bike lock.

From Coquitlam Station or Port Coquitlam Station, take the #C38 Prairie/River Springs bus and alight at the Victoria Dr. and Rocklin St. stop.

For up-to-date information, contact TransLink at www.translink.ca or 604-953-3333.

From the bus stop, locate the nearby three-way Victoria Dr. and Lower Victoria Dr. intersection slightly to the east and choose the left-hand uphill fork; this is the road not used by buses. Cycle northeast along Victoria Dr., which later becomes Quarry Rd., until you reach the Quarry Rd. entrance to the park. This is a pleasant rural route.

Introduction

Minnekhada Regional Park is west of the Pitt River in northeast Coquitlam. This large, 175-hectare (432-acre) park provides great diversity. Seldom does one park offer such varied landscapes. Two large, picturesque marshes, separated by a dike walking trail, are surrounded by forested hills with mountains in the background.

This gem of a park offers 10 kilometres (6.2 miles) of walking trails across marshes where birds abound, through forest and up to rocky knolls with beautiful views. Some trails are reasonably flat, but many hilly trails have steep and rocky sections. The name Minnekhada comes from a Sioux Indian word that means “beside still waters.”

Minnekhada Lodge, a small hunting lodge at the south side of the park, was designed and built in the mid-1930s for BC's 15th Lieutenant-Governor, Eric Hamber. The lodge is often open on Sundays and it is well worth seeing.

Natural History Visit

At the Quarry Rd. entrance a map shows a choice of trails. You can either

Two leaves of the miner's-lettuce are fused together to form a disk around the flowers.
Wayne Weber

stay near the marshes and the lodge or venture farther afield up to Low Knoll, High Knoll or Addington Lookout. This park offers some lovely scenery, so if you have binoculars and a camera, take them along.

The marsh is home to beavers, as their lodges show, and bird life abounds both there and along the dike from the Addington Lookout to the Pitt River. According to season there may be northern shovelers, American wigeons, gadwalls, the ever-present mallards and great blue herons.

In spring many flowers such as miner's-lettuce, foamflower, skunk cabbage, salmonberry and bleeding heart edge the trails. Giant mannagrass thrives around the marsh.

Each of the two knolls has a different view. Low Knoll is a pleasant place to sit and look down on the marsh where, if you are very lucky, you may see a black bear among the rushes. High Knoll faces over blueberry fields that turn a spectacular red in fall. Moss-draped trees are visible from the forest trails, and autumn brings a crop of interesting mushrooms.

Bears are in the park, although seldom seen, and warning signs are posted on trails. Keep a lookout for them, particularly in summer, when

The view is one of your rewards for climbing High Knoll. *Rosemary Taylor*

A beaver lodge is built from chewed-off twigs and other vegetation. *Rosemary Taylor*

they sometimes forage among salmonberry bushes beside the road from Addington Dike to the lodge.

Each season has its charm, bringing different flowers, birds, animals and foliage that you can enjoy in a variety of settings. You will soon forget the proximity to urban sprawl as Minnekhada's peace and tranquility replace the stresses of city life at least for a short time.

Minnekhada is a year-round park where there is always something of interest to see. Trails, although muddy at times, are always in good condition for hiking. In winter enjoy wildfowl on the marsh, and in summer soak up the views from either Low or High Knoll.

Nearby Locations

- DeBoville Slough to the southwest and Pitt River dikes to the southeast are in easy cycling distance on the Traboulay PoCo Trail; they offer more birding and enjoyable walks along the river's edge

Some Alerts

- bears

More Information

Metro Vancouver Regional Parks: www.metrovancouver.org/services/parks_lscr/regionalparks/Pages/default.aspx
Metro Vancouver Regional Parks Central Area Office: 604-520-6442
Map of Traboulay PoCoTrail:
http://www.city.port-coquitlam.bc.ca/Citizen_Services/Parks_and_Recreation/Facilities_Amenities/Traboulay_PoCo_Trail.htm

Grant Narrows Regional Park

by Larry Cowan

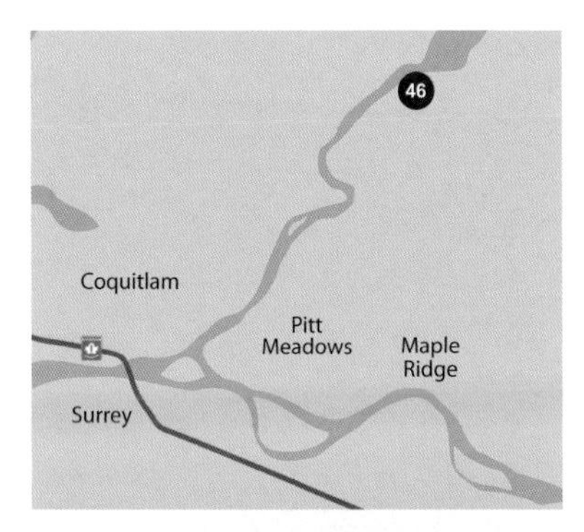

A shrub lichen, leaf lichen and moss thrive on a dry tree trunk in this lichen garden.
Larry Cowan

Placid river and lake to lush valley and mountain peaks

Location

Grant Narrows Regional Park is on the north side of Pitt Meadows at the end of Rannie Rd. off Neaves Rd.

Transit Information

Bring your bicycle for the 15.5-kilometre (9.6-mile) ride to complete your journey; remember a bike lock.

From Coquitlam Centre Station, board the #701 Haney Place/Maple Ridge East bus and alight at the Dewdney Trunk Rd. and 203rd St. stop.

For up-to-date information, contact TransLink at www.translink.ca or 604-953-3333.

From the bus stop, cycle north on 203rd St. for 2.1 kilometres (1.3 miles). Turn right onto Old Dewdney Trunk Rd. and cycle east for 0.8 kilometre (0.5 mile). Then turn left at Neaves Rd., which later becomes Rannie (also spelled Rennie) Rd., and cycle north for 12.6 kilometres (7.8 miles) to the park entrance. Your cycle ride back can be an adventure; dike-top trails provide an option to get off pavement for much of your return to the bus.

Introduction

Grant Narrows Regional Park lies at the end of a flat cycle ride through wide expanses of diked farmlands and nature reserves of the Pitt River Valley. The park, at the south end of Pitt Lake, is at the north end of a narrowing valley between the rugged Golden Ears peaks on the east and the Pitt River and Burke Mountain on the west. The view of the surrounding mountains is spectacular, particularly when they are snow-capped.

The park is small at 6 hectares (14.8 acres). However, it is located within the Pitt-Addington Marsh Wildlife Management Area (PAMWMA), into which several trails lead from the park. Grant Narrows is the focal point of many kilometres of dike-top trails through many different habitat types. Its boat launch facilities provide a jumping-off point for land and water adventures for boaters, kayakers and canoeists travelling up Pitt Lake and beyond. A favourite adventure is to rent a kayak or canoe at the park and enjoy a

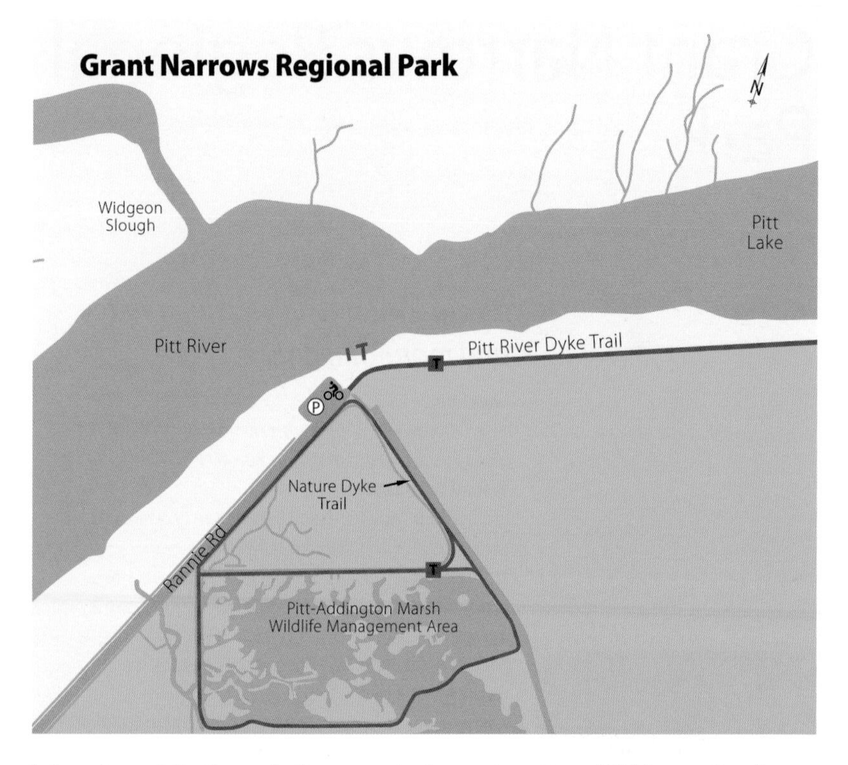

leisurely paddle through the meandering waterways of Widgeon Creek to a public campsite and a short hike to Widgeon Falls.

An attraction of the park is its completely natural location, surrounded by Pinecone Burke Provincial Park, Golden Ears Provincial Park, UBC Malcolm Knapp Research Forest and PAMWMA. Widgeon Slough is just across the Pitt River.

The last remnant of snow on the mountains completes a summer view near Pitt River.
Larry Cowan

Sandhill cranes are often mistaken for herons despite their red colouring. *Mark Habdas*

The park is a stopover spot for many migrating birds such as warblers, thrushes and waterfowl in spring and fall. PAMWMA supports a breeding population of sandhill cranes that you can often see and hear while you are journeying to Grant Narrows.

Natural History Visit

At Grant Narrows Park, the big draw for many is the wooded Nature Dike Trail, which is a walking trail only. Turn right at the food concession; the trail leads southeast toward the mountains. It is home to many species of birds that are hard to find elsewhere in the Lower Mainland, for example, gray catbirds, eastern kingbirds and Bullock's orioles. It has hosted its share of rarities over the years, including American redstarts, Baltimore orioles, black-throated sparrows and veeries. There is a viewing platform 1.8 kilometres (1.1 miles) along the trail.

On another dike the Pitt River Dike Trail continues along the side of Pitt Lake from the parking area. It allows excellent observation of nesting ospreys from May through August from a viewing platform that affords spectacular views of the Katzie Marsh, Pitt Lake and the surrounding mountains. Scanning the marsh through the year provides an opportunity to see most of BC's waterfowl species, with large concentrations of trumpeter swans in spring. The marsh has a small breeding population of mute swans and occasionally trumpeter swans in the summer.

The park also hosts a diverse group of four-legged inhabitants. There have been sightings of black bears, black-tailed deer, beavers, muskrats, otters and coyotes.

Pitt Lake is the second-largest freshwater tidal lake in the world; the lower Pitt River south of the lake changes its flow direction. This effect results from tidal variations in the water level at its confluence with the Fraser River. Northward-flowing water from the Fraser River carries sufficient sand and silt that it has constructed a delta into Pitt Lake. The Pitt River Dike Trail is actually on the delta. Older parts of the delta underlie the flat land that extends south from the Nature Dike Trail.

A western meadowlark sings its heart out.
Virginia Hayes

The park offers things to see and experience year-round but is best enjoyed from April through September, when migrants and nesting species are present in abundance. Fall and winter bring an influx of waterfowl that in turn attract bald eagles, peregrine falcons and usually a gyrfalcon. Winter can be a great time for photography; you can use the snow-topped mountains and lake vistas as your photographic canvas.

Nearby Locations

- Widgeon Slough is an easy paddle across the Pitt River
- Pitt-Addington Marsh Wildlife Management Area (PAMWMA) lies to the south

Some Alerts

- bears
- strong tidal currents at times in the river
- the lake can become very rough in the afternoon

More Information

Metro Vancouver Regional Parks: www.metrovancouver.org/services/parks_lscr/regionalparks/Pages/default.aspx
Metro Vancouver Regional Parks East Area Office: 604-530-4983
Ayla Canoe Rentals: 604-941-2822 or www.aylacanoes.com
PAMWMA: www3.telus.net/driftwood/wmapitt.htm
City of Pitt Meadows Cycling: www.pittmeadows.bc.ca/EN/main/residents/742/10585.html

Brae Island Regional Park

by Jaideep Mukerji

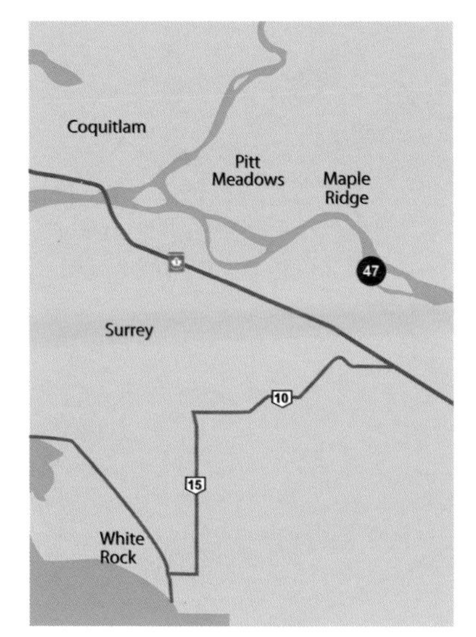

A rural island in the Fraser River near a national historic site

Location

Brae Island Regional Park is in Fort Langley on Glover Rd. just northeast of River Rd.

Transit Information

From the Surrey Central SkyTrain Station, take the #501 Langley Centre bus to Langley Centre. Then transfer to the #C62 Langley Centre/Walnut Grove bus and alight at the Glover Rd. and 96th Ave. stop in historic Fort Langley.

For up-to-date information, contact TransLink at www.translink.ca or 604-953-3333.

Alternatively, from Maple Ridge, take the #C48 Thornhill bus along River Rd. to the Albion Ferry stop and then ride the free Albion Ferry across the Fraser River to Fort Langley.

For ferry information, contact www.bchighway.com/ferry/albion.html or 604-230-5221.

Introduction

There are few places in Greater Vancouver where you can combine riverside walks, woodland trails through mature second-growth forest, wide mountain vistas and a visit to the birthplace of British Columbia. The newly opened Brae Island Regional Park, on an island in the Fraser River off the village of Fort Langley, offers just this opportunity. Archaeological evidence suggests that seasonal settlement in the general area began 9,000 years ago with the Coast Salish or Sto:lo peoples occupying these traditional territories. Today this area is the traditional territory of the Kwantlen First Nation.

Pair of beetles mate on Philadelphia fleabane. Each white ray is a complete flower. *Jaideep Mukerji*

Within this 68-hectare (168-acre) park, forest trails link the parking area to Tavistock Point at the northern tip of the island. Nearby, the 304-hectare (751-acre) Derby Reach Regional Park has a more varied topography, and 9 kilometres (5.6 miles) of trails weave through its shoreline, meadow and woodland features.

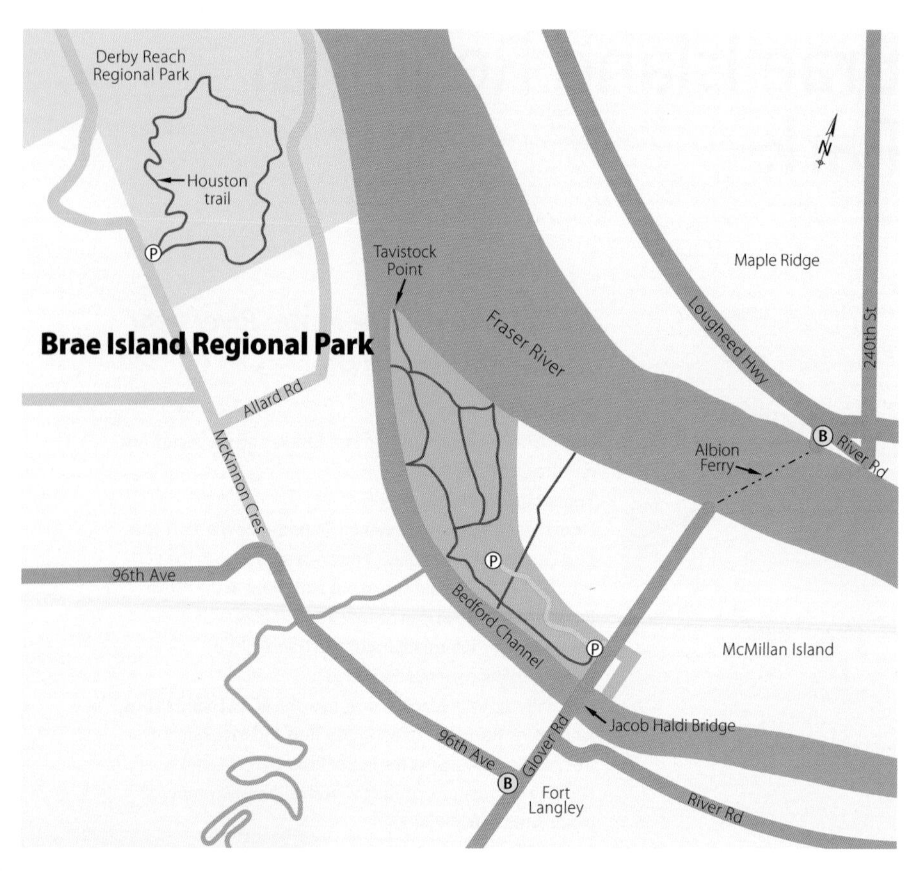

A woodland trail leads down Brae Island to Tavistock Point.
Jaideep Mukerji

The 3.5-kilometre (2.2-mile) Fort to Fort Trail along the Fraser River begins close to the entrance of Brae Island Regional Park. It connects the present Fort Langley National Historic Site to the heritage area of Derby Reach Regional Park and the stone cairn marking the original Fort Langley settlement site.

Natural History Visit

From the bus stop in Fort Langley, a brief walk along Glover Rd. across the Jacob Haldi Bridge and then down a footpath immediately on your left takes you to the park entrance. Alternatively, from the Albion Ferry, walk a short distance south along Glover Rd. to the park entrance on your right.

The Fraser River islands and adjacent shorelines have distinctive vegetation because of the flood plain's rich soils, plentiful water, seasonal flooding and warm microclimate. A community of trees consisting of Pacific willow, red alder and cottonwood—all tolerant to flooding—has developed along the edge zone.

Yellow irises set off expansive river and mountain views from Tavistock Point. *Jaideep Mukerji*

The wide, level main trail on Brae Island meanders through forest for more than 2 kilometres (1.2 miles) to the tip of the island at Tavistock Point, where irises, bulrushes and sedges grow. There are also branch trails that take you right to the river shoreline. In the forested and shoreline sections of Brae Island and Derby Reach parks, birds commonly spotted include downy woodpeckers, hairy woodpeckers, winter wrens and American robins. Occasionally golden-crowned kinglets may be observed, and varied thrushes are seen infrequently. Other species you may see are Steller's jays, bushtits, belted kingfishers, great blue herons, bald eagles, Bewick's wrens, spotted towhees and song sparrows.

After you leave the park and go over the bridge back to Fort Langley, you will cross the scenic Fort to Fort Trail to Derby Reach. The trail begins just before the railway tracks across from the heritage CN Rail train station in the heart of Fort Langley. Derby Reach is 3.5 kilometres (2.2 miles) down the trail to your right. To your left the Fort Langley National Historic Site is a short walk away.

If you decide to take the Fort to Fort Trail, you will come to an access path to the Houston Trail within Derby Reach. This is farther inland and traverses an area where the original forests of western redcedar, Douglas-fir, western hemlock and perhaps Sitka spruce were harvested between the late 1880s and the mid-1930s. The forest has regrown naturally, and succession has progressed to the red alder and bigleaf maple stage. There are stands of other tree species, particularly black cottonwood, western redcedar, western hemlock, grand fir, Sitka spruce and Douglas-fir.

Visit these parks at different times of the year to observe changes in the river flow and see seasonal wildflowers and migrating birds. In late summer you can spot migrating salmon jumping in the waters of Bedford Channel that separates Brae Island from Fort Langley.

Golden Ears and Mt. Judge Howay are over the river from Brae Island and Derby Reach.
Jaideep Mukerji

Nearby Locations

- the Fort Langley National Historic Site, The Langley Centennial Museum, the BC Farm Machinery Museum and the 1915 CN Station are all within easy walking distance in the interesting village of Fort Langley with its art galleries, antique stores and eateries

Some Alerts

- occasional bears
- eroding cliffs
- strong river currents

More Information

Metro Vancouver Regional Parks: www.metrovancouver.org/services/parks_lscr/regionalparks/Pages/default.aspx
Metro Vancouver Regional Parks East Area Office: 604-530-4983
Fort Langley: http://www.fortlangley.com/
Fort to Fort Trail map: www.tol.bc.ca/files/web_files/recreation/FortLangleyTrail.pdf
Albion Ferry: www.translink.ca/Transportation_Services/Albion_Ferry

south of vancouver

Preceding page: In spring, rufous hummingbirds swoop by the Bog Forest Trail. *Richmond Nature Park*

Top: In November a huge flock of snow geese occupies a field near Reifel Bird Sanctuary. *Mark Habdas*

Iona Beach Regional Park

by Peter M. Candido

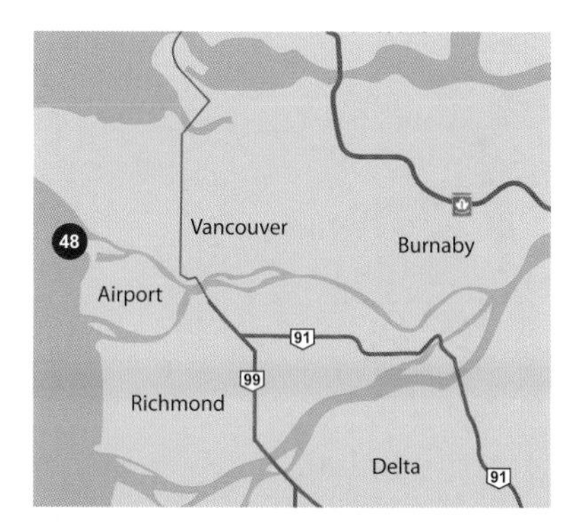

The dazzling male yellow-headed blackbird is a favourite of visitors to the ponds. *Peter M. Candido*

A long shoreline jetty for sightings of rare or unusual bird species

Location

Iona Beach Regional Park is in northwest Richmond at the end of Ferguson Rd. off Templeton St.

Transit Information

Bring your bicycle for the 5.7-kilometre (3.5-mile) ride to complete your journey; remember a bike lock.

From downtown Vancouver, board the #98 B-Line Richmond Centre bus to Airport Station. Transfer to the #424 Airport/Airport Station bus and alight at the Miller Rd. and Templeton St. stop. Note that the very infrequent #C90 Sea Island North bus takes you closer, within 5.1 kilometres (3.2 miles) of the park at its final stop.

For up-to-date information, contact TransLink at www.translink.ca or 604-953-3333.

From the bus stop, cycle north along Templeton Street, which becomes Ferguson Rd. as it continues west to the park entrance. At first a bicycle path will lead you over the traffic-lighted intersections. It goes on for 2.5 kilometres (1.6 miles), then the road narrows and winds past fields and hedgerows. There may be some heavy truck traffic.

Alternatively, when the Canada Line SkyTrain extension is complete, from Templeton SkyTrain Station, it will be an approximately 5-kilometre (3.1-mile) cycle ride along Templeton St. and then Ferguson Rd. to the park entrance.

Introduction

Iona Beach Regional Park is in northwest Richmond, adjacent to the Vancouver International Airport and bordering the Iona Island sewage treatment ponds. Although it is only 30 hectares (74 acres) and within Metro Vancouver, the park includes rare or unique habitats. Two artificial ponds were created to replace habitat destroyed during construction of the sewage treatment plant.

Iona Beach now supports a variety of waterfowl and marsh birds. Adjacent to the ponds are several other habitats: low sand dune, saline dune meadows and a narrow sand beach.

The park includes a federally owned southern jetty that extends 4 kilometres (2.5 miles) into the Strait of Georgia. It provides a level, scenic walk or bicycle ride with views of the distant North Shore mountains and Vancouver Island. It also offers opportunities to observe many species of ducks, loons, grebes, shorebirds and gulls. Harbour seals are often visible at high tide.

The red throat feathers of a red-throated loon grow only in spring and summer. *Virginia Hayes*

The North Arm Jetty is outside the park and managed by Port Metro Vancouver. At low tide you can walk along the beach on its south side, where an interesting sand dune ecosystem has developed.

Natural History Visit

From the parking lot, the base of Iona Jetty lies about 100 metres (328 feet) to the south. You can observe birds on both sides of the jetty by walking on the concrete and gravel surface along the top of the sewage outfall pipe. If you're cycling, stay on the parallel gravel road for safety.

Some waterbirds that spend the winter here, from September or October to March or April, are surf and white-winged scoters, greater scaups, Barrow's and common goldeneyes and northern pintails. You may also see other waterfowl such as horned, red-necked and western grebes and common and red-throated loons. At low tide in fall, large flocks of shorebirds such as western sandpipers and dunlins feed on the mud flats; dunlins spend winter in the area too. With luck you may see a peregrine falcon swooping on these flocks, trying to capture a meal.

On an offshore tower, a nesting colony of double-crested cormorants may be visible in summer. Great blue herons are especially numerous at low tide, and bald eagles frequent the area. In fall, from the end of the jetty, with a telescope you may see migrating parasitic jaegers harassing Bonaparte's gulls.

East of the washrooms and adjacent to the parking lot are the two marshy artificial ponds that you can scan for birds from a short boardwalk and observation platform. Duck numbers and variety are greatest in winter and may include buffleheads, ruddy ducks, lesser scaups, hooded mergansers, canvasbacks, mallards, American wigeons, gadwalls, green-winged teals, ring-necked ducks and northern pintails. Nesting species in summer include pied-billed grebes, gadwalls, mallards, Canada geese and American coots.

The north pond is home to the only colony of yellow-headed blackbirds in the Lower Mainland; the striking males sing their bizarre groaning songs from clumps of reeds and bushes. From the trail between the two ponds in

The boardwalk provides an excellent vantage point to view waterfowl. *Peter M. Candido*

summer, you can hear red-winged blackbirds singing out their loud *on-ka-reee* songs from shrubs and cattails and marsh wrens skulking in the reeds. Along the southeast corner of the north pond is a large beaver lodge, and around the ponds you occasionally see beavers, muskrats, river otters and mink. At the edges of the ponds, turtles may be sunning themselves; these are red-eared sliders, an introduced species. If time allows and the tides are right, you can also explore the sand ecosystems on the North Arm Jetty.

River otters frolic along the water's edge. *Joan Lopez*

This park is interesting at any time. In winter it is a particularly good destination, given the large diversity of birds, the open terrain and the easy walking. Spring and late summer to fall are the best times to see migrating birds. In summer you can observe birds that breed in and around the marshes.

Nearby Locations

- the eastern half of the Sea Island Conservation Area can be accessed from MacDonald Rd, a 4-kilometre (2.5-mile) cycle ride away, or farther east from Grauer Rd.; the dike provides good bird habitat

Some Alerts

- go onto the beach only on a falling tide: consult tide tables
- sharp drop from atop the sewage outfall pipe of the south jetty
- truck traffic en route to the park

More Information

Metro Vancouver Regional Parks: www.metrovancouver.org/services/parks_lscr/regionalparks/Pages/default.aspx
Metro Vancouver Regional Parks West Area Office: 604-224-5739
Habitat information and bird checklist: www.geog.ubc.ca/richmond/city/lona.htm

Terra Nova Natural Area

by Eric Greenwood

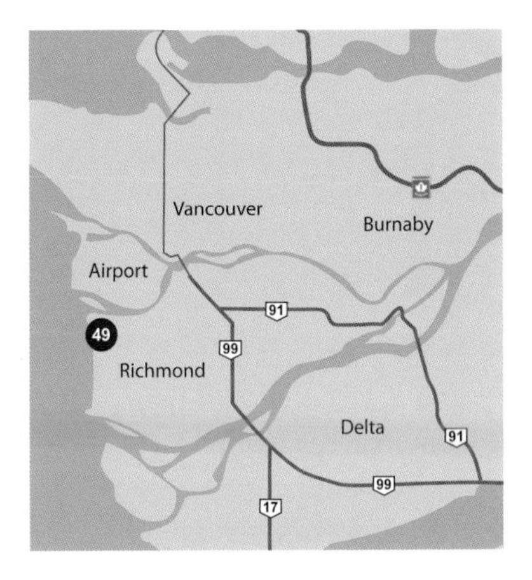

Grassy fields, mountain views, ocean breezes and abundant wildlife

Location

Terra Nova Natural Area is on the west side of Richmond at the west end of Westminster Hwy.

Transit Information

From downtown Vancouver, take the #98 B-Line Richmond Centre bus to Richmond Centre. Then transfer to the #401 One Rd. bus and alight at the No. 1 Rd. and Westminster Hwy. stop. For your return trip east, the stop is one block east at the Westminster Hwy. and Forsythe Cr. intersection. For up-to-date information, contact TransLink at www.translink.ca or 604-953-3333.

Introduction

Owned by Richmond City, the 14-hectare (35-acre) Terra Nova Natural Area preserves old field habitat adjacent to the West Dyke Trail and Sturgeon Banks in Richmond. The natural area lies between Westminster Hwy. to the north and Quilchena Golf and Country Club to the south. It features a pond, native plantings, viewing platforms and pathways. The site provides habitat and food for a variety of wildlife including raptors (hawks), herons and migrating birds.

A ring-necked pheasant ingests gravel as part of its digestive process. *Mark Habdas*

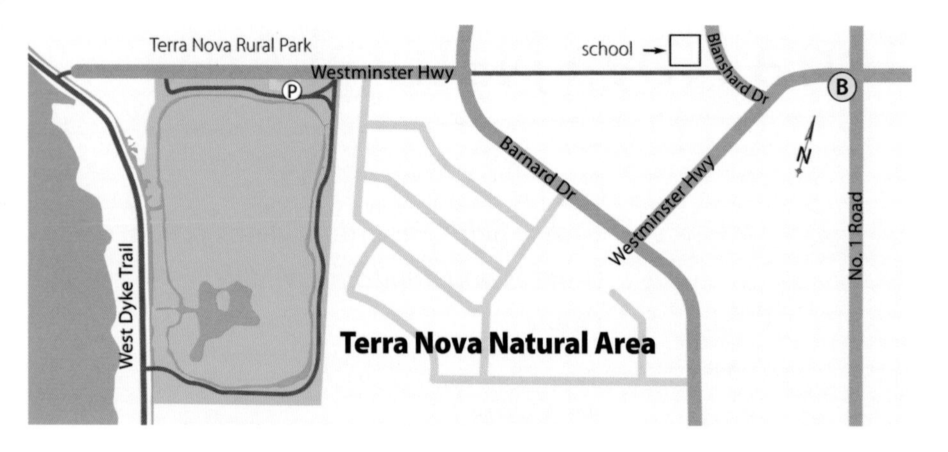

The area was farmed until the late 1980s and then slated for housing development. A public outcry was fuelled by the rapid development of the residential area close by, and eventually the City of Richmond reacquired the site from the developers.

North across Westminster Hwy. is the Terra Nova Rural Park. Occupying the northwest corner of the main island of Richmond, it offers excellent views of the North Shore mountains, Vancouver International Airport, Sturgeon Banks and the Fraser River. Phase One construction of this park began in early 2005. Trails crossing the rural park make the whole Terra Nova area ideal for walks that can make you feel you are out in the country.

Natural History Visit

From the bus stop, walk west along Westminster Hwy. past Terra Nova Village Mall and turn right on Blanshard Dr. Take the path on the left just

Black hawthorn blooms develop into blackish-purple haws that birds love. *Wayne Weber*

before Spul'u'kwuks Elementary School. This path heads west for about 0.3 kilometre (0.2 mile) through Terra Nova Neighbourhood School Park and ends at the Barnard Dr. and Westminster Hwy. intersection. Follow Westminster Hwy. west for another 0.2 kilometre (0.1 mile); Terra Nova Natural Area will be on your left.

The area is surrounded by the slough and bounded by a well-maintained walking path on three sides. As well, the north and south walking paths both connect to West Dyke Trail, so you can take an easy, pleasant walk around the perimeter of the habitat. In the southwest corner an observation deck offers views of a spring-fed pond that hosts ducks year-round.

The old field habitat enclosed by the perimeter trails is ideal for ground-nesting birds such as pheasants and Savannah sparrows, so public access is not permitted. To simulate a cycle of crop rotation, the City of Richmond has maintained the area as a farmer would; the grass has not been harvested from the fields, but areas have been mown and sometimes reseeded.

As you walk around the perimeter, look for the old fence posts that once separated the fields and the more recently erected perches that encourage raptors and owls. In late spring and summer, patches of native wildflowers thrive: cow-parsnip, lupine and Canada goldenrod. Native trees and shrubs include red-osier dogwood, salmonberry, hardhack, red elderberry, black hawthorn, Pacific crab apple, Indian-plum and Douglas-fir.

At Terra Nova, the North Shore mountains are a distant backdrop to old field habitat.
Eric Greenwood

Snow geese normally travel in large flocks and flutter to the ground like snowflakes.
Virginia Hayes

In winter the natural area hosts several species of raptors and ducks wearing their bright mating plumages, and you can see them in the slough and the pond. Spring and early summer herald the arrival of migrants: songbirds passing on their way north, other songbirds that stay to nest, migrant duck species and swallows. The reverse migration in fall brings back numerous songbirds; in their more dowdy fall plumage they are more difficult to identify at this time of year.

On any sunny day the views of the North Shore mountains make the trip to the natural area worthwhile, especially in clear, crisp weather. Seasonal birds can be seen year-round.

Nearby Locations

- a community garden and Terra Nova Rural Park are to the north across the Westminster Hwy.
- the 6-kilometre (3.7-mile) West Dyke Trail to Steveston adjoins the Terra Nova Rural Area to the west

Some Alerts

- small children need supervision near the water

More Information

Terra Nova Highlights:
www.richmond.ca/parksrec/ptc/trails/exploring/terranova.htm
City of Richmond: 604-276-4000 or www.richmond.ca

Garry Point Park, Steveston

by Terry Taylor

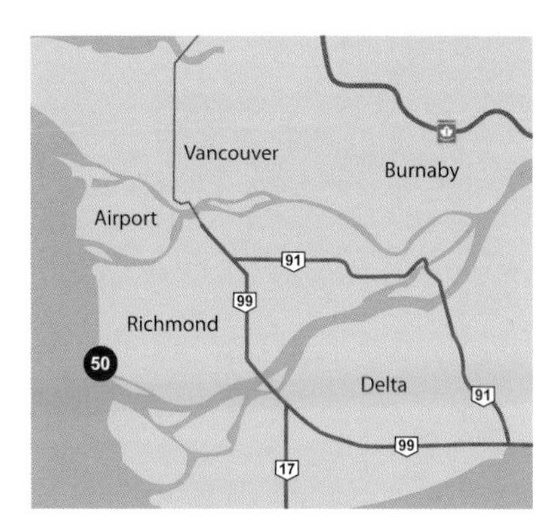

A triple point where ocean, river and land come together

Location

Garry Point Park, Steveston is on the southwest side of Richmond at 7th Ave. and Chatham St.

Transit Information

From the 22nd St. SkyTrain Station or Richmond Centre, take the #410 Railway bus. Alight at the last stop at 7th Ave. and Chatham St. close to Garry Point.

For up-to-date information, contact TransLink at www.translink.ca or 604-953-3333.

Introduction

This 30-hectare (74-acre) Richmond City park is at the southwest corner of Lulu Island, where the South Arm of the Fraser River enters the Strait of Georgia. It offers a sweeping view from the river across the strait to Vancouver Island and north to the North Shore mountains.

Garry Point occupies the southern extremity of Sturgeon Bank, a place where the land becomes the sea. The park, which occupies part of the Fraser River delta, is underlain by sand and silt that the Fraser River has transported from throughout its 233,000-square-kilometre (89,968-square-mile) drainage basin as far away as the Rocky Mountains.

Dunegrass has deep roots that stabilize the foreshore, and its thick leaves slow evaporation.
James Holkko

Natural History Visit

From the bus stop, walk along 7th Ave. to the park entrance. A wide trail encircles the park. At Garry Point pioneer plants are colonizing the sandy soil that has been dredged from the river channel, so this is an excellent place to see how this process begins. Sand is low in nutrients and unstable and dries out rapidly; the plants here are adapted to extremes. They actually require disturbance and instability to survive, being unable to tolerate the shade or competition present in better-drained sites.

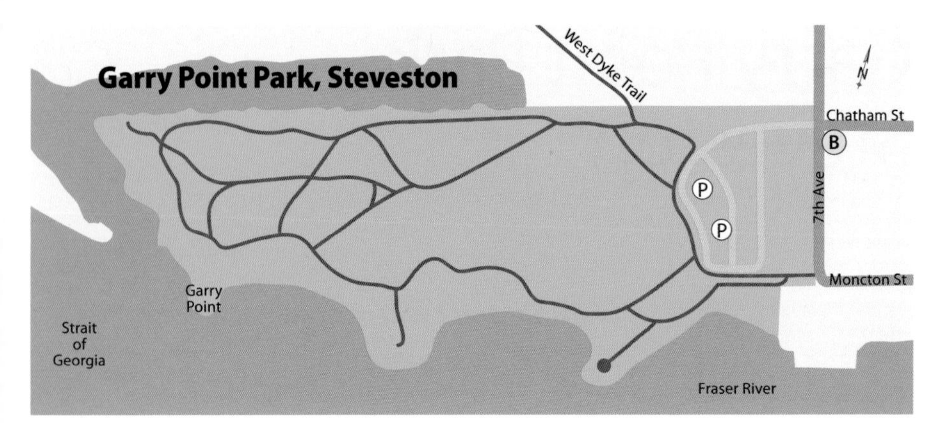

Many of them are annuals that complete their lifecycle early in the year and die when summer drought arrives.

Above: The pinkish flowers of hare's-foot clover resemble a rabbit's foot when they become seeds. *James Holkko*

Below: California sea lions are hauled out on the rocks of Steveston Jetty. *Sheila Byers*

The most striking flowers here are the large-leaved lupines that form extensive colonies. The beautiful purple blooms appear during the summer. These perennials can survive because of their extensive root system; the bacteria in their roots also produce nitrogen fertilizer, which feeds the lupines. Other species growing here are the hare's-foot clover, with soft hairy flower clusters, and the compass plant, with leaves directed north-south to maximize light-gathering power in the morning and evening.

Dunegrass grows among the breakwater boulders on the south side of the park; its thick evergreen leaves are adapted to wind and sand abrasion. Below these rocks the grass-like Lyngby's sedge dominates a small

Logs that have escaped from log booms become a feature of many Lower Mainland beaches.
James Holkko

zone of estuary plants. The plants' decaying leaves provide an important link in the food chain that feeds young salmon.

To the north of the park Sturgeon Bank, visible from the West Dyke Trail, is covered by this estuary vegetation. Here large flocks of snow geese congregate in the winter. The estuary plants grow in distinct zones governed by differences in salinity levels and water depths. Most of them are grass-like and wind pollinated, as insect pollination is not reliable in windy, exposed areas such as river estuaries.

Visit all year. Winter is the best time to see waterfowl, and summer is the best time for flowers.

Nearby Locations

- the West Dyke Trail, which is popular with birders during the winter months, extends northward along the dike for 5.5 kilometres (3.4 miles) to Terra Nova
- the historic fishing port of Steveston is an easy stroll to the east of the park

Some Alerts

- cyclists
- do not venture onto the estuary vegetation because of the environmental impact and the slippery, unstable surface

More Information

Garry Point Park: www.richmond.ca/asp/parks/park.asp?ID=17
City of Richmond: 604-276-4000 or www.richmond.ca

Richmond Nature Park

by Kristine Bauder

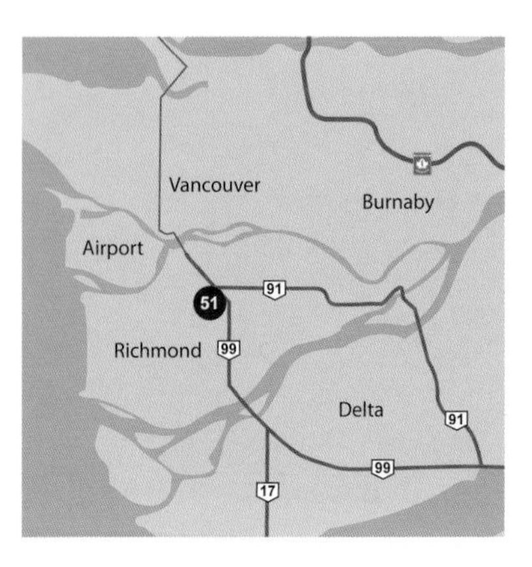

Natural bog environment with an extensive Nature House

Location

Richmond Nature Park is in the centre of Richmond on Lulu Island at Westminster Hwy. and No. 5 Rd.

Transit Information

From downtown Vancouver, take the #98 B-Line Richmond Centre bus to Richmond Centre. Then transfer to the #405 Five Rd. bus and alight at the Westminster Hwy. and No. 5 Rd. stop.

For up-to-date information, contact TransLink at www.translink.ca or 604-953-3333.

Introduction

Richmond Nature Park is owned and operated by the City of Richmond. Admission is free, but donations are appreciated.

Labrador tea is a dominant bog plant. Early settlers dried the leaves for tea. *James Holkko*

The park is on the north side of Westminster Hwy. No. 5 Rd. bisects it, with the Richmond Nature Park and Nature House on the west side and the Richmond Nature Study Centre on the east side. Each part is approximately 43 hectares (106 acres).

Richmond Nature Park is open throughout the year. The Nature House features interpretive exhibits, games and hands-on activities, live animals, a nature library and a demonstration wildlife garden, and organizes programs and special events. Knowledgeable staff members can assist with your visit. Easy trails guide you safely through the park while you explore this unique environment.

Natural History Visit

The entrance to the Richmond Nature Park and Nature House is at the Westminster Hwy. and No. 5 Rd. intersection close to the bus stop. Both the park and the extensive and attractive Nature House are ideal places to experience nature. If you want to explore the natural environment further, take a

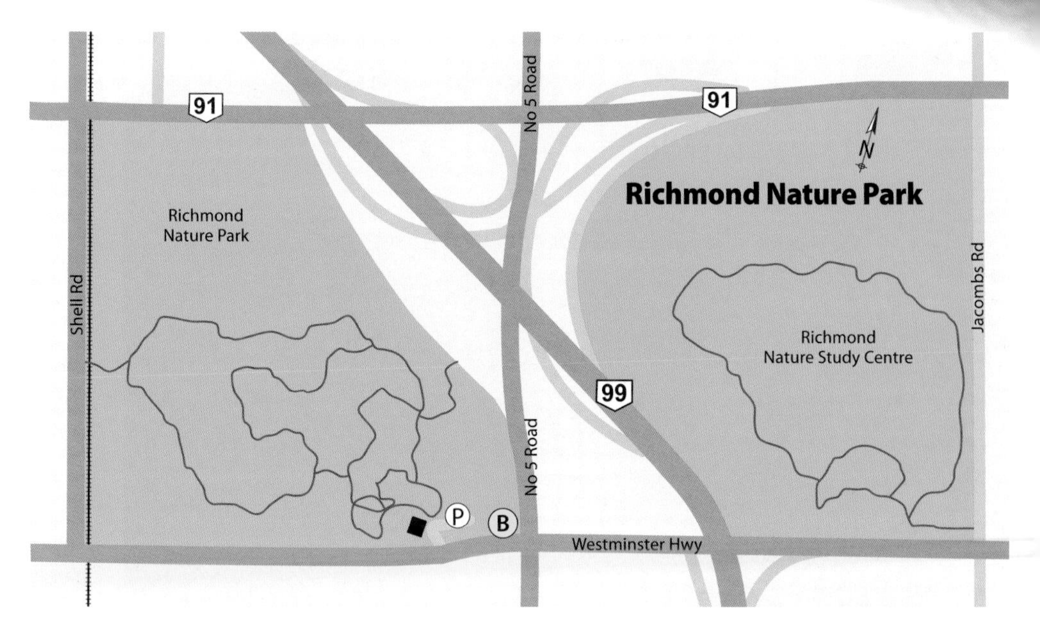

10-minute walk east along Westminster Hwy. to the Richmond Nature Study Centre entrance at Jacombs Rd.

As you walk in the nature park, cast your mind back in time to a Richmond of a simpler day. The air is sweet with the tang of salt water and growing things, not fouled by the spew of vehicles. The forest, bog and slough

Salal is abundant in many habitats. Birds and humans enjoy its berries. *James Holkko*

Visit the Nature House year-round for displays and programs. *Richmond Nature Park*

sing to the music of the world; no roar of planes shatters the stillness. The land is rich in wildlife: otter, mink, muskrat, beaver, bear and deer. Birds by the millions seek the verdant marsh and foreshore to raise their young or rest on long migrations. In the tidal marshes salmon and herring feed on abundant invertebrates. To First Nations people the island is rich in seasonal resources and bursting with the fruits of its life. Blueberry, cranberry and Labrador tea are thick in the island interior, while fish and fowl can be taken from its shores. Plants provide fibre for nets and baskets; others are a source of pharmaceuticals. Even the lowly sphagnum moss finds a role as diapers for infants.

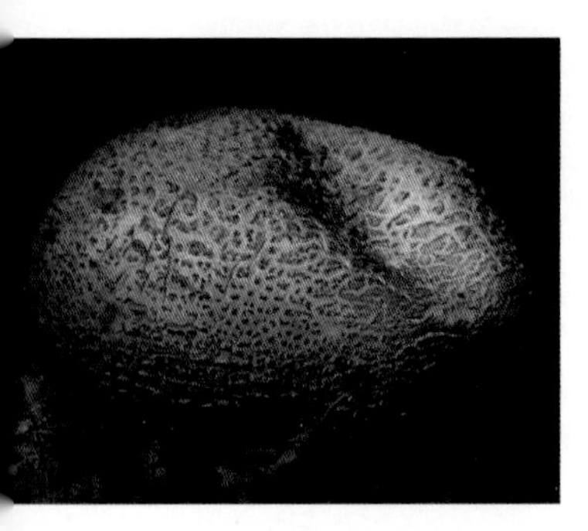

The top of a mature studded puffball opens when touched to release a burst of spores. *James Holkko*

Today Richmond seems only distantly connected to its past. The new landscape is one of highways and high-rises connected by the frenetic activity of a growing community. A close look, however, reveals some remnants of the old Lulu Island. The Richmond Nature Park, foremost among these, preserves a sample of the once extensive bogs in a natural state for all to see and enjoy. The bogs are underlain by sands and silts of the Fraser River delta.

The bog is a place of subtle beauty. Plants grow slowly in the acid environment and are stingy with their flowers. What they lack in size, though, they make up in detail; cranberry flowers are exquisite tiny shooting stars, while bog laurel flowers are miniature satellite dishes that track the sun. Sphagnum moss glows in a dozen shades of green, and blueberries put on a magnificent crimson show of autumn colour. Diminutive winter wrens fill the woods with superlative song, while hummingbirds whiz about their business. Patient garter snakes stalk the edge of the pond waiting for frogs to show themselves.

A paper birch forest now flourishes where shore pine was the dominant species several decades ago. *James Holkko*

As we discover the value of bogs in a world afflicted by climate change, their once lowly image is being redefined. A new appreciation for bogs stems from their capacity to sequester carbon, store water and act as gene banks for rare and endangered species. We also recognize their value as a place to get off the pavement and rediscover nature—a place of fresh air, soft surfaces, gentle sounds and space to restore the soul.

The Richmond Nature Park is open year-round, dawn to dusk.

Nearby Locations

- none close by

Some Alerts

- none

More Information

Richmond Nature Park: 604-718-6188 or
www.richmond.ca/parksrec/ptc/naturepark/about.htm
City of Richmond: 604-276-4000 or www.richmond.ca

George C. Reifel Migratory Bird Sanctuary

by Murray MacDonald

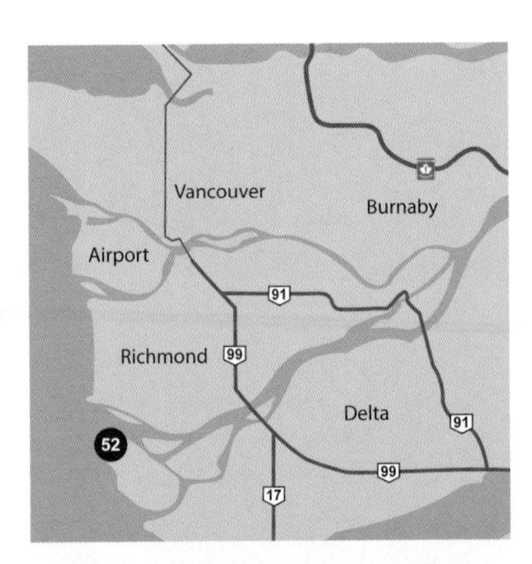

The black-crowned night-heron is a regular visitor and can reliably be found in winter. *Mark Habdas*

Notable bird watching site on the Fraser River estuary

Location

George C. Reifel Migratory Bird Sanctuary is at the west side of Delta at the end of Robertson Rd. off Westham Island Rd.

Transit Information

Bring your bicycle for the 9-kilometre (5.6-mile) ride to complete your journey; remember a bike lock.

From Burrard Station, take the #601 South Delta bus to Ladner Exchange. Alternatively, from Scott Rd. SkyTrain Station, take the #640 Ladner Exchange bus to Ladner Exchange. Then transfer to the #C86 Ladner South/Ladner Exchange bus and alight at the 46A St. and River Rd. West stop.

For up-to-date information, contact TransLink at www.translink.ca or 604-953-3333.

From the bus stop, cycle west along River Rd. for nearly 3 kilometres (1.9 miles) to the Westham Island Bridge on your right. Cross the bridge and cycle down Westham Island Rd. (which later becomes Robertson Rd.) for nearly 5 kilometres (3.1 miles) until it ends at the large black Alaksen property gates. Turn left and follow the sanctuary driveway for 1 kilometre (0.6 mile).

Introduction

Reifel Migratory Bird Sanctuary is just west of Ladner on Reifel Island, next to Westham Island at the mouth of the South Arm of the Fraser River. It is operated by the BC Waterfowl Society, a non-profit organization. It occupies 344 hectares (850 acres) of flat land that is part of the Fraser River delta, and provides 4 kilometres (2.5 miles) of wheelchair accessible trails along dikes and near ponds, sloughs and the ocean.

Reifel Migratory Bird Sanctuary is named after George C. Reifel, who in 1927 acquired, diked and reclaimed the land to create a family farm. When the land was leased to the BC Waterfowl Society in the 1960s, Ducks

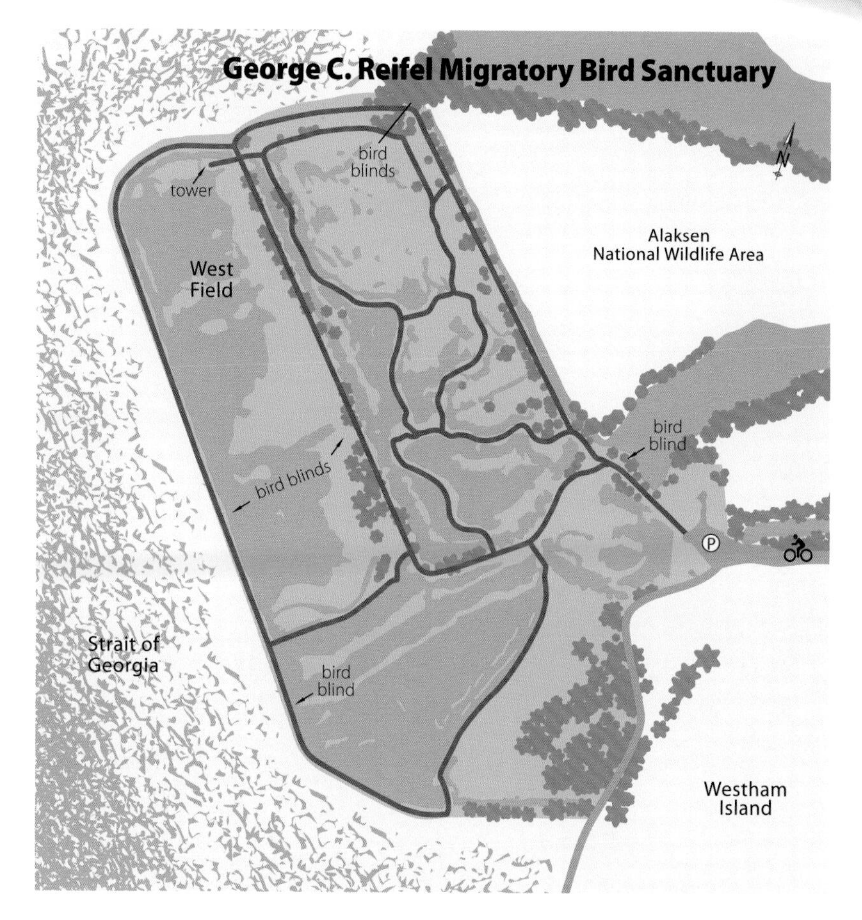

Unlimited enhanced the waterfowl habitat. Now the society leases the area from the federal government.

Westham Island is a rural area with many farms growing a variety of crops. Over the flat, spacious terrain, it affords beautiful views over the Strait of Georgia to the North Shore mountains, Vancouver Island and the Gulf Islands. The sanctuary provides a variety of vegetation including alders, blackberries, Pacific crab apples, Douglas-fir, black cottonwood, much shrub cover and cattail that is sustained by a large salt marsh.

There is a modest admission charge to the sanctuary.

Natural History Visit

At the admission window, you can purchase seed to feed to the birds as you walk through the sanctuary. Also at the entrance, note the posted list of birds observed in the sanctuary during the past week. After you pass the warming hut on your left and a bird blind overlooking the slough on your right, you will have several paths to choose from, each leading to a different area of the sanctuary. You can wander between or around the three

All kinds of waterfowl and shorebirds visit the shallow waters of Reifel Bird Sanctuary. *Mark Habdas*

display ponds, or alternatively, venture out to the perimeter path west of the West Field nearer the ocean.

Throughout the sanctuary, you can shelter in several bird blinds and watch the birds through viewing slots while you remain hidden. There are also raised viewing platforms and an observation tower.

The more unusual birds most frequently associated with Reifel are wintering black-crowned night-herons, resident sandhill cranes, and in the late fall, thousands of snow geese arriving from Wrangel Island in northeast Russia, on their journey south.

Other notable birds seen in the sanctuary are northern harriers, nine sparrow species including swamp sparrows (usually in winter) and seven types of owls including snowy and long-eared owls (mainly in winter). In winter you may see three types of hawks including goshawks and four types of falcons including gyrfalcons. Five types of swallow including bank

The ring on the bill of the ringed-neck duck is more obvious than the neck ring.
Virginia Hayes

swallows may touch down in migration. The sanctuary supports more than 270 species of birds in all.

Mammals that you may see are mink, muskrat, river otter, raccoon, harbour seal and beaver. Beaver families live in lodges, but adult males live apart in bank burrows.

The sanctuary is open every day, and there is always good birding. From September to November the fall migration brings numerous shorebirds, ducks and geese. November is the best time for migrating snow geese. From November to March, birds of prey from the north spend the winter. April to June marks the spring migration of numerous shorebirds and warblers. From June to August you can observe the resident nesting birds.

Nearby Locations

- the Alaksen National Wildlife Area adjoins the sanctuary to the east and is open for visits during weekday business hours; access is from Robertson Rd., and you must check in and check out at the Canadian Wildlife Service office inside the gates

Some Alerts

- dikes can be slippery when wet

More Information

Reifel Migratory Bird Sanctuary: 604-946-6980 or www.reifelbirdsanctuary.com
BC Waterfowl Society: 604-946-6980 or www.reifelbirdsanctuary.com/bcws2.html

Boundary Bay Regional Park at Centennial Beach

by Al and Jude Grass

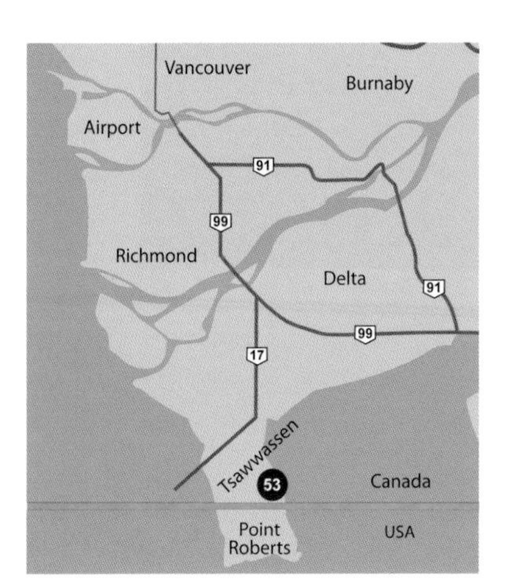

Sand dunes, meadow, sandy beaches, salt marsh and tidal flats

Location

Boundary Bay Regional Park at Centennial Beach is in Tsawwassen on Boundary Bay Rd. just north of 3rd Ave.

Transit Information

From downtown Vancouver, take the #601 South Delta/ Boundary Bay bus to the 56th St. and 12th Ave. (Tsawwassen Town Centre) stop. Then transfer to the #C89 Boundary Bay/ South Delta Exchange bus to either the Centennial Beach Parking lot (in summer) or the final stop at 3rd Ave. and 67th St. at the south end of the beach.

For up-to-date information, contact TransLink at www.translink.ca or 604-953-3333.

Introduction

Centennial Beach, located in the southern portion of Boundary Bay Regional Park, is excellent for nature viewing at all times of the year; every season has its own special rewards. Here you can find salt marsh, marine, tidal flat, beach, meadow and hedge habitats.

Butter clams bury themselves in sand and passively filter water to obtain food.
Al and Jude Grass

Boundary Bay became an Important Bird Area (IBA) in 2001 in recognition of the global, national and provincial significance of its habitat for birds. This makes it a top site in Canada for bird watchers. More than 225 species of birds have been observed within the park, including snowy owls, western bluebirds, western meadowlarks and bald eagles.

The park has a wonderful beach to explore for marine life, marvellous views across Boundary Bay to Mount Baker in Washington state and a fine rural landscape.

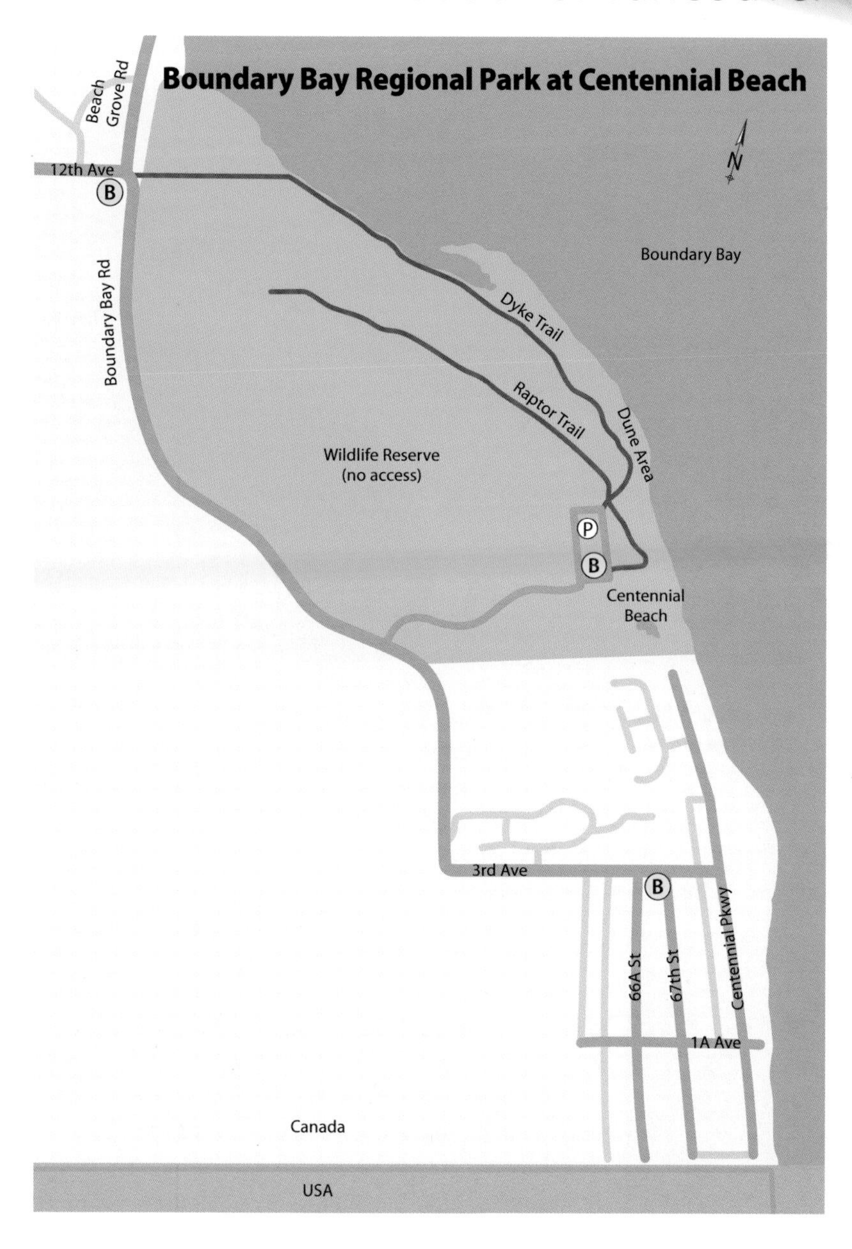

Excellent walking and cycling paths include a viewing platform overlooking Boundary Bay and the tidal flats. Note that these are shared trails for walkers, on-leash dogs and bicycles.

Natural History Visit

Characterized by its rich plant and animal life, the park has tidal flats, salt marsh, meadows, hedges and sand dunes for visitors to explore.

A boardwalk leads through sand dunes and a wetter area where cattails grow. *Al and Jude Grass*

Boundary Bay is renowned for its migrating shorebirds and wintering raptors and owls. Peregrine falcons can be seen chasing flocks of dunlins, which are small sandpipers. Red-tailed hawks and Cooper's hawks are regulars. Bald eagles are a common sight in the park, often perched in trees or sitting on the tidal flats.

Large-headed sedge seed cases are spiny and uncomfortable to walk on. *Al and Jude Grass*

The dunes have a network of trails with interpretive signs explaining this locally rare ecosystem. A stroll on the sand dune trails reveals a marvellous diversity of plants that are growing in desert-like conditions. These include large-headed sedge, which is a featured plant of the dunes, bare-stem desert-parsley, blue-eyed Mary and common draba. Desert-parsley is one of the main larval food plants of the locally rare anise swallowtail butterfly found in the park.

You can beachcomb for cast-up sea life and an excellent variety of seashells, sand dollars, crab skeletons, seaweeds and other treasures. Remember to leave them all as you found them.

All seasons have their special rewards. In winter there are raptors, owls, waterfowl and many different gulls. Look for sanderlings, which are small, pale shorebirds. Their motions on the beach have been compared to those of clockwork toys. You can also see clouds of dunlins; their flight is awesome to watch. Owls seen here include short-eared and great horned owls, and in certain years, snowy owls. Good numbers of brant geese winter here, feeding on eelgrass. Winter botany includes lichens and mosses.

In spring you will see early wildflowers and migrating shorebirds such as western sandpipers, brant geese and peregrine falcons. Summer brings more wildflowers and butterflies including Milbert's tortoiseshells, Lorquin's admirals, western tiger swallowtails and anise swallowtails. On warm summer days, listen for crickets chirping. In fall migrating shorebirds bring birders from around the world to Boundary Bay.

Pink and blue lupines attract bumblebees, butterflies and lots of insects. *Al and Jude Grass*

Nearby Locations

- the Orphaned Wildlife Rehabilitation Society (OWL) is a 9-kilometre (5.6-mile) walk from Centennial Beach along the main Boundary Bay dike trail; OWL, where injured birds of prey are nursed back to health, is near the foot of 72nd St. (road access off Hwy. 10)

Some Alerts

- do not venture far into the tidal flats; these are soft, quicksand-like places
- fast incoming tides are dangerous
- red jellyfish sometimes found on the beach can sting; do not touch

More Information

Metro Vancouver Regional Parks:
www.metrovancouver.org/services/parks_lscr/regionalparks/Pages/default.aspx
Metro Vancouver Regional Parks West Area Office: 604-224-5739
Nature Guide to Boundary Bay, Anne Murray. Nature Guides BC, 2006.
"Boundary Bay: A Special Place," brochure published by the Friends of Semiahmoo Bay Society: 604-536-3552
Birds on the Bay programs: www.birdsonthebay.ca
OWL tours: 604-946-3171 or www.owlcanada.ca
BC Wildlife Watch bird checklist: www3.telus.net/driftwood/bcwwhome.htm

Deas Island Regional Park

by Viveka Ohman

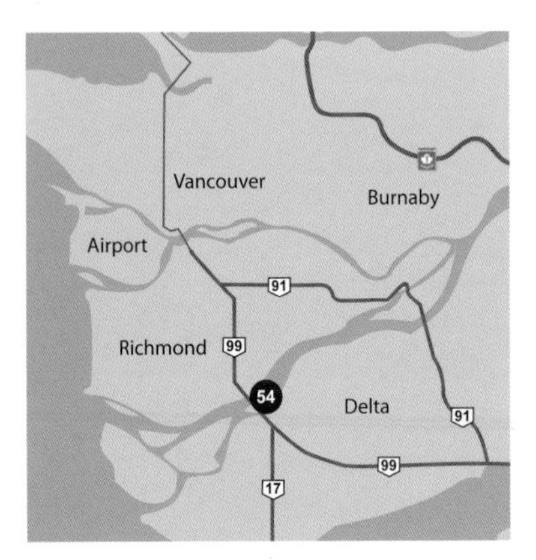

A Fraser River island with meadows, dunes, marshes and heritage buildings

Location

Deas Island Regional Park is on the north side of Delta at River Rd. and 62B St.

Transit Information

From Scott Rd. SkyTrain Station, take the #640 Ladner Exchange bus along River Rd. to the River Rd. and Deas Island Rd. stop near the park entrance.
For up-to-date information, contact TransLink at www.translink.ca or 604-953-3333.

Introduction

Deas Island, part of the Fraser River delta, is a Metro Vancouver park in the Municipality of Delta on the South Arm of the Fraser River. Hwy. 99 crosses the Fraser River by the George Massey Tunnel that passes under the south end of the island. The highway is unobtrusive to the park visitor except from the viewing location.

Indian blanket, an introduced wildflower, is common in dryer parts of North America.
Rosemary Taylor

This 70-hectare (173-acre) park has 5 kilometres (3.1 miles) of trails that let you wander through a large variety of habitats including meadows, dunes and marshes. Deas Slough to the east, a former backchannel of the Fraser River, is known for its rowing sculls; in the spring at dusk you can often watch rowers preparing for upcoming events. Across the Fraser River to the west you can see the BC Ferries Maintenance Yard and Ocean Fisheries Processing Plant, one of the few original salmon canneries left in the Lower Mainland. On a clear day you can see the snow-capped mountain peaks of the North Shore mountains.

John Sullivan Deas was the island's first settler, a black freeman and

tinsmith who in 1873 claimed the island and built a salmon processing cannery. Many families, mostly of Greek origin, made their home on the island, working the Fraser River gillnet fisheries until the early 1950s.

Heritage buildings that maintain some of the Delta settlement history have been moved to the island, where you can visit them. The Burr House, originally built on River Rd. in 1906, is a Queen Anne-style residence open in the spring and summer. The 1909 Inverholme Schoolhouse and 1899 Delta Agricultural Hall, both restored, often host special exhibits and events.

Natural History Visit

From the bus stop, walk past the mounted propeller at the park entrance and down the driveway into the park. On both sides of the driveway, trails lead toward the island's shoreline. By following these trails you can take a circular route around most of the island. Farther south, at the end of the driveway, more branch trails lead to the rocky southwest point.

In the early morning, particularly if there is dense fog, you can smell the woodsy, almost tar-like scent of the native black cottonwoods. The fragrance is noticeable and invigorating. Along with alders, cottonwoods are the most prominent tree in this park. Shrubs such as salmonberry, red elderberry, red-osier dogwood and Pacific ninebark are common on the island. In the Lyngby's sedge marsh at the west end of the island, you may see wildflowers such as marsh-marigold, white rein-orchid, Henderson's checker-mallow and nodding beggarticks.

At Deas Island there is tidal fishing in the Fraser River along the west shore. This area is frequented by local fishermen in the fall when the salmon runs are heading up the Fraser.

A creek runs to the west of the driveway, and wood ducks take cover there all year under the sheltering edges of the overhanging vegetation. Barred owls and great horned owls are seen on the island as well as Cooper's hawks by the slough or circling above. Smaller birds—sparrows and Bewick's and winter wrens—and woodpeckers frequent this island. Skunks, mink, short-tailed weasels and possums are also present. The occasional coyote has been spotted. At dusk visit Deas Island to see and hear bats of at least three species: little brown bat, big brown bat and Yuma bat.

The water off the southwest tip of the island is

On this trail in February, you can appreciate the graceful tree shapes and the view beyond. *Viveka Ohman*

a favourite haunt of red-breasted and common mergansers, which feed on smelts and eulachons that swim just below the surface and close to shore. The rising tide brings the fish upriver to the island, and dabbling ducks such as gadwalls, mallards and wigeons follow them along the shoreline.

Visit anytime, but the park is especially interesting in the fall when the salmon are running.

A double-crested cormorant dries its wings after diving and swimming underwater. *Viveka Ohman*

Nearby Locations

- none within walking distance

Some Alerts

- take care in marshy areas
- fast-flowing river
- at extreme low tides, take care not to be stranded on the rocks at the southwest tip of the island
- the trail at the southwest tip may flood during high tides

More Information

Metro Vancouver Regional Parks:
www.metrovancouver.org/services/parks_lscr/regionalparks/Pages/default.aspx
Metro Vancouver Regional Parks West Area Office: 604-224-5739
Burr House: 604-432-6352

Delta Nature Reserve, Burns Bog

by Val and Anny Schaefer

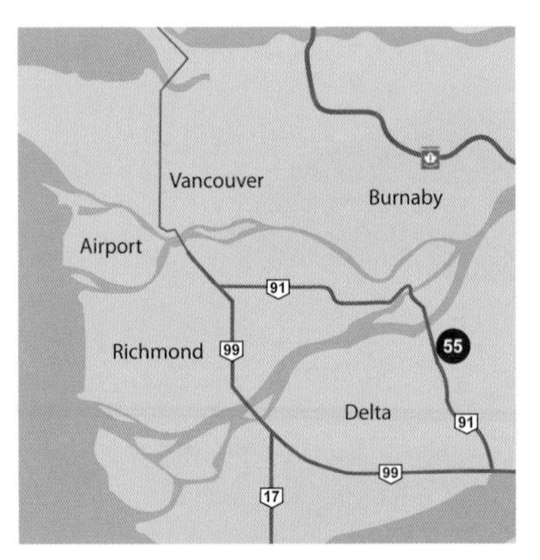

A reserve in Greater Vancouver's largest green space

Location

Delta Nature Reserve, Burns Bog is in northeast Delta at the end of Nordel Court off Nordel Way.

Transit Information

From Scott Rd. SkyTrain Station, take the #640 Ladner Exchange bus or the #314 Surrey Central bus along River Rd. to the River Rd. and Centre St. stop almost under the Alex Fraser Bridge.

For up-to-date information, contact TransLink at www.translink.ca or 604-953-3333.

Introduction

Burns Bog is the largest green space in Greater Vancouver. At 4,000 hectares (9,880 acres), it is about 10 times the size of Stanley Park. It was named after Dominic Burns of Burns Meats, who owned the bog and is reported to have grazed cattle there. Much of Burns Bog is privately owned and not accessible to the public. About 10 percent of the southwest corner is the Vancouver Landfill, used for the region's garbage disposal. About half of the bog was set aside as a protected area in 2004.

The thin, secretive Virginia rail can slide through tall marsh vegetation. *Mark Habdas*

Delta Nature Reserve, the only area of the bog accessible to the public, comprises about 60 hectares (148 acres) in the northeast corner. Two boardwalk trails, an inner loop and an outer loop, were built by volunteers with funding obtained by the Burns Bog Conservation Society. A popular feature is a sunken tractor, still visible beside the shorter inner loop.

Bogs form in areas of little or no external drainage, usually in depressions in the landscape. Burns Bog is unique in the Vancouver area in having

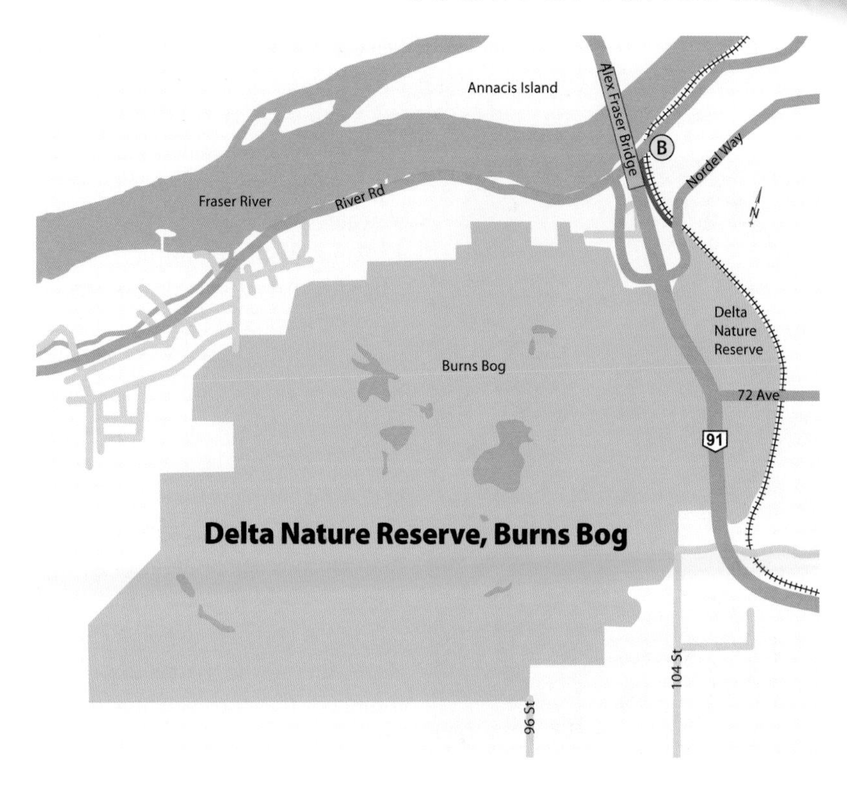

formed a raised dome. Raised bogs rely on rain as their primary source of water and do not have any significant inflow from streams. As a result the acids released from decaying organic matter accumulate, creating a unique acidic ecosystem. A bog is characterized by sphagnum moss, the material that makes peat when it dies. Sphagnum moss not only tolerates acidity but also promotes it to reduce competition from other plants.

In addition to withstanding acidity, bog plants show adaptations to prevent water loss, as the acidic water is largely unusable by the plants; they are living in a liquid desert. Bogs are nutrient-poor environments in which the acidity prevents decomposition of dead plants and the release of their nutrients. Some plants have become insectivorous to obtain nutrients from insects instead of the soil.

Natural History Visit

From the bus stop, walk west along River Rd. for a minute until you are directly under the Alex Fraser Bridge. Go through the gate on your left and take the Metro Vancouver access road that follows the direction of the bridge. Then continue alongside a bird-populated slough to the notice board at the Delta Nature Reserve entrance. Farther on, the trail splits into the two loop trails.

As you walk the trails, you can see many interesting plants. The sundew plant, which traps insects on its sticky leaves, is common in bogs and is a treat to discover. The curled leaves of Labrador tea have red furry undersides to trap moisture. Bog cranberry and swamp laurel have thick waxy cuticles on their leaves that make them tough and shiny and resistant to water loss.

The dense showy clusters of spirea (hardhack) flowers attract many insects. *Val and Anny Schaefer*

Some plants in Burns Bog are considered remnants of the vegetation that first colonized this area at the end of the last ice age. Cloudberry, crowberry and velvet-leaved blueberry arrived as the glaciers receded. A common tree growing in the higher elevations of the bog is the shore pine, a subspecies of the lodgepole pine found in the BC Interior, where it grows straight and tall and is good for building cabins. However, in the harsh bog environment, the tree is stunted and twisted. Also common in the bog are salal, bracken fern and sweet gale. Look for a magical forest of Sitka spruce, western hemlock and western redcedar at the far end of the outer loop trail. In this area several uprooted trees have intriguing dens formed in their root balls, possibly inhabited by amphibians or small mammals such as raccoons.

Burns Bog lies on the Fraser River delta, and many birds migrating along the Pacific Flyway use it. Over 150 species of birds can be seen here, as can 28 species of mammals including black bear, black-tailed deer and beaver. There is plenty of evidence of beaver along the trails. Scientists have recently confirmed that what was previously thought to be a masked shrew is actually a separate species of shrew, *Sorex rohweri*. It has been found only in Burns Bog in Canada and in 13 places in northwest Washington state.

A walk around Delta Nature Reserve is enjoyable year-round. Most plants are in bloom from March to October. Migratory birds pass through in spring and fall. Early in the morning or late at night you are likely to hear owls

Stay on the boardwalk to avoid the deep, perilous pits of water in the bog.
Val and Anny Schaefer

hooting or see great blue herons feeding. Burns Bog Conservation Society offers public, community and school tours; see their website for more information.

Nearby Locations

- none within walking distance

Some Alerts

- the bog can be muddy and wet after rain
- a drainage ditch on the site can be slippery and deep

More Information

Burns Bog Conservation Society: 604-572-0373 or www.burnsbog.org/index.shtml

Blackie Spit Park

by Viveka Ohman

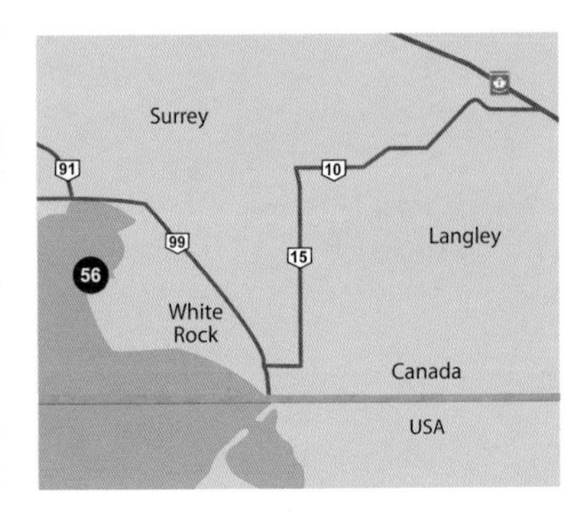

Haven for birds to rest and feed during migration stopovers

Location

Blackie Spit at Crescent Beach is in southwest Surrey at the end of McBride Ave. off Sullivan St.

Transit Information

From downtown Vancouver, take the #351 Crescent Beach bus. Alight at the final stop at Sullivan St. and Kidd Rd. For up-to-date information, contact TransLink at www.translink.ca or 604-953-3333.

Introduction

Blackie Spit Park, in the City of Surrey, is 25.5 hectares (63 acres). Extending into Mud Bay—the eastern part of Boundary Bay—as a small peninsula, it attracts shorebirds, seabirds and accompanying predators on their migration route. It offers protection from the elements and food from the mud flats, enabling shorebirds to rest and fatten up for the next leg of their journey.

Cormorants rest on pylons where purple martin nest boxes have been established. *Viveka Ohman*

The spit was formed through the deposition of sand and gravel over long periods of time. Eroding and reforming with the tides and weather, the spit changes shape often but not always noticeably. A narrow channel on the west side with markers must be kept deep enough for vessels to sail through and is dredged from time to time.

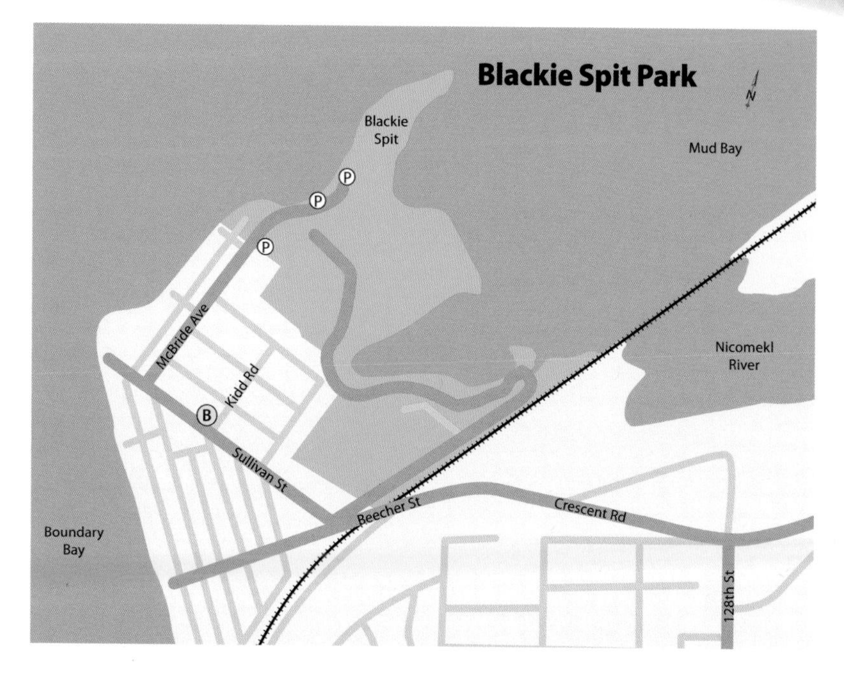

The east side, facing the mouth of the Nicomekl River, is recognized as an environmentally sensitive area. The flow of the river combined with the tidal action in Mud Bay makes it a favourite stopover for birds. The mud flats support numerous invertebrate organisms that provide a rich source of protein and calories for the starving sandpipers when they arrive in May and August.

Natural History Visit

From the bus stop, walk a short distance west along Sullivan St. and turn right onto McBride Ave. to the spit, where the bay and its vistas unfold in front of you.

At Blackie Spit you may see flocks of dunlins flying in tight formation. As the birds twist and turn in unison, the flock looks like smoke one minute and like a white cloud the next. This behaviour helps to protect them from predation by falcons, notably peregrines.

The spit has an exposed western shore and a protected lee on the east side. On the spit itself you can find a host of introduced weedy plants as well as native plants such dunegrass, American searocket, silver burweed and tall pepper-grass. In the salt marsh on the lee side of the spit, look for the same plants as those found in the Boundary Bay salt marsh: American glasswort, seashore saltgrass, sea plantain, sea arrow-grass, Baltic rush, Gerard's rush, Pacific alkali grass, orache, entire-leaved gumweed and Douglas' aster. In August the large yellow flowers of gumweed put on one the best wildflower displays to be seen anywhere in the Lower Mainland.

Blackie Spit is a bird watcher's paradise in winter. *Viveka Ohman*

One of the most interesting plants at Blackie Spit is an English elm. The elm consists of hundreds of trees all connected by an underground root system, all part of the same plant and all genetically identical. The trees form a dense thicket, with the taller trees at the centre and the smaller ones on the edge. If left unchecked, the elm would spread over a very large area. The corky ridges on the twigs are a distinctive feature of this plant.

The marbled godwit, one of BC's largest shorebirds, is named after its godwit call. *Mark Wynja*

The low shrub and grassy areas attract grassland birds at certain times of the year. You may spot Savannah sparrows, with their insect-like buzz and habit of flying up and landing in the grass. Rarer sightings include snow buntings and longspurs. The "three amigos" are a dependable sight in late fall and early winter: willets, marbled godwits and long-billed curlews. At present long-billed curlews are residents here.

In the environmentally sensitive area to the east, take time to read the plaque about Rene Savenye's contribution to protecting the spit. A shore

Western sandpipers crowd together for safety and protection. *Mark Habdas*

pine has been planted in the naturalist's honour. Then follow an unmarked trail toward the promontory, where you can view the site of the Purple Martin Recovery Program. Across from the fence, purple martin nest boxes sit atop posts in the water. From April to August you can hear and see these large swallows flying around this established nesting site.

Visit all year, though spring and fall are the best time to see shorebirds. Seabirds are present November to February, and you can see and hear purple martins from early May to August.

Nearby Locations

- Elgin Heritage Park is a few kilometres to the northeast
- Kwomais Park is 3 kilometres (1.9 miles) south along side roads

Some Alerts

- strong current on the west side of the spit
- avoid soft mud flats on the east side; they are dangerous to walk on

More Information

City of Surrey: 604-591-4011 or www.surrey.ca/default.htm

Serpentine Wildlife Management Area

by Al and Jude Grass

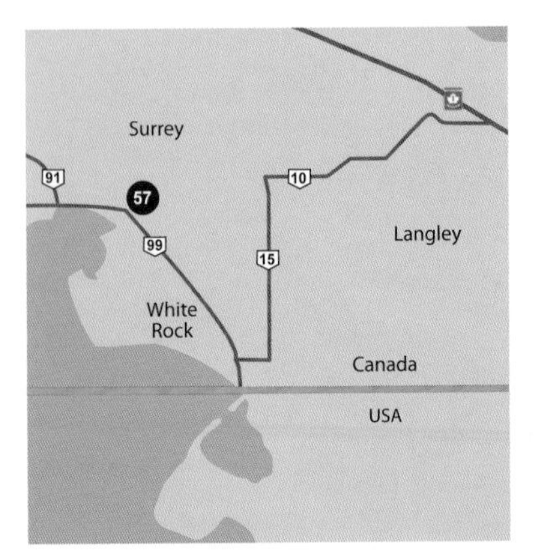

Easily observable meadow and wetland harbouring a wide variety of birds

Location

Serpentine Wildlife Management Area is on the west side of Surrey at King George Hwy. and 44th Ave.

Transit Information

From the Surrey Central SkyTrain Station, board the #321 White Rock bus and alight at the plant nursery at the King George Hwy. and 44th Ave. stop.

For up-to-date information, contact TransLink at www.translink.ca or 604-953-3333.

Introduction

Serpentine Wildlife Management Area (WMA) just off Hwy. 99 in South Surrey is under the jurisdiction of the BC Ministry of Environment and managed by Ducks Unlimited Canada. The entrance is at 44th Ave. and King George Hwy. There is no entrance fee.

The site covers 106 hectares (262 acres) of river flood plain and former tidal flats, with 80 hectares (198 acres) of diked freshwater marsh and 4 hectares (9.9 acres) of undiked salt marsh. The north side is bordered by the Serpentine River, a major geographical feature of the site. It is one of two rivers that feed nearby Mud Bay, the eastern part of Boundary Bay. Silt brought down by the Serpentine and Nicomekl rivers over thousands of years has built up the Serpentine tidal flats, a major shorebird and waterfowl habitat.

An American coot has green lobed feet. It pumps its head to and fro as it swims.
Al and Jude Grass

The many habitats in the sanctuary include grassy meadows, marsh, fresh-water ponds and hedges. Pond habitats have been enhanced by Ducks Unlimited for breeding and wintering waterfowl. Pacific crab apple, red elderberry and blackberry are typical hedge plants attractive to birds.

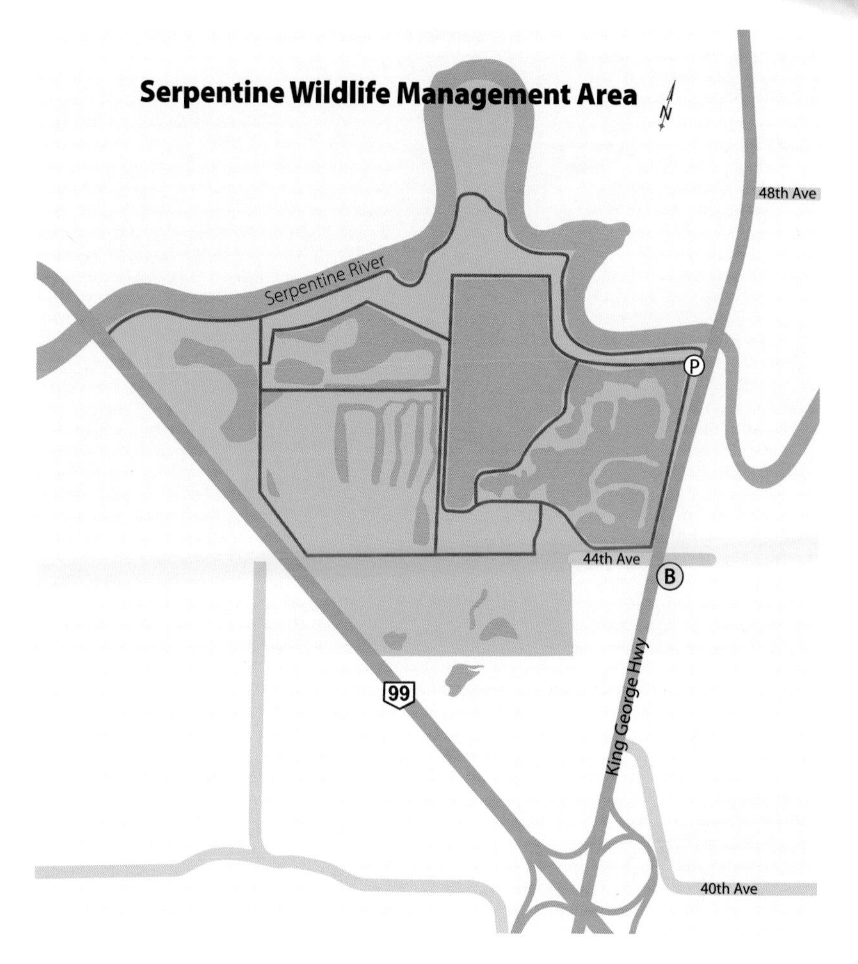

Natural History Visit

From the bus stop, walk down 44th Ave. to the Serpentine WMA entrance; the notice boards and picnic area will be on your left. Continuing down the unpaved road, you will soon see the trail access and observation tower on your right. The sanctuary's trails afford good views of all habitats, and from the three observation towers you can get wonderful views of the surrounding area.

Check the high tension transmission towers for raptors like bald eagles, red-tailed hawks and peregrine falcons; there is a good chance of seeing a falcon here. Watch in hedges for a variety of songbirds including sparrows, Bewick's wrens, cedar waxwings, Bohemian waxwings, northern shrikes and (in winter) common redpolls. Hedges are excellent places to check for wintering sparrows including golden-crowned, white-crowned and fox sparrows as well as spotted towhees.

Fields attract Savannah sparrows, American goldfinches, western

A barn swallow stretches its wings, ready to launch into the air after insects. *Virginia Hayes*

Viewing towers afford panoramic views of the sanctuary and its surroundings.
Al and Jude Grass

meadowlarks and northern harriers. In winter look for short-eared owls and rough-legged hawks. Meadows are habitat for red-tailed hawks, along with short-eared owls and sandhill cranes. Cattail marshes are home to red-winged blackbirds, marsh wrens and rails.

The ponds are an excellent habitat for a variety of ducks and geese including gadwalls, northern pintails, American wigeons, buffleheads, hooded and common mergansers, ring-necked ducks and lesser and greater scaups. Additional waterfowl species to see include rare Eurasian wigeons, green-winged teals and common goldeneyes. The waterfowl mix depends on the season; winter brings the best selection. In autumn 2007 a locally very rare great egret spent several weeks at the sanctuary.

Muskrat, beavers, Canada river otters, coyotes and bats are mammals commonly observed at the Serpentine WMA. In summer evenings, bats fly over the fens. Also in summer, watch for

The serene Serpentine River winds through fields and wetlands to emerge in Mud Bay.
Al and Jude Grass

butterflies including western tiger swallowtails, Lorquin's admirals and Milbert's tortoiseshells.

The wetlands provide good year-round bird watching, and every visit should be a rewarding one. The best waterfowl and raptor viewing is in winter. In summer watch the skies for swallows, swifts and common nighthawks; in late summer, look for purple martins from the nearby Blackie Spit colony. Migrating sandhill cranes appear in fall.

Nearby Locations

• downtown White Rock and Crescent Beach are a bus ride away

Some Alerts

• slippery trails on rainy days
• respect any closure of interior trails

More Information

Serpentine Wildlife Area: http://www3.telus.net/driftwood/wmaserp.htm
Bird Checklist:
www.env.gov.bc.ca/wld/documents/wldviewing/birdlistserpentine.pdf
Wildlife Viewing Brochure:
www.env.gov.bc.ca/wld/documents/wldviewing/wvserpentine.pdf

White Rock Pier and Promenade

by Al and Jude Grass

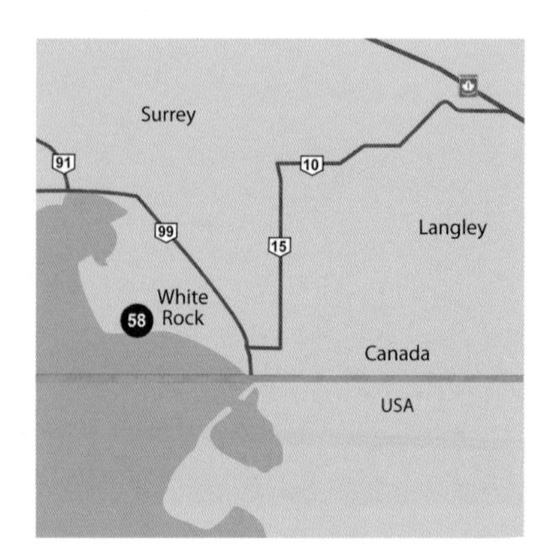

Beachcombing with close-up views of seabirds and sea mammals

Location

White Rock Pier and Promenade is in south Surrey at Marine Dr. and Martin St.

Transit Information

From downtown Vancouver, take the #351 Crescent Beach bus to White Rock Centre. Then transfer to the #C52 Seaside bus or the #C51 Ocean Park bus and alight at the Marine Dr. and Martin St. stop at the museum.

For up-to-date information, contact TransLink at www.translink.ca or 604-953-3333.

Introduction

The City of White Rock's 472-metre (1,548-foot) pier and 2.2-kilometre (1.4-mile) seawalk promenade provide an excellent wildlife viewing site for shorebirds, waterfowl, grebes and loons. It is a fine place to get close views of these birds, and the pier is a favourite local crab fishing site.

Any time of year, White Rock Promenade is an excellent place for a seaside stroll. *Al and Jude Grass*

The pier also offers a fine view of Mount Baker, a towering snow-covered volcanic cone in Washington state. It is often spectacular in winter, with a lovely pastel glow. The breakwater at the end of the pier is a habitat for cormorants, black turnstones and black oystercatchers. You can also observe many sea mammals from here. Stairs provide access to the sandy shore below the pier, where beachcombing is excellent. From the pier you can stroll in either direction along the seawalk promenade, which extends west to Bay St. and east to Finlay St.

Natural History Visit

From the bus stop, walk 5 minutes east to the pier, one of the Lower Mainland's best sites for viewing wintering waterfowl. These include three

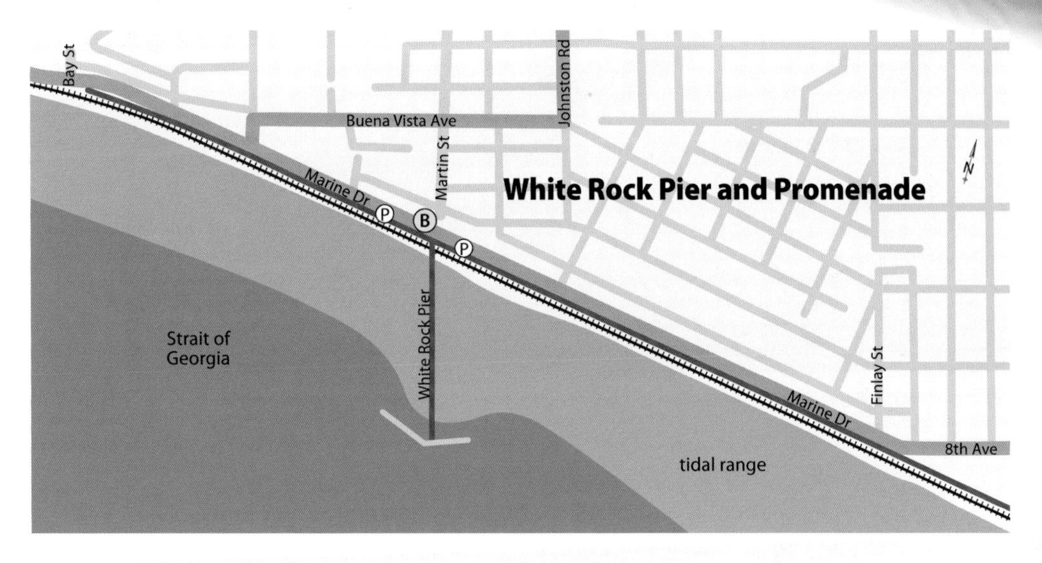

The western grebe, a superb fisher, uses its pointed yellow bill to catch its prey.
Virginia Hayes

scoter species and long-tailed ducks that often gather in large numbers offshore, and several loon species such as common, red-throated and Pacific loons. As well, you may see horned and eared grebes, beautiful harlequin ducks and a fine variety of gulls including western, Thayer's, glaucous-winged, ring-billed, mew and rarely herring gulls. You can have fun sorting out the gull species; in winter many hybrids show up here, including western x glaucous-winged gulls and herring x glaucous-winged gulls. Marine mammals seen here include river otters, harbour seals, orcas, California sea lions and rarely gray whales.

Descend the steps from the pier to the beach, where you can beachcomb

A stroll down White Rock Pier can lead you to a rich diversity of marine bird life. *Al and Jude Grass*

for various mollusks such as basket cockles, bent-nose macomas and mud clams. Take photos but don't collect. Also look for washed-up marine plants including various species of seaweed and eelgrass. Eelgrass, which is not seaweed, is a vital component of offshore ecosystems and supports various invertebrates including bubble snails. It is also a vital food source for brant geese. Forests of eelgrass lie offshore.

The black scoter is distinguished from other scoters by its "butter nose." *Al and Jude Grass*

From the pier, as you stroll east along the seawalk promenade, notice the white rock which gives the town its name. This boulder is a huge erratic that was carried here by glacier ice thousands of years ago and remained when the ice melted. It is said to weigh 486 tonnes (536 tons).

Winter and spring are best for birding, but all seasons have their special rewards. There is good beachcombing anytime. A walk on a warm summer evening is magical, especially when Mount Baker is aglow. Sunsets can be spectacular over Boundary Bay.

Nearby Locations

- the Little Campbell River enters Semiahmoo Bay at the east end of town; this estuary provides excellent birding

Some Alerts

- do not walk along the railway tracks; cross with care only near the washrooms at the pier

More Information

City of White Rock: 604-541-2181 or www.city.whiterock.bc.ca/
Georgia Basin Habitat Atlas: www.georgiabasin.net
Birds on the Bay: www.birdsonthebay.ca

Campbell Valley Regional Park

by Viveka Ohman

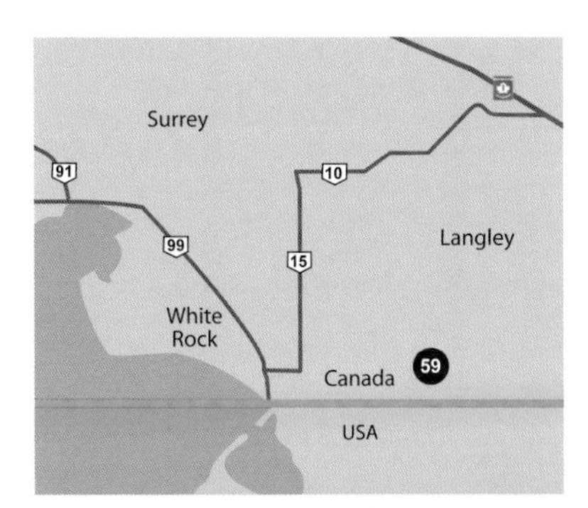

The tiny winter wren has a wonderful, complex song in spring or summer.
Mark Habdas

Rich in habitats and bird life, with a listening bridge

Location

Campbell Valley Regional Park is in southwest Langley on 16th Ave. just east of 200th St.

Transit Information

Bring your bicycle for the 2.5-kilometre (1.6-mile) ride to complete your journey; remember a bike lock.

From the Surrey Central SkyTrain Station, take the #502 Aldergrove/Brookswood/Langley Centre bus to Langley Centre or to Brookswood. Transfer to the #C63 Fernridge bus and alight at the 200th St. and 20th Ave. stop.

For up-to-date information, contact TransLink at www.translink.ca or 604-953-3333.

From the bus stop, cycle south along 200th St. to 16th Ave. Then turn left and cycle east along 16th Ave. to the North Valley entrance to the park.

Introduction

Campbell Valley Regional Park in Langley is large at 535 hectares (1,321 acres) of diverse scenery. Here it is easy to feel far removed from the urban world. Originally a farm, cleared and homesteaded in 1886 by Alexander Annand, it was owned by Len Rowlatt between 1918 and 1973 and then acquired by Metro Vancouver. The park was opened in 1979.

The park features historical buildings including the 1898 Annand Rowlatt Farmstead that has been restored and is a designated historical site. The 1924 Locheil Schoolhouse was moved to the park from 16th Ave. and 227th St. after serving as a school until 1975 and then as a community hall.

The park, with 20 kilometres (12.4 miles) of walking trails and 14 kilometres (8.7 miles) of horseback and walking trails, is rich in diverse habitats including marsh, coniferous forest, mixed forests and meadows. One of its most interesting features is the Listening Bridge over the Little Campbell River where you can relax, slow down and take in the variety of sounds around you.

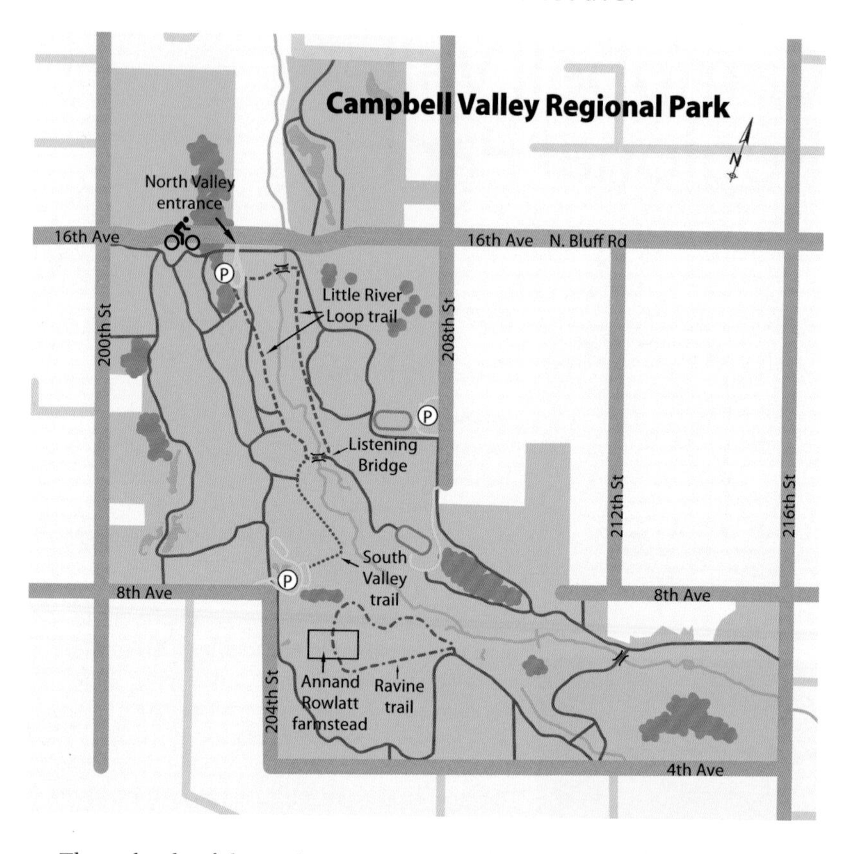

The uplands of the park area overlie stony sand and clay deposited near the end of the last great glaciation. The valley of the Little Campbell River, including its steep slopes, was eroded by a glacial meltwater stream originating from ice that extended to a few kilometres east of the park.

You may hear the common yellowthroat's witchy call near the Listening Bridge.
Mark Habdas

Natural History Visit

From the parking lot at the North Valley entrance, walk through a grove of cottonwood trees and cross the bridge over the Little Campbell River. Following the Little River Loop Trail south down the river's eastern bank, you will pass through a mixed conifer and deciduous forest often alive with birdsong. In spring you may see migrant western tanagers, black-headed grosbeaks or Swainson's thrushes, all fine songsters. Downy woodpeckers, Douglas squirrels and numerous black-capped chickadees live here all year long.

The Listening Bridge is a lovely corner of the park to sit and relax. *Viveka Ohman*

The trail passes over the Listening Bridge, a wonderful place to stop for a while and pay attention to the sounds from the marshland and river below. Over the marshes, listen for the calls and look for flashes of yellow as American goldfinches, yellow warblers, common yellowthroats and cedar waxwings fly by or perhaps stop to perch.

Continuing down the river's western bank along South Valley Trail, you will pass the meadow in front of the Annand Rowlatt Farmstead about 2 kilometres (1.2 miles) from the North Valley entrance. Here look for marsh birds and maybe a red-tailed hawk, Cooper's hawk or a raven soaring overhead above the forest.

The Ravine Trail, a 2-kilometre (1.2-mile) loop, takes you into second-growth forest of beautiful western redcedar, Douglas-fir and hemlock trees. On a spring morning under dappled sunlight, the carpets of bleeding heart, false lily-of-the-valley, fringecup, foamflower and queen's cup are a joy to behold.

It is magical to listen to the birdsong. The winter wren's complex warbling sound cascades through the forest like a babbling brook, while the Pacific-slope flycatcher's distinctive but simpler *su-wheet* call identifies its presence. Both birds are difficult to see but can be identified by their songs. You may spot a barred owl perching quietly above, almost hidden near the tree trunk. The trail leads out to a viewing platform where you can look both over the marsh and back into the forest.

In spring you can often hear the wreck-it mating call of male treefrogs. *Les Leighton*

To return to the North Valley entrance, follow South Valley Trail and the Little Loop Trail on either side of the river. Alternatively, choose a longer route from the trails shown on the park map. Avoid the Shaggy Mane Trail, which is suitable only for equestrian traffic.

Spring is the best time to visit for birding, but the park is a wonderful refuge all year long.

Nearby Locations

- Aldergrove Lake Regional Park is 10 kilometres (6.2 miles) east of the park
- White Rock Pier is about 8 kilometres (5 miles) to the west

Some Alerts

- horses on the equestrian trails
- it is easy to lose your bearings in this large park; the river flow can be a good orientation aid

More Information

Metro Vancouver Regional Parks:
www.metrovancouver.org/services/parks_lscr/regionalparks/Pages/default.aspx
Metro Vancouver Regional Parks East Area Office: 604-530-4983

Lighthouse Marine Park, Point Roberts, WA

by John Chandler

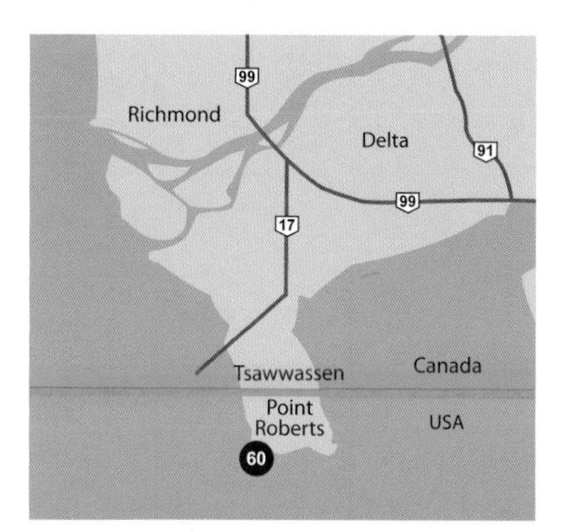

A common loon almost in full breeding plumage swims offshore. *Virginia Hayes*

Pre-eminent site for watching seabirds and whales from shore

Location

Lighthouse Marine Park in Point Roberts, Washington state, is south of Tsawwassen in the southwest corner of the Point Roberts peninsula.

Transit Information

Bring your bicycle for the 5.5-kilometre (3.4-mile) or 4.3-kilometre (2.7-mile) ride to complete your journey; remember a bike lock. Also bring identification required to enter the USA; you may also wish to bring some US dollars.

The #601 South Delta/Boundary Bay bus provides a one-bus trip to the 54th St. and 4th Ave. stop a few blocks from the border. To get closer to the border, at the South Delta Exchange, transfer to the #C84 English Bluff bus and alight at the 56th St. and 1st Ave. stop.

For up-to-date information, contact TransLink at www.translink.ca or 604-953-3333.

First cycle south on 56th St. to the Canada-US international border, one block south of the 56th St. and 1st Ave. intersection. After clearing US Immigration, cycle south on Tyee Dr., which later skirts the marina and becomes Marina Dr. Then bear right onto Edwards Dr. and cycle west to the Lighthouse Marine Park entrance at the southwest corner of the Point Roberts peninsula.

Introduction

Point Roberts is a small peninsula in Washington state, USA, south of the 49th parallel. You can access it from Vancouver through Tsawwassen, BC, along 56th St. As you arrive and as you leave, you must pass through the Canada-US border, where you must provide the required identification.

The rural peninsula has the air of a relaxed oceanside resort area. Because of its mild climate, the range of birds and plants found here is a little different from those found in Metro Vancouver.

Lighthouse Marine Park is a Whatcom County park. This relatively small park, about 16 hectares (40 acres) at the southwest corner of the Point Roberts peninsula, provides panoramic views of the Strait of Georgia. It is one

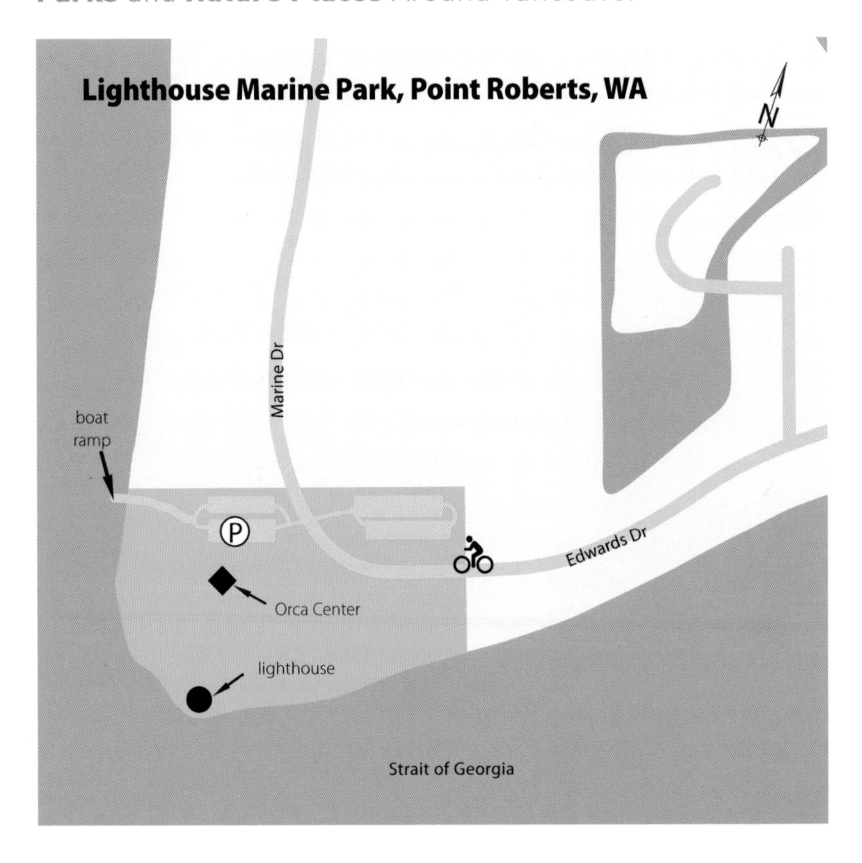

of the best places in the area to see seabirds and whales from land, as it protrudes into fairly open ocean. The beaches provide opportunities to beachcomb and spot marine life. Be sure to visit the Orca Center in the park to read about the mammals' behaviour.

A harbour seal rests on the pebble beach before another fishing trip.
www.lifeforcefoundation.org ©

Whatcom County now has four parks on the Point Roberts peninsula, one in each corner. Lily Point Marine Reserve in the southeast, recently purchased from developers, is a renowned natural area with 36 hectares (89 acres) of undeveloped marine shoreland and 16 hectares (40 acres) of tideland. Monument Park in the northwest and Maple Beach in the northeast are two smaller parks.

From Lighthouse Marine Park there are stunning views across Boundary Bay to Mt. Baker. *Ben VanBuskirk*

Natural History Visit

There is very little shelter as you walk along the shore at Lighthouse Marine Park, where it is often windy and colder than you might expect, so dress for the weather. You can see some birds on the beach or close to shore, but take binoculars or a viewing scope, as many birds will be offshore or flying by.

From the parking lot, scan the pilings by the boat launch and also those to the north for gulls and bald eagles. In fall and winter loons, grebes, cormorants and scoters are common, and you may see harlequin ducks, sanderlings and black turnstones feeding along the waterline.

Walk a short distance south along the gravel path to the point. Here you can watch birds as they fly by the peninsula heading in or out of Boundary Bay to the east. It's a good place to set up a spotting scope. In spring look for loons in breeding plumage. Cormorants and parasitic jaegers are common from August to October.

The bright red bill is an identifying feature of the noisy Caspian tern.
Virginia Hayes

Harbour porpoises and other sea mammals are often visible from the point. In summer orcas from the J, K and L pods—with a combined population of over 80—are often offshore. In July and August they are generally spotted every day, but sightings are much less frequent in May, June, September and October. By November the orcas have left. Gray whales pass by from March to May on their 19,000-kilometre (11,800-mile) journey from their breeding grounds in Mexico to their feeding grounds in Alaska. They return in the fall.

From the point, follow the gravel path east to the park boundary and take one of the many paths that meander through the campground past large shrubs bearing blackberries and other berries. Songbirds, often sparrows and juncos, are common in this area.

For bird watching, the best times to visit are spring and fall.

Nearby Locations

- three other parks are on the Point Roberts peninsula in Washington state: Lily Point Marine Reserve in the southeast, Monument Park in the northwest and Maple Beach in the northeast

Some Alerts

- dress warmly for this windy, cool park
- bring identification and maybe US currency

More Information

Lighthouse Marine Park: 360-945-4911 or
www.co.whatcom.wa.us/parks/lighthouse/lighthouse.jsp

over the water

Previous page: A graceful arbutus tree grows on a sunny, rocky oceanside slope.
James Holkko

Top: From the Bowen Island Ferry, don't miss wildlife watching or the views of Howe Sound. *Will Husby*

Crippen Regional Park, Bowen Island

by Will Husby

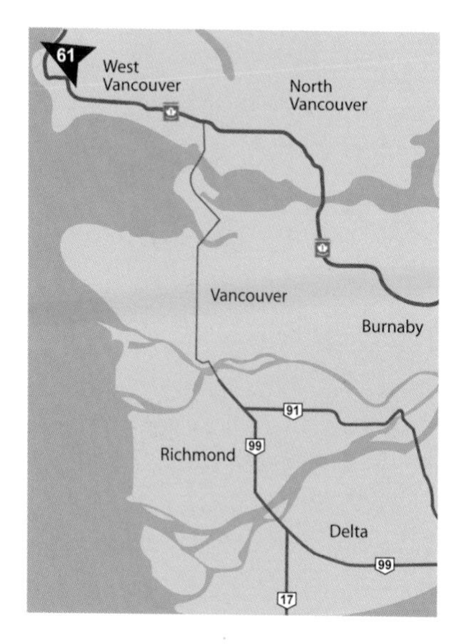

Island rain forest and one of Vancouver's first resorts

Location

Crippen Regional Park, Bowen Island is in Howe Sound west of West Vancouver, on Cardena Dr. off Government Rd. and close to the BC Ferries terminal.

Transit Information

From Downtown Vancouver, take either the #257 Horseshoe Bay Express bus or the #250 Horseshoe Bay bus to Horseshoe Bay. Arrive well ahead of the ferry's sailing time.
For up-to-date information, contact TransLink at www.translink.ca or 604-953-3333.
At Horseshoe Bay, take the 20-minute BC Ferries ride to Bowen Island. You will pay a fare to Bowen Island, but the trip back to Horseshoe Bay is free!
For up-to-date information, contact BC Ferries at www.bcferries.com or 1-888-BCFERRY.

Introduction

Crippen Regional Park on Bowen Island is part of the Metro Vancouver Regional Park system and contains 240 hectares (593 acres) of coastal forest. Killarney Creek, the island's main salmon stream, drains Killarney Lake, the island's largest lake. A trip to Bowen Island will take you to the site of one of the earliest resorts to serve Vancouver.

In the summer, watch for red-legged frogs in the ferns beside the trails. *Will Husby*

In any weather, start your nature watching right at the Horseshoe Bay ferry terminal. In late fall, winter and early spring look for rafts of hundreds of goldeneyes and surf scoters loafing on the surface near the ferry dock. They come to Howe Sound to spend the winter before migrating north to the Arctic or east to the Prairies for the summer breeding season. Don't miss the spectacular view up Howe Sound; maybe you'll see a bald eagle or catch a very rare glimpse of a pod of transient killer whales that occasionally visits Howe Sound to hunt seals.

Natural History Visit

You are almost at Crippen Regional Park when you get off the ferry at Snug Cove. Follow the other foot passengers up the walkway on the right side of Government Rd. At the intersection turn right at Cardena (also spelt Cardina) Dr. Walk past the historic Union Steamship Company Store and pick up a trail brochure at the Info Centre.

Continue up Cardena Dr. You will soon see the entry sign for Crippen Regional Park on your left. Take the main trail and look to your right to catch glimpses of Killarney Creek lagoon, which hosts great blue herons, common and hooded mergansers, the occasional bald eagle and a large, vicious mute swan.

A little farther up the trail listen for rushing water and look for a short side trail on your right down to the Bridal Veil Falls viewpoint on Killarney Creek. Note the fish ladder system to help salmon pass the waterfall. You may see one or two small grey American dippers plunging into the rushing water to hunt for aquatic insects and fish eggs. In late fall witness the spawning of chum salmon at the base of the fish ladder; you may even see a

coho attempt the ascent. This is about 1.5 kilometres (0.9 mile) from the ferry.

In fall you may see salmon attempting an ascent of the fish ladder to detour the waterfall. *Will Husby*

When you return to the main trail, proceed to Miller Rd. and cross it. Then either take the longer meandering Hatchery Trail, directly across the road, or take a short jog up the road to the right and cross onto the main Killarney Creek Trail. It runs 1.5 kilometres (0.9 mile) to Killarney Lake. In spring or early summer watch for the riot of salmonberries that line the trail and note the throngs of robins and varied thrushes feasting on the plump fruit. Also keep an eye out for barred owls lurking in the alders. Listen for the frantic calls of Steller's jays, crows and robins. If these birds find an owl, they join together in an angry mob and try to evict the predator from their home territory.

At Killarney Lake enjoy the still waters reflecting the green rain forest. In spring and summer look and listen for nesting American coots and pied-billed grebes among the yellow water lilies, watershields, cattails and rushes. In late spring listen for the symphony of red-legged frog song as these amphibians set up mating territories in the shallows of the lake.

You can walk the 4-kilometre (2.5-mile) loop trail around Killarney Lake to get better views of the lake from some high viewpoints. Look for signs of beaver as you walk along a boardwalk through a flooded forest. Returning to Snug Cove along the main Killarney Creek Trail, count the coastal rainforest tree species you find: Douglas-fir, western hemlock, western redcedar, Sitka spruce, cascara, bigleaf maple and red alder. While you are looking at the trees, you may see at least one of the shy native Douglas squirrels and maybe a pileated woodpecker.

A walk in Crippen Park is enjoyable at any time of year.

Barred owls are seen along the trail to Killarney Lake year-round. *Will Husby*

Nearby Locations

- you can swim at Sandy Beach, about 0.5 kilometre (0.3 mile) northeast from the ferry terminal, near the end of Cardena Dr.
- Dorman Point is a 2.5-kilometre (1.6-mile) uphill walk south from the ferry; it offers a spectacular view over the ocean
- Mount Gardner is the highest point on Bowen Island; trail suitable for expert and fit hikers only

Some Alerts

- occasional bears and cougars
- horses and mountain bikes on trails
- trails and boardwalks are slippery when wet
- use the small washroom beside the ferry terminal; note that the washroom water is not safe to drink
- avoid hiking during high winds and immediately after heavy snowfall
- check ferry schedules and allow plenty of time for every stage of your trip

More Information

Metro Vancouver Regional Parks:
www.metrovancouver.org/services/parks_lscr/regionalparks/Pages/default.aspx
Metro Vancouver Regional Parks West Area Office: 604-224-5739
Mount Gardner map and trail directions:
www.trailpeak.com/trail-Mount-Gardner-Bowen-Island-near-Vancouver-BC-636#

Index

Index

Index

More great *nature* titles from HARBOUR PUBLISHING

Wilderness on the Doorstep: Discovering Nature in Stanley Park
by Vancouver Natural History Society (Nature Vancouver), edited by Alison Parkinson

From evergreen forest to marshy wetland to rocky seashore, Stanley Park offers a number of different habitats teeming with an amazing variety of wildlife. Detailed descriptions, stories, photos, maps, artwork and colour photography by local naturalists makes this a fascinating guidebook and treasured souvenir for park visitors.
978-1-55017-386-4 · Paperback · 5.5 x 8.5 · 168 pp

Exploring the BC Coast by Car
by Diane Eaton & Allison Eaton

This indispensable book shows how you can use BC's ferry and coastal road system to reach the coast's most spectacular places in the comfort of your family car. Newly revised and updated in 2008, each chapter has "getting there" directions, information on recreation opportunities, local points of interest, anecdotes and facts on local plants, trees, wildlife and sea life.
978-1-55017-415-1 · Paperback · 5.5 x 8.5 · 400 pp

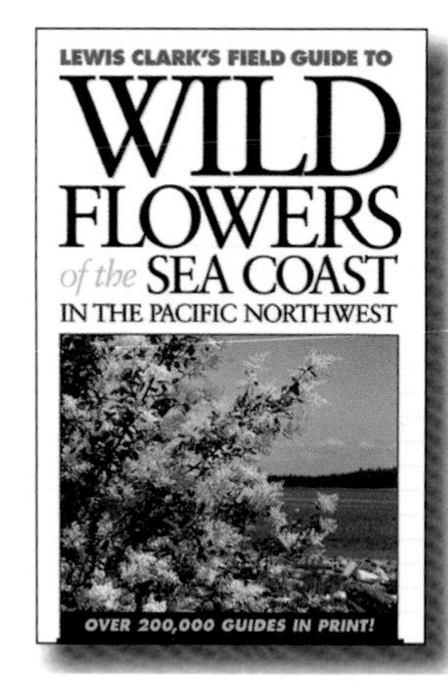

Wild Flowers of the Sea Coast In the Pacific Northwest
by Lewis J. Clark, edited by John Trelawny

Descriptions, diagrams and surprisingly large colour photos of almost 100 flowering plants of the coastal region from northern California to southern Alaska. Combining scholarly rigour with a conversational prose style, this easy-to-use guide will appeal to experienced botanists and afternoon strollers alike.
978-1-55017-307-9 · Paperback · 5.5 x 8.5 · 80 pp